SEQUOIA & KINGS CANYON

LEIGH BERNACCHI

Contents

SEQUOIA AND KINGS CANYON NATIONAL PARKS

© MOON.COM

To Visalia

To Fresno

GENERAL GRANT TREE
★ KINGS CANYON
i VISITOR CENTER
i Grant Grove Village

Badger

Pinehurst

Lake Kaweah

180

198

GENERALS

GENERALS HIGHWAY

Three Rivers

South Fork

Kaweah River

Oak Grove

Dennison Mountain 8,650ft

Sheep Mountain 10,050ft

Quinn Peak 10,168ft

Coyote Pass 10,160ft

Coyote Peaks 10,892ft

Little Kern River

Great Western Divide

Tower Rock 8,469ft

FOOTHILLS VISITOR CENTER

ASH MOUNTAIN ENTRANCE STATION

Admiration Point

Yucca Mtn 5,937 ft

Crystal Cave

GENERALS HIGHWAY

198

Hospital Rock

GIANT FOREST MUSEUM

Sequoia National Park

LOOKOUT POINT ENTRANCE STATION

ATWELL MILL

Farewell Gap 10,587ft

Mt. Florence 12,432ft

Mineral King

MINERAL KING RANGER STATION 7,700ft

Sawtooth Peak 12,343 ft

Black Rock Pass 11,600ft

Kaweah River

Moraine Lake

Rattlesnake Cr.

Kern

Kern Canyon River

Funston Lake

Boreal Plateau

Siberian Pass 10,950ft

Cottonwood Lakes

New Army Pass 11,475ft

Big Baldy 8,209ft

Kings Canyon NP

GENERAL SHERMAN TREE

Panther Gap 8,640 ft

LODGEPOLE VISITOR CENTER

Little Baldy 9,044 ft

Alta Peak 11,291 ft

Stony Creek Village

Twin Peaks 10,463 ft

J.O. Pass

Mount Stewart 12,205ft

Kaweah Gap 10,700ft

Black Kaweah 13,765ft

Kaweah Basin

Mount Kaweah 13,802ft

Triple Divide Peak 12,634ft

Cloud Canyon

Centennial Peak 13,251ft

Table Mountain 13,630ft

Kings-Kern Divide

Mount Genevra 13,055ft

Forester Pass 13,160ft

Sequoia National Park

Mount Guyot 12,300ft

Mount Hitchcock 13,184ft

Mount Whitney 14,494ft

Trail Crest 13,680ft

Mt. Langley 14,042ft

Whitney Portal

Avalanche Pass 10,040ft

Sphinx Creek

Mount Brewer 13,570ft

Mount Bradley 13,289ft

Mount Tyndall 14,018ft

Mount Barnard 13,990ft

Shepherd Pass 12,050ft

University Peak 13,632ft

To Lone Pine

Tulainyo Lake

N

0 5 km
0 5 mi

DISCOVER

Sequoia & Kings Canyon

CONGRESS
TRAIL

Your experiences in Sequoia and Kings Canyon can be like the features of the parks themselves: the biggest, highest, and deepest.

Sequoia National Park houses the two largest living trees in the world: General Sherman and General Grant. The tallest peak in the contiguous United States is Mount Whitney, soaring above the Sierra Nevada at 14,505 feet high. Driving the Kings Canyon Scenic Byway drops you into one of the deepest canyons in the United States, even deeper than the Grand Canyon. From the top of the Sierra Nevada down to the Kings River, countless waterfalls hurtle off cliffsides. Towering above the giant trees are granite spires and marble walls, carved by glaciers into nature's immense sculptures.

Most of the parks' two million annual visitors come for the giant sequoias. Of all the denizens of earth, sequoias are among the oldest, rarest, and largest. The sheer magnitude of these giants defies description and confounds cameras. These remnants of an ancient time once covered the northern hemisphere. Most of the groves remaining in the world persist in a narrow band in Sequoia and Kings Canyon. You can't help but be awestruck when you're standing at the base of General Sherman Tree, the largest living thing on earth.

Clockwise from top left: tourists standing inside a giant sequoia; Grizzly Falls; Sequoia visitor; Wuksachi Lodge in winter; taking a rest on General Grant Trail; Congress Trail.

The natural world awaits around every bend of river, road, and trail. Wild-flowers paint hillsides along the Kings and Kaweah Rivers in spring. Squirrels chatter and jays shriek. Bears shuffle along the same trails as we do.

Human history is preserved here, too: Among the oaks are grinding stones, where Native Americans once processed acorns to feed their families. Underneath it all lies a system of 200 caves, many of which remain untouched by humans.

These are your parks. Get out there and explore! Gawk up at thousands of giant sequoias. Find unparalleled solitude in the open expanses of windswept granite in the backcountry. Walk along narrow wooded trails, glimmering gold meadows, or snowy paths. Peer up at ink-dark skies and try to count all the stars. Sequoia and Kings Canyon contain enough adventure for a lifetime.

Clockwise from top left: stream fed by Sierra snowmelt; staircase up to Moro Rock; Indian paintbrush flower; General Sherman Tree.

10 TOP EXPERIENCES

1 **See Giant Trees:** Behold the two largest living trees on earth: the General Sherman Tree (page 72) and the General Grant Tree (page 102).

2 **Venture Underground:** Explore the otherwordly rock formations inside Crystal Cave (page 74).

3 **Go Stargazing:** The ink-black skies of Sequoia and Kings Canyon are framed by granite peaks. Stare in awe and try to spot a shooting star or the Milky Way (page 28).

>>>

4 **Take a Hike:** Take a short stroll to a waterfall or spend the whole day on the trail (page 32).

5 **Feel the Spray of a Waterfall:** Hear the boom of Roaring River Falls (pictured) or hike all day to Mist Falls (page 36).

6 **Go Snowshoeing:** In the winter, the parks are quiet, covered in a blanket of snow. See for yourself how different the landscape looks by strapping on a pair of snowshoes (pages 87 and 114).

>>>

7 **Go Backpacking:** To immerse yourself in the wilderness of these magnificent parks, pack up your gear and hit the backcountry trails. There's nothing quite like the solitude here (page 35).

8 **Drive Kings Canyon Scenic Byway:** Explore one of North America's deepest canyons from the comfort of your car on this gorgeous winding road (page 130).

9 **Wander Through Wildflowers:** You'll find gorgeous displays in meadows, along river banks, and in countless other spots throughout the parks (page 138).

>>>

10 **Take in the Views at Moro Rock:** It's a steep climb up 400 stairs to reach the top of this granite dome, but it's worth it for the expansive views, stretching from the valley floor to the mountain peaks (page 72).

Planning Your Trip

Where to Go

Foothills

The foothills of the Sierra Nevada are often overlooked as visitors race to the sequoias. But this area, rich in **Native American heritage** and filled with **oak trees,** deserves your time and exploration, too. Pleasant **hiking, bird-watching, fishing,** and hotel and dining options create an ideal **year-round** escape. Spring is an especially wonderful time to visit this area, with countless **waterfalls** and colorful **wildflowers.**

Giant Forest and Lodgepole

Giant Forest and Lodgepole are the most popular parts of the park, and it's easy to see why. Not only does the largest living being on earth, the **General Sherman Tree,** preside over the thousands of surrounding sequoias, but there are over 50 miles (81 km) of trails for **hiking** and exploring.

Lodgepole grants quick access to high country **lakes** and unforgettable **backpacking** trips. Staying at **Wuksachi Lodge** is a treat, but you can also sleep under the stars at one of the popular **campgrounds.**

Grant Grove

Bustling Grant Grove offers all the amenities you need for a comfortable trip, including cabins, a lodge, a restaurant, and an excellent visitors center. It's also home to the world's second largest tree, the **General Grant Tree,** and a network of **hiking trails.** Grant Grove has something for everyone: **scenic vistas**

base of the General Sherman Tree

GENERAL SHERMAN

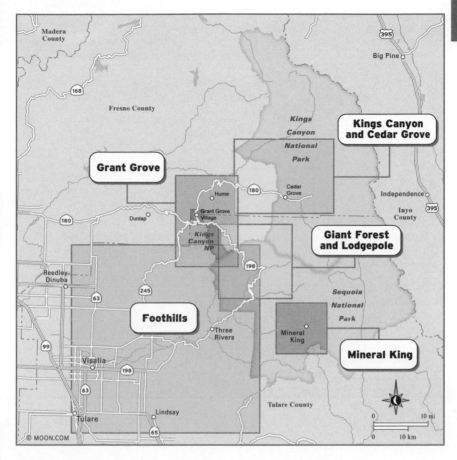

for photographers, the activity-filled **Hume Lake** for families, and **Redwood Mountain Grove,** for those looking to lose themselves in nature.

Kings Canyon and Cedar Grove

Kings Canyon, one of the deepest canyons in the country, is an ideal **backpacking** destination, containing hundreds of miles of **wilderness.** Granite basins are dotted with idyllic **lakes** and **waterfalls,** accessible via **day hikes** as well as multiday treks. If it gets too hot in the summer,

you can duck underground and explore **Boyden Cavern.** This is also a great area for **camping.**

Mineral King

In this **remote** area, the least visited of either park, you'll encounter peaceful **lakes,** brightly colored metamorphic **rock formations,** and a bounty of wildflower-lined **waterfalls. Camp** at one of two campgrounds, either by a stream or under sequoias, or stay at a **rustic resort.** This is an excellent place for **backpacking, fishing,** and **bird-watching.**

Before You Go

When to Go

Sequoia and Kings Canyon are open every day of the year, though some areas close in the winter.

HIGH SEASON (MAY-AUG.)

Summer, from **May to August,** is the high season for both parks. Plan ahead for **lodging reservations** and tours of **Crystal Cave,** especially on weekends. Lines to get into the park can be long, so arrive early. The shuttles that traverse Giant Forest and Lodgepole will be packed, so don't wait for the last bus of the day. To escape the crowds, visit less trafficked parts of the parks, like Cedar Grove or Mineral King.

MID-SEASON (MAR.-APR. AND SEPT.-NOV.)

The **shoulder seasons** are when you can get great deals on hotels, first pick of backcountry campsites, and enjoy temperate weather. **Fall,** from **September to November,** is gorgeous in Cedar Grove, Grant Grove, Lodgepole, and

Mineral King, when the leaves of riparian trees and the grasses brighten to gold. The streams of the Foothills run low, but you'll enjoy cool weather for strenuous hiking.

Springtime, from **March to April,** is a delight in Grant Grove, Lodgepole, and the Foothills, when snowmelt trickles into waterfalls, hiking trails start to thaw, and the blooms of redbud trees blaze along the river. Spring is peak **wildflower season** in the Foothills.

LOW SEASON (DEC.-FEB.)

Lodgepole and Grant Grove are at perhaps their most photogenic in **winter,** which spans from **December to February,** with white snow contrasting against the red bark and green needles of the giant sequoias. Cozy up at the hearth of a park lodge, or join a ranger on a snowshoe walk.

The Foothills don't see snow in winter, so you'll have your pick of trails, many of which offer total solitude. Cedar Grove and Mineral King are closed in winter.

wildflowers in the Foothills region

Sequoia and Kings Canyon In-Park Lodging

	Location	Price	Season	Lodging Type
Potwisha Campground	Foothills	$22	year-round	tent and RV sites
Buckeye Flat Campground	Foothills	$22	Mar.-Oct.	tent sites
South Fork Campground	Foothills	$6	year-round	tent sites
Wuksachi Lodge	Giant Forest and Lodgepole	from $140	year-round	hotel rooms
Lodgepole Campground	Giant Forest and Lodgepole	$22	Apr.-Nov.	tent and RV sites
Dorst Creek Campground	Giant Forest and Lodgepole	$22	June-Sept.	tent, RV, and group sites
John Muir Lodge	Grant Grove	from $200	year-round	hotel rooms
Grant Grove Cabins	Grant Grove	$40-150	early spring-early fall (Tent Cabins); year-round (Camp Cabins)	cabins
Crystal Springs Campground	Grant Grove	$18	mid-May-early Sept.	tent and RV sites
Azalea Campground	Grant Grove	$18	year-round	tent and RV sites
Sunset Campground	Grant Grove	$22	mid-May-early Sept.	tent and RV sites
Cedar Grove Lodge	Kings Canyon and Cedar Grove	from $140	mid-Apr.-mid-Nov.	hotel rooms
Sentinel Campground	Kings Canyon and Cedar Grove	$22	mid-Apr.-mid-Nov.	tent and RV sites
Sheep Creek Campground	Kings Canyon and Cedar Grove	$18	mid-Apr.-mid-Nov.	tent and RV sites
Moraine Campground	Kings Canyon and Cedar Grove	$18	mid-Apr.-mid-Nov.	tent and RV sites
Canyon View Campground	Kings Canyon and Cedar Grove	$30-60	mid-Apr.-mid-Nov.	group sites
Atwell Mill Campground	Mineral King	$12	mid-June-late Oct.	tent sites
Cold Springs Campground	Mineral King	$12	May or June-late Oct.	tent sites

If You're Looking for...

rock climber above Kings Canyon

- **Backpacking:** For a unique experience, sleep under the sequoias of **Redwood Mountain Grove.**

- **Bird-watching:** Along **Marble Falls Trail** in the Foothills region, watch for colorful passerines and listen for the lovely songs of thrushes and wrens.

- **Fishing:** Ply the emerald waters of the **Kings River** in **Cedar Grove** for trout.

- **Hiking:** A trip to Kings Canyon in the summer can be sweaty, but the cool spray of **Mist Falls** is worth the effort.

- **Horseback riding:** The **Cedar Grove Pack Station** will take you on a trip that lasts a few hours—or a couple of days.

- **Geologic wonders:** Take a tour of **Crystal Cave,** and don't miss the mesmerizing folds of marble, visible just off the road in **Kings Canyon.**

- **Rock climbing:** In **Kings Canyon,** you can climb some big walls—or watch others scamper up the granite.

- **Scenic drives:** Spanning from Grant Grove to Giant Forest, the **Generals Highway** provides vistas and links the General Sherman and General Grant Trees before it takes a thrilling drop down to the Foothills.

- **Solitude:** Pack up your bear canister and head into the backcountry of **Cedar Grove** or **Lodgepole.** Nearly any trail will do, but Cedar Grove's **Granite Lake** offers a special peace after a tough climb.

- **Swimming:** In Three Rivers, check out the **Slick Rock Recreation Area.**

- **Views:** Visit **Big Baldy** or any of the **granite domes** at sunset.

- **Winter recreation:** Snowshoe among the sequoias along the **North Grove Loop** in Grant Grove. For a bigger adventure, ski to the **Pear Lake Winter Hut** and spend the night in the backcountry.

Before You Go

Visit the official website for **Sequoia and Kings Canyon National Parks** (www.nps.gov/seki). There's even an official (and free!) **smartphone app** offered by the National Park Service. The site and app give you access to the park map and newsletter, among many other resources and tools. For more ideas, check out the website for the **Sequoia Parks Conservancy** (www.sequoi-aparksconvervancy.org) and follow the nonprofit group on social media.

Park Fees and Passes

To cruise through the park entrance stations without waiting in a long line, buy your entrance pass online in advance. Passes last for up to seven days and cost $35 per vehicle, $30 for motorcyclists, and $20 for pedestrians and bicyclists. Other options include:

- an **annual pass** to Sequoia and Kings Canyon, which costs $70 and covers all passengers in your car

- the **America the Beautiful pass,** which costs $80 for a year and covers all passengers in your car

- a **senior pass** ($20 for a year or $80 lifetime), if you're a U.S. citizen or permanent resident and 62 or older

- the **Access Pass** (free), which is available to U.S. citizens and permanent residents with disabilities

- the **Every Kid Outdoors Annual 4th Grade Pass** (free), which is available to children in fourth grade (and their families) and lasts the length of the school year

Entrance Stations

The southern entrance to the parks is the **Ash Mountain Entrance Station** (Hwy. 198, open year-round), near the town of Three Rivers. It provides easy access to the Foothills, Giant Forest, and Lodgepole.

Big Stump Entrance Station

Escape the Crowds

Sequoia and Kings Canyon have a few areas that get very crowded. Solitude is available in abundance here, though, especially if you're willing to explore during dawn and dusk or visit in fall, winter, or spring. If your trip is scheduled for a summer holiday weekend, here are some options to decrease time with crowds and increase time with nature:

- Instead of crowded Moro Rock, climb another **granite dome** like **Little Baldy.**

- For a quiet **sequoia grove,** visit **Muir Grove** rather than General Sherman or General Grant.

- **Fish** in the high country by hiking out to one of Mineral King's many lakes, like **Eagle Lake** or the **Franklin Lakes.** At Cedar Grove's lower elevations, try your luck in the **Kings River.**

- Rather than hiking a long way to popular Mist Falls, take the shorter and less crowded stroll to **Sheep Creek Cascade.**

- Though **Crystal Cave** is well known, the group size for the Discovery Tour is kept small. Or choose another cave entirely: **Boyden Cavern** doesn't require advance reservations.

- For a quiet dinner in crowded Lodgepole, avoid the restaurant at Wuksachi Lodge. Instead, buy some picnic supplies at **Lodgepole Market** and have a sunset dinner at **Wolverton Picnic Area.** (Bring a flashlight for the walk back!)

hiker in the backcountry

- To explore a remote part of the park, visit **Mineral King.** Few people venture to this area, so you may just have the trail to yourself.

- To get up close with **Kings Canyon** itself, make stops along the curvy, winding highway into **Cedar Grove** to **Road's End.** Far fewer people take this scenic drive than the one along the Generals Highway.

Also near Three Rivers is the **Lookout Point Entrance Station** (Mineral King Rd. and Hwy. 198, late May-mid-Oct.), which provides access to Mineral King.

For access to Grant Grove, Cedar Grove, and Kings Canyon, head to the **Big Stump Entrance Station** (Hwy. 180, open year-round), the northern entrance to the parks.

Reservations

If you're visiting in summer, you'll want to reserve most activities in advance, especially tours of **Crystal Cave** and **horseback riding excursions.** Ranger activities are free and do not require reservations.

Reserve a **campsite** on www.recreation.gov. For the park-based **lodges** and **cabins,** you can make reservations on www.visitsequoia.com. If you plan on taking the **shuttle** into the park from Visalia, reserve your seat in advance at www.sequoiashuttle.com.

In the Park

Visitors Centers

The parks' four major visitors centers house educational exhibits and bookstores with souvenirs. They also host ranger programs and are where you can obtain a wilderness permit.

- **Giant Forest Museum** (Generals Hwy., 16 mi/26 km north of the Ash Mountain entrance, 559/565-4480, 9am-6pm daily mid-May-mid-Nov., 9am-4:30pm daily mid-Nov.-mid-May) is in the heart of Sequoia's big trees. There's a shuttle stop and a large parking lot, a picnic area, access to hiking trails, and enough information about giant sequoias to make you an expert.

- **Lodgepole Visitor Center** (63100 Lodgepole Rd., 559/565-4436, 7am-5pm daily May-Nov.) hosts a wilderness permit desk, a bookstore, and ranger programs in a centralized location near the Marble Fork of the Kaweah River. Nearby are a restaurant and shuttle stop.

- **Kings Canyon Visitor Center** (Hwy. 180, 559/565-3341, ext. 0, 8am-5pm daily late May-early Sept., 9am-4pm daily late Sept.-Dec. and early Mar.-May, 10am-3pm daily Jan.-early Mar.) is the most detailed in the park. Located in Grant Grove Village, the center has interesting displays and staffs enthusiastic rangers.

- **Foothills Visitor Center** (Generals Hwy., 559/565-4212, 8am-4:30pm daily Apr.-Nov., 9am-4pm daily Dec.-Mar.) features displays about the area's flora and fauna, as well as its human history. It's small, but it packs in a lot, including a self-registration desk for off-season backcountry trips, a bookstore, and lots of handouts about the parks.

The parks have three other informational facilities, though these are more rudimentary than the main visitors centers. In Cedar Grove, the one-room **Cedar Grove Visitor Center** (Hwy.

Giant Forest Museum

180, 559/565-3793, 9am-5pm daily May-Sept.) offers historical photographs and information. The **Road's End Permit Station** (Hwy. 180, 559/565-3341, 7am-3pm daily May-Sept.) in Kings Canyon functions as a wilderness station where you can rent bear canisters. In Mineral King, the one-room **Mineral King Ranger Station** (mile 24/km 39, Mineral King Rd., 559/565-3768, 8am-3:45pm daily late May-mid-Oct.) doubles as the wilderness permit office and bookstore.

Where to Stay

If you're looking for a place to stay in Sequoia and Kings Canyon at the last minute, here are some tips:

- Check www.recreation.gov for campsite **cancellations.** Sometimes you can snag a last-minute reservation at Lodgepole or Dorst Creek Campgrounds.

- **Call the park** (559/565-3341) to see if all campgrounds are full.

- Pick an area where you'll have a better chance of success, and try your luck at **first-come, first-served campgrounds.** You'll find the most options at **Azalea** and **Crystal Springs Campgrounds** in Grant Grove. In Cedar Grove, try **Sheep Creek** or **Moraine Campgrounds.** If you're set on camping in Lodgepole, try for a spot in **Stony Creek** or **Upper Stony Creek,** both of which are in nearby Sequoia National Forest.

Getting Around

A **personal vehicle** is recommended to optimize your ability to move around and between the parks. There is a free **park shuttle,** but it's limited to just the Giant Forest and Lodgepole areas of Sequoia National Park. There's also a **long-distance shuttle** that transports riders to Giant Forest from Visalia; it costs $20. Both shuttles run only on holidays and in the summer.

Best of Sequoia and Kings Canyon

Over a long weekend in Sequoia and Kings Canyon, you can see the highlights and get some solitude. Whether you want to camp or stay in a hotel, be sure to make reservations in advance.

Day 1

Pack a picnic lunch for today, so that you can stop to eat whenever hunger—or the scenery—calls. Enter **Sequoia National Park** via **Ash Mountain Entrance Station.** Just past the entrance station is the Indian Head sign, carved in the 1930s, which marks the entrance to Sequoia. Pop into the **Foothills Visitor Center** to get your passport stamped and to get oriented.

Continue up the Generals Highway until you reach **Hospital Rock.** At this large rock outcropping, you can see pictographs left by the Patwisha people who once lived here. It's about an hour's drive to the next stop: the **General Sherman Tree,** a giant sequoia that's also the world's largest living tree. Explore more of the surrounding Giant Forest by hiking the **Congress Trail.**

Backtrack along the highway a bit to the **Giant Forest Museum.** Park your car here and explore the museum, learning all about giant sequoias. Take the **shuttle** to **Moro Rock,** then climb 400 stairs to get a stunning view of the park, overlooking the forest canopy.

Head back up the Generals Highway to **Wuksachi Lodge,** where you'll retire for the night. Make reservations in advance for dinner at the lodge's restaurant, **The Peaks.** Sip an aperitif on the deck and enjoy the sunset views. If you'd rather sleep under the stars, you'll need to make reservations in advance for a spot at the **Dorst Creek** or **Lodgepole Campgrounds.**

the view from Moro Rock

Go Stargazing

the night sky in in Sequoia National Park

Every section of Sequoia and Kings Canyon boasts beautiful, inky black skies. Light pollution is minimal here and the Milky Way is perfectly framed by granite peaks. For three days every August, the **Dark Sky Festival** (www.sequoiaparksconservancy.org) celebrates the parks' starry skies with more than 50 programs.

EVENTS AND PROGRAMS

Though the best part of the festival is sharing what you see in the sky with the people around you, there are other fun activities, too. The festival puts on daytime and evening **talks** on topics like the solar system, star formation, telescopes, and bats. Astronauts and astrophysicists are often featured speakers. Attend a **concert** or take free **photography workshops** where you can learn how to shoot the stars from expert photographers.

During the festival, there are several special **ranger programs,** including stargazing, of course, but activities can also include **nighttime hikes** under the sequoias and looking for bats with an infrared camera.

Most of the programs take place in the **Foothills** and **Giant Forest**—specifically **Potwisha Campground** and the **Foothills Visitor Center.** Most activities are free; some cost $20.

PLANNING TIPS

The exact dates of the festival vary and are set around the phase of the moon. The festival is very popular, so reserve your **hotel room** in **spring.** Sometimes it's possible to nab a **campsite** during the festival by **volunteering** to work the busy event.

If you have a **telescope** or **binoculars,** bring them. If you don't have either, it's likely that one of your fellow stargazers will let you take a look. Park rangers are often stationed with telescopes, too, and they can help identify what you're seeing.

OTHER WAYS TO STARGAZE

If you're not able to visit during the festival, you can still enjoy the parks' dark skies on your own. In **mid-August,** you can stare in amazement at the **Perseid Meteor Shower,** when around 80 shooting stars per hour streak across the night sky. The best times to go are during crescent and gibbous moon phases.

Of all the parks' regions, **Mineral King** is the perfect place for stargazing, with the best skyscape and least light pollution. By **backpacking** to one of your favorite lakes, you can get excellent views of the Milky Way, constellations, and planets. Typically the air is clearer in early summer than late because of agricultural harvests and vehicle exhaust in the Central Valley below.

Pack a **star chart,** to help you orient yourself, and a telescope or binoculars for truly stunning sky views in this High Sierra wilderness. No matter where you are in the parks, be sure to go outside at night and look up!

Day 2

You've got a couple hours of driving ahead of you today, so start the day early by stretching your legs with a hike. There are countless options, but some of the best include the ones that take you atop a granite dome: **Little Baldy, Big Baldy Ridge,** and **Buena Vista Peak** offer incredible views of the surrounding forests and valleys in less than five miles of hiking.

Get back in the car and take the scenic Generals Highway west and north until you reach **Grant Grove.** You can stop for a buffet lunch at **Montecito Sequoia Lodge,** or wait until the end of your drive and eat at the full-service **Grant Grove Restaurant.**

Take the stunning drive along the **Kings Canyon Scenic Byway,** which descends into **Kings Canyon.** If it's a summer afternoon, take a break from the heat by exploring **Boyden Cavern.** Continue east toward **Cedar Grove,** being sure to stop at **Grizzly Falls** along the way. The misty waterfall is just off the highway and makes for a great photo op.

Check into **Cedar Grove Lodge** or set up camp at one of Cedar Grove's four **campgrounds.** Enjoy a sunset meander through **Zumwalt Meadow.** Find a bench and watch the Kings River roll by. Have dinner at the Cedar Grove Grill. After dark, spend some time **stargazing.** You're in one of the darkest places in the park, so the views are especially good.

Day 3

Pick one big activity for today. If you want to hike, you can enjoy the water at **Mist Falls** or take in the views from the **Cedar Grove Overlook.** To hit the trail on horseback, visit the **Cedar Grove Pack Station.** Or maybe sightseeing is more your speed: both **Knapp's Cabin** and **Roaring River Falls** are a short distance off the highway.

Take the highway up and out of the canyon and return to Grant Grove. Visit the **General Grant Tree,** the world's second largest tree, and admire the other sequoias that surround this giant. Stop in at the **Grant Grove Market** for picnic supplies, then enjoy a sunset dinner at **Panoramic Point.** Watch the skies above the Sierra fade from pink to purple to slate. Spend your last night at one of the **Grant Grove Cabins** and dream of your next trip to these magnificent parks.

Roaring River Falls

Family Fun

Sequoia and Kings Canyon offer families the chance to unplug: Watch for animals, take in the sunset, and count shooting stars. Smell wildflowers, pine needles, and bay leaves. In these parks, you can combine entertainment and education, all while enjoying time together in nature.

Ranger programs are offered throughout the parks and provide engagement for children of all ages. Younger kids will love animal-themed talks, like a discussion of the area's resident bears, while teenagers will enjoy the living history programs and guided stargazing. Goal-oriented kids can spend their time in the parks completing a set of activities, then be sworn in as a **Junior Ranger.**

Montecito Sequoia Lodge is a great spot for families to stay, as its central location means you're less than an hour's drive from both Grant Grove and Giant Forest. The lodge even offers an all-inclusive family camp with meals and activities.

Big Trees

Visit the two largest living trees in the world: **General Sherman** in **Giant Forest** and **General Grant** in **Grant Grove.** Ask someone to snap a photo of your family at the base of either, and you'll end up with a great souvenir of your time here.

To see the giants in a more peaceful setting, get off the beaten path by taking a hike through **North Grove Loop, Redwood Mountain Grove,** or **Muir Grove.**

Caves

Explore the underground world of the parks at **Crystal Cave.** Learn about geology, rare cave creatures, and cool down from the summer heat. The **Family Tour** is 50 minutes long and appropriate for all ages. There are more in-depth and adventurous tours for ages 10 and up, including the **Family Caver Tour,** the **Discovery Tour,** and the **Wild Cave Tour.** Buy tickets in advance.

a Junior Ranger being sworn in

the Big Trees Trail in Sequoia National Park

If you aren't able to get tickets, or if you want to escape the crowds, visit **Boyden Cavern** in **Kings Canyon.** The 50-minute tours are suitable for all ages and don't require advance reservations.

Hiking

Giant Forest and **Lodgepole** offer high-reward and low-mileage wilderness experiences for the whole family. Hike a couple miles to **Tokopah Falls** through the forest along the river to awesome views and a towering **waterfall.** Keep your eyes peeled for **pikas,** cute critters that live among the piles of rock.

The **Big Trees Trail** traces **Round Meadow,** where wildlife and sequoias are accompanied by helpful **interpretive signs.**

For the daring, **Moro Rock** will give young hikers a sense of accomplishment after climbing 400 stairs to the top. Other **granite domes,** like **Big Baldy** and **Buena Vista Peak,** also offer big rewards in short distances.

In **Grant Grove,** get **great views** at the easily accessible **Panoramic Point.** Or venture onto the **North Grove Loop** for a quiet experience in a **sequoia grove.**

In **Cedar Grove,** look no further than the short walk to **Roaring River Falls.** Butterflies and crickets jump along the paved path to this booming **waterfall.** The trail can also be connected to the **River Trail,** where you can get away from the road, explore a **boulder field,** and connect to **Zumwalt Meadow** for a longer, but flat wander among a forest and a wildflower-laden meadow.

Horseback Riding

In Sequoia and Kings Canyon, there are two places to hop on a horse: **Grant Grove Pack Station** and **Cedar Grove Pack Station** will take you and your family on trips of varying lengths. Note that children must be 8 or older; all children need to be able ride independently.

Swimming

Near the **Buckeye Flat Campground** in the Foothills region are several popular **swimming holes.** Outside the parks, in **Three Rivers,**

hiking to Eagle Lake

FOOTHILLS

- **Marble Falls Trail** (7.4 mi/11.9 km round-trip): Year-round, this is one of the best hikes in Sequoia, gradually climbing to a whitewater cascade and providing views of the canyon below (page 50).

GIANT FOREST AND LODGEPOLE

- **Lakes Trail** (8.2-12.4 mi/13.2-20 km round-trip): It's a rare opportunity to be able to hike to an alpine lake not far from a major road; this trail gives you the chance to stop at a few smaller ones on the way to Pear Lake (page 78).

- **Big Trees Trail** (1 mi/1.6 km loop): Join a ranger on a paved loop that circles Round Meadow to enjoy sequoias, wildflowers, and wildlife (page 79).

- **Crescent Meadow and Tharp's Log** (2.2 mi/3.5 km round-trip): This dazzling alpine meadow hike gets you up close and personal with a fallen sequoia that was converted into a home in the 1860s (page 81).

GRANT GROVE

- **North Grove Loop** (2 mi/3.2 km loop): Descend into this peaceful area for a hike among sequoias at all stages of life (page 106).

- **Redwood Mountain Sequoia Grove:** You will have the place to yourself as you hike among the largest standing sequoia grove. **Hart Tree** (7.3 mi/11.7 km loop) and **Sugarbowl** (6.8 mi/10.9 km loop) are two excellent loop trails (page 109).

- **Big Baldy Ridge** (4.2 mi/6.8 km round-trip): This straightforward hike takes you to the highest point in Grant Grove—the top of a granite dome known as Big Baldy. The payoff is an excellent vista of Redwood Canyon and the Great Western Divide (page 112).

KINGS CANYON AND CEDAR GROVE

- **Zumwalt Meadow** (1.8 mi/2.9 km loop): On this loop trail, you'll have your eyes full no matter which direction you look: looming granite faces above, a green river below, and wildflowers all around (page 137).

- **Mist Falls** (9.1 mi/14.6 km round-trip): After the hot hike to this popular waterfall, you're rewarded with the refreshing snowmelt spray. This is the most popular day hike in Cedar Grove (page 139).

MINERAL KING

- **Eagle Lake** (6.8 mi/10.9 km round-trip): This trek climbs out of Mineral King Valley along waterfalls and springs lined with wildflowers to an unsurpassed view of multicolored mountains and a serene Sierra lake. This is an adventure that hikers of all ages will enjoy (page 162).

spend a day playing in the boulder-encased pools of **Slick Rock Recreation Area.** Stay at the lakeside **Montecito Sequoia Lodge,** located right on the Generals Highway, for built-in swimming time.

Wildlife-Watching

Most people, not just kids, want to see wildlife in their natural habitat when they visit Sequoia and Kings Canyon. Generally, the best time to spot wildlife is in the morning or evening. One exception is the late-rising **marmot,** who waits until the sun is high in the sky to bask on warm rocks.

If you sit and wait in quieter parts of the parks, you might get the chance to see **black bears.** Bring a pair of binoculars and look for them grazing in **Crescent Meadow** and **Round Meadow,** foraging along dusty trails in **Giant Forest,** or searching for grubs in fallen logs near **Zumwalt Meadow.**

In addition to marmots and bears, keep your eyes peeled for **deer, squirrels, chipmunks,** and a variety of **birds,** especially the **pileated woodpecker,** the largest of its kind in North America.

Winter Recreation

If you're staying in Grant Grove, Lodgepole, or at the Montecito Sequoia Lodge, don't miss the chance to go on a **guided snowshoe walk** with a park ranger. Though conditions are best just after a storm, these walks are always fun for the whole family. Once a month, you can even go on a **full moon snowshoe walk,** and take in the peaceful parkland at night. Snowshoeing doesn't require previous experience. Call ahead to ensure smaller-sized snowshoes are available.

Sequoia and Kings Canyon have a few **sledding** and **snowplay areas.** These spots are set back from the road, so they're safe from traffic. If you're staying in Giant Forest or Lodgepole, visit the **Wolverton snowplay area.** Sleds are available for rent from the **Wuksachi Lodge.** If you're in Grant Grove, choose between the **Big Stump Picnic Area** or the **Columbine Picnic**

a black bear in Sequoia National Park

If you have just one day (and night) to spend in Sequoia and Kings Canyon, you'll need to choose one park or the other to avoid spending the majority of the day driving.

SEQUOIA NATIONAL PARK

Enter the park at the **Ash Mountain Entrance Station** and ascend the **Generals Highway.** Park at the Giant Forest Museum and take the shuttle to **Moro Rock.** Climb the rock's 400 stairs to obtain some famous Sierra Nevada views, the earlier in the day, the better.

Take the shuttle back to Giant Forest Museum and switch to the General Sherman shuttle. Visit the largest tree on earth, the **General Sherman Tree.** Meander through the **Giant Forest** on the **Congress Trail** before hopping back on the shuttle.

Return to the **Giant Forest Museum** to learn more about the sequoias and pick up souvenirs. You can also walk there from the General Sherman Tree.

Pick up your car, then head to the **Wuksachi Lodge.** Its restaurant, **The Peaks,** offers comfort food and great views from the deck. Spend the night in one of the lodge's comfy rooms or retire to your campsite.

KINGS CANYON NATIONAL PARK

Kings Canyon can be visited in a long day of driving with plenty of great stops along the way. Be sure to fill up on gas and pack snacks and water.

Start your morning from Fresno by climbing up Highway 180 into **Grant Grove.** Take the short, paved trail to the **General Grant Tree** and observe the sequoias in a forest that looks much like it would have thousands of years ago.

General Sherman Tree

Grab the makings of a picnic at the **Grant Grove Market** before hopping back on Highway 180, where you'll make your way toward **Cedar Grove.** Make stops at **Grizzly Falls** and **Roaring River Falls.** Bask in the late afternoon light of **Zumwalt Meadow.**

Spend the night at **Cedar Grove Lodge** or one of the **campgrounds** here and let the river lull you to sleep. The next day, hop back in the car and drive up and out of the deepest canyon in the country. Stop at **Boyden Cavern** on your way out for a cool (literally) conclusion to your trip.

Area. Between the two parks is the **Montecito Sequoia Lodge,** which has ski trails and snowshoeing paths.

Sweet Treats

In **Three Rivers,** the confectioners **Reimer's Candies and Gifts** take the phrase "kid in a candy store" to a whole new level. With housemade ice cream, fudge, and lollipops as big as their head, kids will have a hard time deciding what to choose.

If you're near Grant Grove and need to sate your sweet tooth, stop at the **Hume Lake Snack Shop** for one of their popular milkshakes.

Backpacker's Paradise

Backpacking is the best way to explore the wilderness of Sequoia and Kings Canyon. There are things you can only see by getting off the beaten path, including glacier-carved peaks and passes, unique geologic features, and rare flora and fauna. The parks offer options that are ideal for novices and expert backpackers alike, with varying mileage and elevation.

All backcountry trips require a **wilderness permit,** which can be reserved in advance on the official park website or in person at the Foothills, Lodgepole, and Kings Canyon Visitor Centers, as well as the Road's End Permit Station. If you have your own bear canister, bring it with you. Otherwise, you can rent one from one of the visitors centers.

Rae Lakes Loop is a popular trip, but it gets crowded and it's hard to obtain a permit. Instead, try one of the trips in this section for a taste of the parks—with less crowding. These options offer the best of Sequoia and Kings Canyon: beautiful views, solitude, and starry skies.

Paradise Valley

Basking in the heaven that is **Paradise Valley** (11.4 mi/18.3 km round-trip, 1,600 feet elevation gain) is the best way to spend a summer afternoon. The trail follows the sandy Bubb's Creek Trail before turning up to popular **Mist Falls.** You'll have done most of the climbing by the time you reach the waterfall, and you're not likely to have much company as you continue past this point.

The **campsites** for Paradise Valley are along the verdant South Fork of the Kings River and come equipped with **campfire rings** and **bear boxes.** This means you don't have to bring a bear canister and you can keep your pack lighter.

Paradise Valley can be done as a **one- or two-night trip.** There's a **two-night limit** on

view of Kings Canyon along the Rae Lakes Loop

Best Waterfalls

Sequoia and Kings Canyon are home to varied and dramatic waterfalls. Some are just a few steps from the road, while others require long hikes—but the payoff is always worth it, especially in the spring and early summer. Here are some of the best you'll find in the parks.

FOOTHILLS

- **Marble Falls:** This frothy whitewater cascade rushes over time-polished granite. The hike here is one of the best in Sequoia National Park (page 50).

- **Panther Creek Falls:** This waterfall drops 100 feet into an emerald pool surrounded by granite shores (page 51).

GIANT FOREST AND LODGEPOLE

- **Tokopah Falls:** It's a fairly flat hike out to this ripping waterfall, where you might hear pikas chirping (page 77).

KINGS CANYON AND CEDAR GROVE

- **Grizzly Falls:** Stop at this popular roadside waterfall for its cooling mist. You can get quite close for photographs (page 132).

- **Roaring River Falls:** This seemingly short waterfall exits with great force out of a tight tunneled curve, resulting in the booming noise that gave the cascades their name (page 132).

- **Sheep Creek Cascade:** A brief uphill hike leads to this short cascade, elegantly flowing among mossy rocks (page 135).

Mist Falls

- **Mist Falls:** This 800-foot waterfall gushes and bursts forth with a power few western falls can claim. You'll feel the fall's mist long before you can hear or see it. That's a good thing, as the hike here is long and sunny (page 139).

MINERAL KING

- **Black Wolf Falls:** Just minutes from the road, you will find a perfect cold, white waterfall set amid yellow wildflowers (page 154).

---

camping here because the sites are on the popular Rae Lakes Loop. Try to allow for some flexibility in your desired dates, so that you're more likely to get a **wilderness permit** for this trail.

Redwood Mountain Sequoia Grove

Near Grant Grove, the steep hillsides of **Redwood Mountain Sequoia Grove** are home to densely packed **giant sequoias,** perfect for a **late spring** trip. The grove offers two main loop trails, which you can do as **overnight** trips.

The **Hart Tree Loop** (7.3 mi/11.7 km round-trip, 1,000 feet elevation gain) has rocky views and a small meadow. The **Sugarbowl Loop** (6.7 mi/10.8 km round-trip, 600 feet elevation gain) is slightly easier. It offers views of Big Baldy.

The easiest way to reach the trailhead is via

Upper Monarch Lake

the Big Stump Entrance Station. Pick up your **wilderness permit** and **bear canister** at the Kings Canyon Visitor Center and hit the trail.

Monarch Lakes

For a multi-day adventure, get your friends together and nab a reservation for a trip to **Monarch Lakes** (9 mi/14.5 km round-trip, 2,500 feet elevation gain) in Mineral King. This trip is for people who are comfortable with higher elevations and cold nights.

You'll be doing a lot of climbing, so pack as light as possible. The early part of the trail overlooks **Black Wolf Falls.** After hiking up for a while, you'll reach the namesake **Upper** and **Lower Monarch Lakes.** Set up camp on the shores of your preferred lake, set in the shadow of Sawtooth Peak.

It's a 1.5-hour drive to the trailhead from **Three Rivers,** but you can crash at the **Cold Springs Campground** for an early start. Get a **bear canister** and **maps** at the Mineral King Ranger Station before taking off.

High Sierra Trail to Bearpaw Camp

The trip along the **High Sierra Trail** (11.5 mi/18.5 km one-way, 1,000 feet elevation gain) to **Bearpaw High Sierra Camp** is ideal for beginner backpackers. It's steadily graded, so you won't encounter any surprise switchbacks or stairs. It follows a ridgeline all the way to Bearpaw, so you'll have impressive views the whole trip. Best of all, you get to stay at Bearpaw High Sierra Camp, where you'll sleep in a real bed and be served delicious food. Space is limited at Bearpaw and reservations are very hard to come by, so try to book as far in advance as possible.

Romantic Getaways

Few places are as romantic as Sequoia and Kings Canyon: the red bark of the sequoias reflecting the warm sun, the natural perfume of mint plants and pine trees, and the glorious sight of entire meadows of wildflowers. Though any time of year is perfect for celebrating an anniversary or just taking some time together, winter proves the coziest, and you'll have the parks practically to yourselves. Here are three weekend options.

Grant Grove

In Grant Grove, choose from the cozy **John Muir Lodge,** or get more solitude by opting to stay in one of the **Grant Grove Cabins.**

On your first day, visit **Panoramic Point,** a pretty overlook that's a short drive from the lodge. Next, stretch your legs on the **Sunset Loop** hike to see sequoias and waterfalls. Have a nice dinner and a glass of wine at the **Grant Grove Restaurant.** Try for a table by the windows for lovely meadow views.

The next morning, beeline for the **General Grant Tree.** Be sure to pack a selfie stick so you can get a photo at the base of the tree together. Next, explore the sequoias on the nearby **North Grove Loop** hike. In the afternoon, take a **scenic drive** to **Junction View** along Highway 180, and take in the magnitude of Kings Canyon.

Giant Forest and Lodgepole

In Lodgepole, the top romantic spot is the **Wuksachi Lodge.** It offers unparalleled sunset views and a high-end restaurant, as well as bed-and-breakfast packages.

On your first day, start with a hike through **Crescent Meadow,** then work your way over to the **Giant Forest Museum.** Finish with a sunset picnic at **Beetle Rock** before retiring for the night.

The next morning, enjoy the buffet breakfast at **The Peaks.** Spend the day hiking the **Lakes Trail** for beautiful alpine lakes and wildflower vistas.

Sequoia National Park

Budget Tips

Sequoia Shuttle

These tips for visiting Sequoia and Kings Canyon on a shoestring budget will allow you to have a nice long weekend in the parks for under $100.

- **Leave your car behind.** Enter the park by taking the **Sequoia Shuttle** from Visalia. A ticket costs $20 and includes your park entrance fee. If you drive your own car, expect to spend at least $20 worth of gas climbing up and down the parks' mountain roads. (If you want to visit Grant Grove, you'll need your own vehicle.)

- **Sleep under the stars.** Make reservations in advance for a spot at **Lodgepole Campground,** which is located in the most central and popular part of the parks. Sites run $22 per night and offer easy access to the Lodgepole Market, which sells the most affordable food in the parks.

- **Ride the park shuttle.** The shuttles, which serve Giant Forest and Lodgepole, stop at all the major sights in the area. Best of all, they're **free** to ride!

- **Head to the backcountry.** Wilderness permits cost just $5, and **backcountry campsites** are free.

Mineral King

Perhaps the best Sequoia and Kings Canyon getaway is Mineral King, the most remote area of the parks. Stay at **Silver City Mountain Resort,** which is made up of cabins, a restaurant, and a bar.

Spend your first day hiking to **Timber Gap** and back, stopping to view **Black Wolf Falls** along the way. For dinner, enjoy a beer and pizza on the resort's patio, then play a game of horseshoes.

On your second day, take the challenging hike to **Eagle Lake.** You'll be rewarded with more waterfall views, as well as panoramic vistas and the chance to take a rejuvenating dip in the lake. Visit the giant sequoias at Atwell Mill and Grove on your way home.

Foothills

Many park visitors pass through the Foothills region in a rush to get to the big trees, but this is like showing up half an hour late to a movie. A visit to this area sets the stage for your journey to the higher elevations of the Sierra Nevada. The Foothills contain a rich assortment of plant and animal life, as well as evidence of human habitation across millenia.

Populated with oak trees, the Foothills look very different from what you might expect of a park named after the giant sequoia. In fact, Sequoia National Park preserves a vast acreage of rare oak woodlands and chaparral ecosystems. The land is home to California quail, woodpeckers, black bears, and other animals, many of whom rely on oak trees and their acorns for sustenance.

Highlights

Look for ★ to find recommended sights, activities, dining, and lodging.

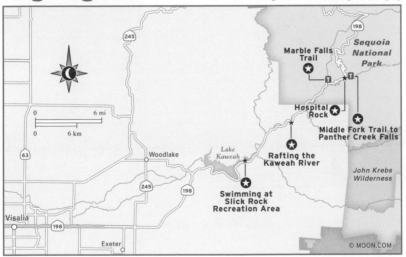

245

198

Marble Falls Trail ★

Sequoia National Park

Hospital Rock ★

Middle Fork Trail to Panther Creek Falls ★

Rafting the Kaweah River ★

Lake Kaweah

Woodlake

63

245   198

Swimming at Slick Rock Recreation Area ★

John Krebs Wilderness

Visalia

198

Exeter

0   6 mi
0   6 km

© MOON.COM

★ **See Pictographs at Hospital Rock:** The indigenous Patwisha people once traded and lived in a village here, near the Kaweah River. Their art is preserved on an overhanging rock minutes from the Generals Highway (page 46).

★ **Hike Marble Falls Trail:** On one of the best hikes in Sequoia, you will gradually climb to a whitewater cascade and enjoy views of the canyon below (page 50).

★ **Follow Middle Fork Trail to Panther Creek Falls:** Get inspired on this all-season hike that boasts views of Moro Rock and the Sierra Nevada (page 51).

★ **Raft the Kaweah River:** Experience the wild rapids of the Kaweah River on a half- or full-day guided trip (page 54).

★ **Swim at Slick Rock Recreation Area:** Plunge into pools surrounded by large, smooth boulders at this popular swimming spot (page 56).

Foothills

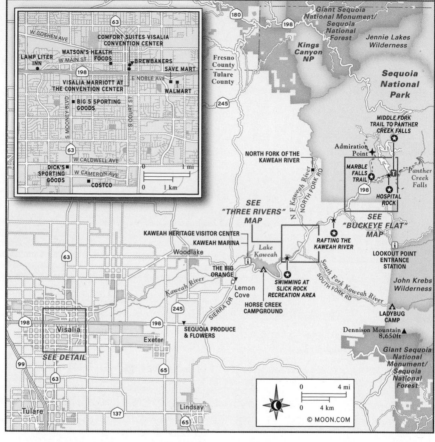

Visiting the Foothills is a great way to learn about the people who thrived here long ago. There is abundant evidence of many Native American groups who lived along the banks of the Kaweah River. Among the oak trees, it's possible to find grinding mortars, used to process acorns into edible food. At Hospital Rock, pictographs from hundreds of years ago depict snakes, birds, and celestial symbols. For a fuller understanding of Native American history and life in this area, stop into Foothill Visitor Center.

Though winter may mean closed roads through the rest of the park, the Foothills are a wonderful experience during this time—and the rest of the year, too. In the winter, you can hike to storm-powered waterfalls, like the booming Marble Falls. Visit from February to July for profusions of spring wildflowers, including the California poppy.

Previous: bridge across the Middle Fork of the Kaweah River; Three Rivers Brewing Company; Paradise Creek.

Where Can I Find...?

- **Accessible campgrounds:** The **Potwisha** and **Buckeye Flat Campgrounds** have accessible sites. At each campground is a vault restroom, the doors of which are heavy and can be difficult to maneuver.

- **ATM:** There are no ATMs in the park. In **Three Rivers,** there's an ATM at **Valley Oak Credit Union** (40870 Sierra Dr., 559/561-4471, http://valleyoak.org) and at the **Three Rivers Market** (41729 Sierra Dr., 559/561-4113), part of a Shell gas station.

- **Electric vehicle charging stations:** There are no EV chargers in this part of the park.

- **Gas:** There are no gas stations inside the park. The nearest gas is at **Stony Creek Lodge,** 12 miles (19 km) north of Lodgepole on the Generals Highway. Before entering the park, you can fill up in **Three Rivers** at **Shell** (41729 Sierra Dr., 559/561-4113).

- **Showers:** The nearest showers inside the park are in **Lodgepole Village.**

- **Shuttle:** For $20 per person, round-trip travel from Visalia and Three Rivers to Giant Forest is available on the **Sequoia Shuttle** (reservations required, 877/287-4453, http://sequoiashuttle.com, multiple trips daily summer). Pickup locations are in Visalia, Exeter, Lemon Cove, and Three Rivers.

- **Supplies:** Load up on groceries in **Fresno, Visalia,** or at the **Three Rivers Village Market** (40869 Sierra Dr., 559/561-4441, http://threeriversvillagemarket.com, 8am-8pm daily). For camping supplies like firewood, there is a small selection at **Kaweah General Store** (40462 Sierra Dr., 559/561-3475).

- **Telephones:** Within the park boundary there are pay phones at the **Hospital Rock picnic area** and **Foothill Visitor Center.**

- **Wi-Fi:** Free Wi-Fi is available at **Foothills Visitor Center.**

In the summer, splash around in the area's rivers. Return in the fall for the picture-perfect golden cottonwoods.

PLANNING YOUR TIME

In the Foothills area of Sequoia National Park, there are several hikes, sights, and dining options in close proximity to each other. Hospital Rock, 6 miles (10 km) from the Ash Mountain Entrance Station, marks the northern boundary of this part of the park. Within 30 minutes, you could be back in Three Rivers, having dinner by the river. From Three Rivers, it's another 30 minutes to reach Visalia.

For weekend warriors, it's easy to pair **one day** in the Foothills with a day in Giant Forest in any season. Arriving on a Friday evening, enjoy a nice meal in **Three Rivers** and retire to your campsite or hotel. On Saturday, enter the park early and spend the day in Giant Forest. Before driving back to Three Rivers, stop at **Hospital Rock.** On Sunday, spend the day hiking either the Marble Falls Trail or the **Middle Fork Trail to Panther Creek Falls.** If it's summer, end the day with a refreshing dip in the **swimming holes** near **Buckeye Flat Campground** before heading home.

If you have **four days,** take a more leisurely approach and explore some lesser-known parts of the Foothills. Plan for one day to explore **Hospital Rock,** peruse the **Foothills Visitor Center,** and hike to **Marble Falls.** On your second day, go **rafting** on the **Kaweah River.** On the third day, take the quiet hike to **Paradise Creek.** Spend your fourth day splashing around the natural pools at the boulder-lined **Slick Rock Recreation Area.**

There are several ways of approaching Grant Grove from the Foothills. The Generals Highway (Hwy. 198) is the most popular and scenic way to travel north, but, due to construction, traffic, and weather conditions, it may be faster to use Highways 216, 63, and 245, leaving the park via Three Rivers, then looping north to reach the Big Stump entrance, which leads to Grant Grove.

The Foothills area is open year-round. **Summer** (May-Sept.) is the busiest—and the hottest—time to visit. Temperatures regularly soar above 100°F (38°C) during the day, cooling off to 60-70°F (16-21°C) after sunset. Plan to hike in the early morning, visiting museums, swimming, rafting, or caving in the heat of the afternoon.

Autumn (Sept.-Nov.) and **spring** (Feb.-May) see cooler, more comfortable temperatures (60-80°F/16-27°C) and the weather is usually clear of storms. These are times when the park is generally less crowded and you are more likely to encounter wildlife like the coveys of quail or families of deer.

Winter (Dec.-Feb.) is a prime time for hiking. Despite temperate climes, there are few travelers except on holiday weekends. Precipitation usually comes as short bursts of rain, making the rare snowstorm an aesthetic treat.

Exploring the Foothills

VISITORS CENTERS
Foothills Visitor Center

Located 1 mile (1.5 km) northeast of the Ash Mountain entrance, the **Foothills Visitor Center** (Generals Hwy., 559/565-4212, 8am-4:30pm daily Apr.-Nov., 9am-4pm daily Dec.-Mar.) is staffed with rangers ready to answer visitor questions. Exhibits focus on ecology and how animals have adapted to this land of harsh summers and little water. This is a great place to identify the wildflowers, birds, and trees you have seen or want to see. Part of the visitors center is a bookstore and gift shop.

Also on site are restrooms, vending machines, and a water fountain. Outside you'll find a pay phone, plus RV parking and a water hookup. Self-serve wilderness permits are available at the visitors center. National Park Passport holders will want to stop in to collect one of five stamps available in the parks.

The visitors center also sells tickets for tours of Crystal Cave. It's a 45-minute drive to Crystal Cave from the visitors center. Tickets are not sold at the entrance of the cave.

Kaweah Heritage Visitor Center

For a quick introduction to dam construction, local wildlife, and Native American history, check out the **Kaweah Heritage Visitor Center** (34467 Sierra Dr., Lemon Cove, 559/597-2005, 10am-4pm Mon.-Fri., 7am-4pm Sat.-Sun., $4 day-use), which lies outside the park, southwest of Three Rivers. A vantage point from atop Lemon Hill affords views of the Lake Kaweah reservoir, the terminus dam, the steep foothills, and the nearby peaks. Stop in to admire the real bedrock mortars and taxidermied wildlife at the entrance. Also on-site is a Sequoia Conservancy bookstore (sales benefit the national parks).

ENTRANCE STATIONS

The **Ash Mountain Entrance Station** (Hwy. 198, open year-round, $35 vehicles, $30 motorcycles, $20 on foot or bike) is the Foothills entrance to the park. Past the entrance station, Highway 198 becomes the Generals Highway, leading north to the Giant Forest and Lodgepole regions of Sequoia National Park. Wait times at the entrance station vary, but can last up to 30 minutes in summer. Get here early, before 9am, to avoid a line on a summer weekend. The entrance station is not staffed 24 hours daily.

SCENIC DRIVES

During the summer, driving through the Foothills region can be a pleasant way to pass the hot afternoons. By car, you can witness what would otherwise take days of hiking to see: the landscape transitions from farms and orchards to oak-laden canyons and conifer forests. This drive on the Generals Highway, which spans 17 miles (27 km) from the Ash Mountain entrance to Crescent Meadow Road, takes approximately one hour. Note: Vehicles longer than 22 feet (6.5 m) are not advised on the section of highway from Potwisha Campground north to the Giant Forest Museum.

Start from the **Ash Mountain Entrance Station** and reset your odometer to better follow along with the mile markers described here.

At 0.8 mile (1.2 km), your first stop is at the tiny but beautiful **Foothills Visitor Center.** Inside, there is an abundance of information, including how species have adapted to the desert-like conditions in the Foothills, and books on every topic in the park. Get your parks passport stamped here before continuing north up the Generals Highway.

In 3.5 miles (6 km) you'll have another photo opportunity. At **Tunnel Rock,** a couple of boulders form a natural ledge that you can walk through. There are parking spots on either side of the rock.

At this point, the road climbs higher and gets curvier, all while the sun glints off of pools in the Middle Fork of the Kaweah River. There are vistas in every direction, and all are worth pausing for. After 3.7 miles (6 km), you'll reach one of the best attractions in the whole park. **Hospital Rock** is a large overhanging boulder with perfectly preserved pictographs made by the Patwisha people who once lived here. There's a picnic area with restrooms across the highway from the pictographs.

From here, you'll continue winding slowly northward, adding nearly a mile in elevation, from 1,700 feet (520 m) to 6,400 feet (1,950 m) by the time you reach Giant Forest. You'll get unparalleled views of Moro Rock above. There are two spots to safely pause for a view. Five miles (8 km) north from Hospital Rock is **Amphitheater Point.** This vista is located just after an extremely sharp hairpin turn in the highway. It offers magnificent views of Moro Rock and Castle Rocks. Continue up the Generals Highway another 1.5 miles (2.5 km) to reach the **Eleven Range Overlook.** Here, you can get a good view of Switchback Peak and Ash Mountain. On a clear day, you can see all the way west to the Coast Ranges, over 100 miles (160 km) away as the crow flies.

It's just 4 miles (6.5 km) farther along the Generals Highway until you reach the Giant Forest Museum and Crescent Meadow Road. (For more information about the scenic drive north of the Foothills region, see the *Giant Forest and Lodgepole* chapter.)

Sights

Most sights in the Foothills area are concentrated within 10 miles (16 km) along the Kaweah River.

TUNNEL ROCK

This massive boulder balanced on a precarious pillar somehow fights time and gravity. In the 1930s, the Civilian Conservation Corps dug beneath **Tunnel Rock** to create part of the Generals Highway. At the time, only one car at a time could pass beneath it. Though the road was eventually widened, today you can only walk underneath or on top of Tunnel Rock. Short trails climb to the top. There is room for parking on either side of the rock, but beware of traffic. From Ash Mountain Entrance Station, Tunnel Rock is 3.6 miles (6 km) north on Generals Highway.

★ HOSPITAL ROCK

Shaded by blue oaks and located within earshot of the Kaweah River, **Hospital Rock** was once the site of a vibrant indigenous Patwisha village. From 1350-1865, this was a bustling multi-lingual and multi-cultural site that was home to as many as 500 Patwisha people, a subset of the Western Monache (or Western Mono) group. Today, visitors can admire preserved Patwisha pictographs and artifacts from their daily life.

Hospital Rock is 6 miles (10 km) northeast of the Ash Mountain entrance. Visitor services include a telephone, potable water, flush toilets, and picnic tables, making this the best, last stop before ascending Generals Highway farther into the park.

From the picnic area, you can take a narrow dirt path that leads to an overlook of a small **waterfall** on the Middle Fork of the Kaweah.

Pictographs

Hospital Rock is the most spectacular and accessible **pictograph site** in the Foothills area. Across Generals Highway is a large, granitic boulder cleaved on one side. The overhanging slab is covered with Patwisha-created pictographs of snakes, birds, people, and celestial designs. Each measures 18-24 inches in length, painted with fingertips or brushes. Never touch pictographs—the oils from your hand can destroy them.

The pictographs are located across the highway from the Hospital Rock parking lot and picnic area. You'll need to climb a short set of steps to reach the pictograph viewing area.

Grinding Mortars

About 20 feet from Hospital Rock is a flat bedrock slab with notable depressions. These depressions, known as **grinding mortars,** were likely created by Patwisha women, who used river rocks as pestles to grind acorns into flour—a staple food.

The grinding mortars are located across the Buckeye Flat Campground entrance road, on the same side of Generals Highway as the pictographs.

AMPHITHEATER POINT

Many people breeze past this incredible vista, but a quick stop at picturesque **Amphitheater Point** should not be missed. Look to the east to spot the rounded dome of Moro Rock. Gaze south and across the canyon to Castle Rocks, a set of spindly granite towers. Amphitheater Point is located at an extremely sharp hairpin turn in the highway, 10 miles (16 km) north of the Ash Mountain entrance to the park. There's a small parking area on the north-bound side of the road. To get here from northern points in the park, you must cross traffic near a blind turn to park, so it's better to stop on your way into the park instead. This is one of the few places to stop on Generals Highway.

THREE RIVERS HISTORICAL MUSEUM

Just outside the Ash Mountain entrance, the **Three Rivers Historical Museum** (42268 Sierra Dr., 559/561-2707, www.3rmuseum. org, 9am-3pm daily Oct.-Mar., 9am-5pm daily Apr.-Sept., free, donations appreciated) greets travelers with a gigantic tribute to a fictional character of lumber lore: a burly statue of Paul Bunyan, complete with Babe the Blue Ox, carved from 40 tons of a sequoia tree. Inside, curated exhibits detail the story of the town of Three Rivers through historical housewares, braided rugs, and items of clothing. Special exhibits on nearby Mineral King include mining history and artifacts from the Wukchumni and Wuksachi indigenous groups, including burden baskets, baby carriers, and dwelling reconstructions.

1: the approach to Hospital Rock 2: pictographs at Hospital Rock 3: Tunnel Rock 4: Amphitheater Point

Foothills Hikes

Trail	Effort	Distance	Duration
Indian Head River Trail	easy	0.5 mi (0.8 km) rt	15-20 min
Potwisha to Hospital Rock via Middle Fork Trail	easy	2.5 mi (4 km) one-way	1 hr
Potwisha River Walk	easy	0.5 mi (0.8 km) rt	15-20 min
Marble Falls Trail	moderate	7.4 mi (11.9 km) rt	4 hr
Middle Fork Trail to Panther Creek Falls	moderate	6 mi (10 km) rt	3 hr
Paradise Creek	moderate	5.8 mi (9 km) rt	3-4 hr

Recreation

DAY HIKES

Rich in wildflowers and wildlife, the Foothills provide year-round beauty and solitude. The best season to hike is in autumn, when riverside cottonwoods turn gold. In spring, poppies paint the hillsides, but the weather is less predictable. You will find yourself mostly alone on many trails and nearly every hike ends with a stream to soak your feet in. To beat the summer heat, start hiking early in the morning. Although this is a warm area, wear long sleeves and pants to prevent exposure to ticks and poison oak.

Indian Head River Trail

Distance: 0.5 mile (0.8 km) round-trip
Duration: 15-20 minutes
Elevation change: 100 feet (30 m)
Effort: Easy
Trailhead: Indian Head River Trail
Directions: Drive 0.1 mile (160 m) past the Ash Mountain entrance. The trailhead is in a pullout on the east side of the road.

This trail offers a great introduction to the park, with views of Moro Rock, and is a good place to stretch your legs after a long drive. The trail leaves the bustle of the road and follows a narrow dirt path through California buckeye and oaks, down cement stairs to the swirls of the Kaweah River.

The trail is accessible from a pullout right after the Ash Mountain entrance to the park, but there is no signage for it. To find the trailhead, look for the historic Indian Head sign, which marks the entrance for Sequoia National Park. The sign was carved from a fallen sequoia in the 1930s. The image, a Native American's face in profile, was based on the Indian Head nickel and has no direct connection to the park itself.

Potwisha to Hospital Rock via Middle Fork Trail

Distance: 2.5 miles (4 km) one-way
Duration: 1 hour
Elevation change: 600 feet (180 m)
Effort: Easy
Trailhead: Potwisha Campground overflow parking
Directions: From Potwisha Campground, cross Generals Highway and enter the overflow parking lot. To find the trail, walk uphill 50 yards to the RV dump station and look for the small "Middle Fork Trail" sign.

This route once connected two Patwisha villages, following the Middle Fork of the Kaweah River. It's a gentle walk among the oaks that offers river views and leads to one of the area's best attractions, Hospital Rock.

Foothills Area Hikes

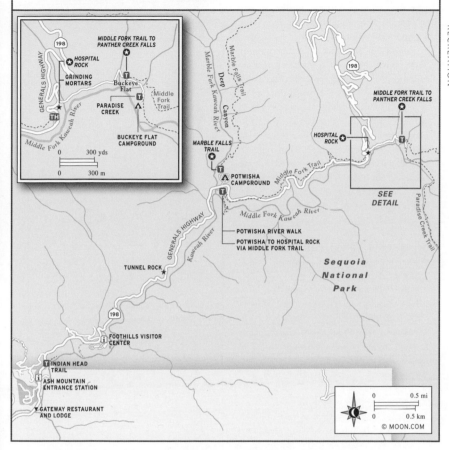

Starting from the overflow lot of Potwisha Campground, follow the trail as it heads east. At 0.5 mile (0.8 km), the trail crosses the Generals Highway and begins a more exposed journey above both the road and the river. The views are better here, but the sounds from the road are a bit more noticeable. Yucca, buckeye, and sacred datura, with their massive white blooms, line the trail as you approach the **Hospital Rock picnic area.** After a scenic woodland, the trail ends at the restrooms.

Unfortunately, there's no shuttle. Arrange for a pick up at Hospital Rock or return the way you came. It's also possible to hike this trail in the reverse direction, starting from the Hospital Rock picnic area.

Potwisha River Walk

Distance: 0.5 mile (0.8 km) round-trip
Duration: 15-20 minutes
Elevation change: None
Effort: Easy
Trailhead: Potwisha Campground overflow parking
Directions: From Potwisha Campground, cross Generals Highway and enter the overflow parking lot. The trailhead is at the south end of the lot.

Enjoy a quiet walk along the Middle Fork of the Kaweah River. This unmarked but well-worn trail leads to the river and well-preserved examples of Patwisha grinding mortars. As you examine the mortars, it's easy to imagine women seated by the river, working acorns into flour.

Across the river, look for an overhanging rock, which showcases some preserved pictographs. After tracing the shores of the river for 0.25 mile (0.4 km), the trail leads to a photogenic suspension bridge with wooden slats. Meander along the river banks or stop for a swim by the small sandy beach on the far side of the bridge. Be careful on the wet granite slickrock along the shore. The trail continues up the hillside, but it becomes brushy and peters out shortly after the climb. Return the way you came. This walk is beautiful year-round.

★ Marble Falls Trail

Distance: 7.4 miles (11.9 km) round-trip
Duration: 4 hours
Elevation change: 2,550 feet (780 m)
Effort: Moderate
Trailhead: Marble Falls
Directions: From the Ash Mountain entrance, drive 3.7 miles (6 km) on the Generals Highway. Turn left onto the Potwisha Campground road. Take the first left, then turn left again to reach the trailhead parking lot.

No matter the time of year, this long walk to Marble Falls is worth the trek. It is a mostly gradual, steady climb except for a short butt-kicking set of stairs near the end. Find the trailhead near site 14 at the northern end of Potwisha Campground. The exposed beginning of the trail follows a utility road for a short distance to a diversion dam. From there, the Marble Falls Trail veers right to a narrow uphill and brushy path. There are seven small canyons that you will pass, alternating through dry hillsides of shrubs and damp forests of big-leaf and vine maples. The scent of California bay laurel fills the air for the first 0.5 mile (0.8 km). Watch for colorful passerines and listen for the lovely songs of thrushes and wrens. Listen to the rush of the Marble Fork of the Kaweah River. At around 3.5 miles

Marble Falls Trail

(6 km), there is a bare rocky expanse. Open views lure you upward, along switchbacks. In 0.2 mile (0.3 km), you'll reach an overlook that offers a view of **Marble Falls,** where frothy water rushes over time-polished granite. Although several game trails continue up the canyon, this is your turnaround point. Return the way you came.

Poison oak is common along this trail, so wear long pants and sleeves to avoid it (and ticks). There's a small parking lot at the

Middle Fork Trail

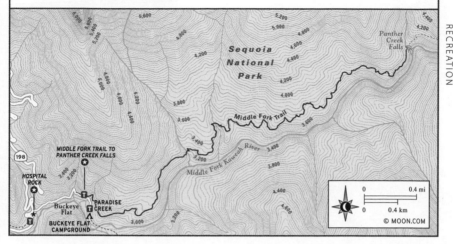

trailhead. If it's full, park across Generals Highway at the campground's overflow parking lot.

★ Middle Fork Trail to Panther Creek Falls

Distance: 6 miles (10 km) round-trip
Duration: 3 hours
Elevation change: 550 feet (170 m)
Effort: Moderate
Trailhead: Middle Fork
Directions: From the Ash Mountain entrance, drive 5.8 miles (9 km) northeast on the Generals Highway to Hospital Rock. Turn right onto the road to Buckeye Flat Campground. At 0.4 mile (0.6 km) down the road, veer left onto the dirt road. Follow this for 1.3 miles (2 km) to a parking area for the trailhead.

Few trails offer such an extensive experience within a few miles. The Middle Fork Trail provides broad views of the upper canyon of the Middle Fork of the Kaweah, Moro Rock, and spindly Castle Rocks. Panther Creek Falls—a 100-foot (30-m) drop to a large emerald pool surrounded by granite shores—provides a great picnic spot and a natural turn around point, though the trail continues eastward and upward. This trail also makes a great spring or fall backpacking

trip. (For more details, see the *Backpacking* section.)

From the trailhead to the waterfall is a single track trail that takes you along several miles of sunny chaparral. Oaks and buckeyes fill in the small canyons you pass, and drought-tolerant plants paint the hillsides. The exposed trail parallels the Middle Fork of the Kaweah. You won't always see it, but you'll be within earshot of it.

After 3 miles (5 km), the trail crosses just above **Panther Creek Falls,** overlooking the staggering 100-foot (30-m) flume. Look down and watch the water splashing into the granite pool below. After you've rested a bit, turn around and head back the way you came.

In winter, the road to Buckeye Flat may be closed. You'll need to park at Hospital Rock and walk to the trailhead. This will add 2.6 miles (4 km) to the hike's round-trip distance.

Paradise Creek

Distance: 5.8 miles (9 km) round-trip
Duration: 3-4 hours
Elevation change: 1,100 feet (340 m)
Effort: Moderate
Trailhead: Hospital Rock

Directions: From the Ash Mountain entrance, drive northeast for 5.8 miles (9 km) on the Generals Highway. Park in the lot for Hospital Rock.

This popular (but not crowded) Foothills hike features creekside beauty, a waterfall, and a unique view of Moro Rock—one that makes climbing it seem even more precarious. From the Hospital Rock parking lot, cross the Generals Highway and walk east down the road for 0.6 mile (1 km) to the southern part of Buckeye Flat Campground.

Join the Paradise Creek trailhead, across from campsite 28, and continue south along the trail. You'll pass an old fish hatchery and arrive at a bridge 0.2 mile (0.3 km) down the trail. Cross the Middle Fork of the Kaweah and continue following Paradise Creek Trail.

Wildflowers of every color dot the path and the smells of oak and bay laurel trees fill the air. At 0.8 mile (1.2 km) the trail enters a sparse pine and cedar forest. Look north to see Moro Rock's massive face gazing over the San Joaquin Valley a mile below.

You'll cross Paradise Creek at 1.3 miles (2 km) and again 0.1 mile (0.2 km) later. Continue uphill to a small, 15-foot waterfall. The toughest part of the trail is here, but the trek is worth it to stand at the base of the peaceful **Paradise Creek Falls.** Once you've had your fill of waterfall views, turn around here.

On the return, retrace your path along Paradise Creek Trail. Take the left before the bridge that's 0.2 mile (0.3 km) from the trailhead. This leads to a peaceful spot for a picnic and you can rest your feet in the Paradise Creek swimming hole. From there, it's just one final hill back to the trailhead.

BACKPACKING

In autumn, many of the Foothills' creeks will be empty, so bring plenty of water. In the spring, these creeks require careful crossings: Always unbuckle your backpack's hip belt (so that you can quickly remove it if you fall in), wear shoes, and walk with a buddy if you can. These two trips are beginner-friendly, but the start of Lady Bug is very remote. They both offer access to wilderness and solitude, and are great in the off-season.

Redwood Meadow via Middle Fork Trail

This is a trip for someone who wants to know the park from bottom to top, and experience its plethora of wildlife and plants along the way. This 22.6-mile (36-km) out-and-back trek starts in dry, oak-populated chaparral and climbs 3,000 feet (910 m) to Redwood Meadow, a secluded sequoia grove. This is the kind of wilderness experience that Sequoia is known for.

Starting from the Middle Fork trailhead near Buckeye Flat Campground, you will walk above the Middle Fork of the Kaweah River on a gradual climb—with some steep spurts and a couple of switchbacks. At 3 miles (5 km), you'll hear the splashes of **Panther Creek Falls,** which soon comes into view. Here, on the south side of the river is the first allowed spot for camping. Just below the falls is a large pool, a good place to stop for a break before continuing uphill.

As you approach the next creek crossing, observe the wilderness as it transitions from arid foothills to forest. A couple of nice **campsites** can be found at **Mehrten Creek** (6 mi/10 km in) and **Buck Creek** (9 mi/14 km in).

Just past Buck Creek, views of the Great Western Divide will accompany you as you climb for another mile to a trail junction. Turn right, enjoying the shade as you go. At the next trail junction, stay to the right again. Finally, after a half dozen switchbacks and 0.9 mile (1.5 km) of climbing, you've made it to **Redwood Meadow,** your final destination and turnaround point. There's a lot of brush on this narrow trail, so wear long pants to protect against poison oak and ticks.

1: view from the Indian Head River Trail 2: Middle Fork Trail

Ladybug Trail to Whiskey Log Camp

This 8.4-mile (13.5-km) round-trip journey offers seclusion and spring wildflowers. On this moderate out-and-back trip, you'll climb 1,600 feet (490 m) in a few short sections. The beginning of the trail crosses the South Fork of the Kaweah and graceful little waterfalls before quickly arriving at the barred entrance of Clough Cave, one of Sequoia and Kings Canyon's 200 limestone caverns. The trail continues east, traveling along the north shore of the South Fork. This part of the trail is a little faint and overgrown at times. In 1.9 miles (3 km), you'll arrive at **Ladybug Camp,** a flat camping spot along the river. Ladybugs, or ladybird beetles, gather here in the winter in such dense clusters that when they finally disperse in spring, they are picked up by radar.

From Ladybug Camp, the trail turns north to face Homer's Nose—a bulbous outcropping where a cluster of sequoias gather at the base. For the next 1.4 miles (2.2 km) you will be climbing and traveling above the river. At **Cedar Creek,** you'll encounter the lowest elevation sequoia—a singleton probably planted by a land slide in 1876. **Whiskey Log Camp** is down a short hillside at 4.2 miles (6.8 km) into the hike. This campsite is a great place to spend the night. In the morning, head back the way you came to return to the Ladybug trailhead.

The Ladybug trailhead is in a secluded part of the park. To get there from Three Rivers, turn onto South Fork Drive from Highway 198 in town. Follow this road for 12.7 miles (20 km) to South Fork Campground. The trailhead is on the east end of the campground. Pack sufficient drinking water; there's none at the campground.

BOATING AND RAFTING

When the temperatures heat up, there's no better way to experience the park than by getting on or in the water. Try paddling through rapids down the small but mighty Kaweah River or lounge on a party barge in Lake Kaweah with views of the mountains.

★ Rafting the Kaweah River

The **Kaweah River** is the steepest river in North America, which means that it drops faster in elevation per mile than any river on the continent. Whether this is your first time in a raft or you're an experienced river rat, the Kaweah makes for a nonstop aquatic adventure. The typical rafting season lasts from April to June; the season may extend if snowpack levels are higher than usual.

There are a few rafting outfitters in Three Rivers. Each offers half- and full-day trips, typically in 4- to 8-person rafts. For beginners and families, explore the lower 3 miles (5 km) on one of the many half-day trips. The more adventurous can try the full river or the upper half, where continuous class IV and higher rapids will keep your paddles busy.

For a down-to-earth adventure, sign up with **Kaweah Whitewater Adventures** (Mountain Rd. 349, Three Rivers, 559/740-8251, www.kaweah-whitewater.com, $40-80). The owner has been rafting and kayaking every crevice of this river since the 1970s, and most of the guides are locals. **Mountain Descents** (41667 Sierra Dr., Three Rivers, 559/601-0256, http://mountaindescents.com, $50-130) has great equipment and safety records, friendly guides, and a passion for rafting. This outfitter offers four trip options, ranging from an easy half-day to a full-day adventure.

Kayaking the Kaweah is another option, but it's not for the faint of heart. There are no whitewater kayak rentals available nearby; bring your own and drop it in at Hospital Rock in May for a trip to remember.

Boating

As far as reservoirs go, **Lake Kaweah** is a pretty great one, boasting mountain views, ample swimming and fishing spots, campgrounds, and a marina where you can rent boats. It's also relatively close to the park, located just 7 miles southwest (11 km) of Three Rivers. Early in the year (Feb.-May), the reservoir is fuller, making it feel more like a natural lake, and the hillsides are green from winter rains and full of golden poppies. This reservoir is relatively peaceful, with several coves that are shielded from the mountain winds.

The **Kaweah Marina** (34467 Sierra Dr., Lemon Cove, 559/597-2526, http://kaweah-marina.com, 8am-6pm daily May-Sept., 8am-4:30pm daily Oct.-Apr.) provides access to affordable, quality recreation options. Save the trouble of towing a boat on these mountain roads, and rent a patio boat (from $130) for a family barbecue or a fishing boat (from $70) to try for some of the lake's chunky bass and cautious trout. You can try stand-up paddleboarding, go kayaking, or head out on a four-person Aqua Cycle. Rates for SUP, kayak, and Aqua Cycle rentals start from $30 for one hour. There is a snack bar, fishing and tackle supplies, and convenience store at the marina. Always wear your life vest. The marina includes vests with boat rentals only. If you do not have a vest of your own, borrow one from the **Kaweah Heritage Visitor Center** (34467 Sierra Dr., Lemon Cove, 559/597-2005, 10am-4pm Mon.-Fri., 7am-4pm Sat.-Sun.). Borrowing a vest is free, but you'll need to show your drivers license and return the vest by the time the visitors center closes.

SWIMMING

The Foothills region offers a fine set of swimming holes, especially in the summer when temperatures soar over 100°F (38°C). In low-water years, you may be able to swim from April to August. Be careful: Swimming in winter and spring during peak runoff is hazardous. Every year people are injured or killed in Sierra streams, especially in the spring when water is swift and cold. Keep within arm's reach of children. Do not dive into the river from bridges. Life jackets are very helpful in this natural and unpredictable area. If you do not have one, borrow one for free at the **Kaweah Heritage Visitor Center** (34467 Sierra Dr., Lemon Cove, 559/597-2005, 10am-4pm Mon.-Fri., 7am-4pm Sat.-Sun.), on the southwest side of Lake Kaweah.

Buckeye Flat Swimming Holes

The Buckeye Flat Campground is close to some of the finest—and most popular—swimming holes in Sequoia. Several large, deep-green pools are surrounded by granite boulders and cascades. There are two solid options for swimming. The **main pool** is west of the campground. Several other **pools** lie along Paradise Creek Trail. To reach them, look for the Paradise Creek trailhead near

Lake Kaweah

campsite 28, cross a swinging bridge, and head upstream (left) on an unmaintained trail for your pick of pools. Many people bring inner tubes and party supplies.

To get to Buckeye Flat Campground from the Ash Mountain entrance, drive 6 miles (10 km) northeast on the Generals Highway. Park at the Hospital Rock picnic area (unless you have a reserved site at Buckeye Flat). Walk 0.6 mile (1 km) to the campground.

North Fork of the Kaweah

The area of the **North Fork of the Kaweah River** close to Yucca Creek and Old Colony Mill Road makes for a secluded swimming spot year-round, but especially from September to November. Sandy beaches speckle the black rock shores. Explore the shores of this river, beach towel in hand. This is also a good spot for fishing.

From Three Rivers, the 11-mile (18-km) drive takes over 30 minutes, traveling on paved and dirt roads. From Highway 198 in Three Rivers, turn onto North Fork Drive and cross over the Kaweah River. The pavement ends in 8 miles (13 km), after a hairpin turn. Keep going for another 2 miles (3 km) until you reach a notable split, which marks the western end of the Old Colony Mill Trail. Park at the left hand side of the fork or try your luck by heading farther up the left road for another 300 yards. On the left (west) is a driveway and a parking lot.

To the north is Yucca Creek (when it is running), but the swimming is better in the North Fork, directly west of the parking lot. You'll walk about 100 feet parallel to the boulders in the lot. Continue upstream until you find the water.

★ Slick Rock Recreation Area

Located at the upstream end of Lake Kaweah, 9 miles (14 km) southwest of the Ash Mountain entrance, the **Slick Rock Recreation Area** (39883 Sierra Dr., Three Rivers, 559/597-2301, 7am-6:30pm daily, $5) offers several options for enjoying nature: boating, fishing, hiking, barbecuing, birding, and especially, swimming. Several large flat boulders lend the area its name, forming a variety of pools that are perfect for swimming.

There are accessible restrooms, ample parking, potable water, pay phones, a boat ramp, and picnic tables here. Slick Rock can be crowded in spring and summer with sometimes-raucous visitors. Dogs are permitted. An easy 1-mile (1.5-km) trail will satisfy birdwatchers (look for Bewick's wrens in the parking lot). The area known as "The Boulder Beach" has a few top rope anchors for rock climbers. No alcohol or glass is allowed. Pay the day-use fee at one of two parking areas near the boat ramps.

FISHING

There are two main spots for fishing in this area: river and reservoir. In the springtime, go fly-fishing among the deep pools and rapids of the **Middle Fork of the Kaweah,** for small but colorful trout. Try the Middle Fork Trail from Potwisha Campground for easy access. Or rent a boat from the Kaweah Marina, tie on a spinner, and go trolling through the coves of **Lake Kaweah.**

A California fishing license is required and can be purchased online or in Three Rivers at the **Kaweah General Store** (40462 Sierra Dr., 559/561-3475) or **Three Rivers Mercantile** (41152 Sierra Dr., 559/561-2378), which carries plenty of tackle and camping gear. They even have grills to cook your buttered trout on!

BIRD-WATCHING

This area may not yield any especially exotic species of bird, but it does house the greatest diversity of birds anywhere in the park. The most common birds of the Foothills region are two cousins: the **California towhee,** a large drab sparrow with a red bottom that drags its tail through the brush, and the black-winged, white-speckled **spotted towhee,** with a long flicking tail and a reddish belly.

1: Slick Rock Recreation Area 2: bird-watching along the Kaweah River

Great blue herons skulk along the brush in the fall, **American dippers** flit in and out of the water and light along the creeks, even in winter, and **California quail** are ubiquitous, but difficult to see with their camouflage against the brush.

Take a trip along the **Marble Fork of the Kaweah River** for **passerines** and **wrens** hiding in the brush and **ravens** and **hawks** hovering above. The **Slick Rock Recreation** **Area** is home to many of the valley's birds, like pipits, gnatcatchers, and California quail, and it makes a great winter habitat for water birds like **mergansers.**

Winter migrants frequent the foothills and flock together: **chickadees, kinglets,** and **juncos** create a cacophony of chirps, feeding on the ground as early as November. Pick up a list of the area's birds at any visitors center and see how many different types you can spot.

Entertainment and Events

RANGER PROGRAMS

Ranger programs are held in two locations: **Potwisha Campground** and the **Foothills Visitor Center** (Generals Hwy., 559/565-4212, 8am-4:30pm daily Apr.-Nov., 9am-4pm daily Dec.-Mar.). To attend the free ranger programs at Potwisha Campground and the visitors center, just show up. No advance reservations are needed.

In summer (late May-early Sept.), ranger programs explore ecology, geology, and human history within the park. In winter, there are evening programs at **Potwisha Campground** (7pm Sat.) and a daily feature at **Foothills Visitor Center** (11am daily). Schedules are typically posted in the park newsletter or on bulletin boards in the area.

Outside of the park, the Army Corps of Engineers hosts campfire programs on a range of topics at **Horse Creek Campground** (37843 Sierra Dr., Lemon Cove, 559/597-2301, 7pm Sat. June-Aug.).

EVENTS

The rich tapestry of California foothills tribes comes alive at the annual Native American cultural celebration, **GO NATIVE!** (first weekend in May, free). Hosted by the National Park Service in collaboration with local tribal groups like the Yokuts, this public event occurs at the Foothills Picnic Area (near the Foothills Visitor Center). Opening with ceremonial drumming and a blessing, the event presents demonstrations of handicraft-making, traditional games, and other skills. Bring your own food and drink.

The Kaweah River keeps a steady beat behind the blast of brass and banjos at the annual **Three Rivers Jazz Affair** (www.jazzaffair.com, mid-Apr., $50-100). The celebration includes performances from a dozen live bands across three open-air venues throughout Three Rivers.

The annual **Redbud Arts & Crafts Festival** (Three Rivers Memorial Building, 43490 Sierra Dr., Three Rivers, 559/799-1473, www.artsalliancethreerivers.org, mid-May, free) showcases the region's best artists and artisans in a fun outdoor space with food and music. Proceeds from the event go to scholarships for local art students and to support art events in Three Rivers.

Food

The nearest food inside the park isn't until Giant Forest or Lodgepole. Stock up on snacks, sandwiches, boxed lunches, and groceries in Visalia and Three Rivers, or the farm stands between them.

OUTSIDE THE PARK
Three Rivers

No sport coat is needed for Three Rivers' swankiest dining and best river vistas at the **Gateway Restaurant and Lodge** (45978 Sierra Dr., 559/561-4133, http://gateway-sequoia.com, 8am-midnight daily, $25-50). The sports bar at the entrance is very casual, but farther in, the Visalia-raised chef prepares refined entrées: osso buco, surf and turf, and escargot—as well as homemade chips and hearty burgers. The restaurant offers solid brunch options, too. Reservations are recommended for holidays and summer, especially if you want to nab one of the romantic outdoor tables lit by candlelight.

At **The Buckaroo Diner** (41695 Sierra Dr., 559/465-5088, www.olbuckaroo.com, dinner Thurs.-Fri., breakfast, lunch, and dinner Sat.-Mon., $9-25), a sun room and picnic tables afford views of the Kaweah River. The restaurant serves artful comfort food, from ramen to grilled cheese, local beer, and fancy desserts, like earl grey crème brulée. Reservations are recommended. The owners also run the food truck **Ol' Buckaroo** (hours and days vary), parked right next door to the diner. The truck's globally inspired menu is different from the diner's, serving delightful dishes like lemon ricotta pancakes and Tex-Mex burritos.

Sierra Subs and Salads (41717 Sierra Dr., 559/561-4810, www.sierrasubsandsalads.com, 10:30am-6pm Tues.-Sat., 10:30am-3pm Sun., $10) has twice been deemed one of Yelp's Top 100 Places to Eat in the US (in 2017 and 2018), and it deserves the accolades. At this humble sandwich shop, choose from garlicky mayonnaise or housemade cilantro spread to adorn a sub piled with melty havarti, a garden of veggies, and a stack of meat on fresh bread. They also offer take-and-bake pizzas, gorgeous salads, and an assortment of bottled drinks. Eat in the air-conditioned/heated dining room or picnic by the riverside.

The **Pizza Factory** (40915 Sierra Dr., 559/561-1018, www.pizzafactory.com, 11am-9pm Mon.-Sat., noon-9pm Sun., $8-24) is a western US chain known for their small-town atmosphere and hand-tossed dough. When most other places are closed, you can get a fresh, generously sized pizza in about 20 minutes. This family-friendly spot also offers chicken wings, salads, pastas, and an arcade for kids. Choose from eight draft beers and grab a table outside to round out a big day of hiking.

Located next door to the Pizza Factory, **Casa Mendoza** (40869 Sierra Dr., 559/561-7283, 10am-8pm Sun.-Thurs., 10am-9pm Fri.-Sat., $9-14) is a family-run and family-friendly Mexican restaurant. Everything is made fresh to order, including the monster-sized burritos, taquitos, and chimichangas, which can all be made with any meat or grilled veggies. Breakfast is served until noon. There is Mexican bottled beer and wine available.

After a hard day of hiking, slake your thirst with a beer from one of five fresh taps at **Three Rivers Brewing Company** (41763 Sierra Dr., no phone, 11am-9pm Sun.-Mon., 11am-11pm Thurs.-Sat.). The owner, trained by master beer brewers, combines snowmelt, hops, and barley in his hand-built tanks for a perfectly balanced beer. Try the IPA that is made with Central Valley hops grown just 30 miles (48 km) away or the flagship Gravy Baby Stout. There's live music every Friday night and an awesome riverside patio. Wine is also available, but food is not—so bring your own.

Reward yourself on a hot day with homemade ice cream. **Reimer's Candies and Gifts** (42375 Sierra Dr., 559/561-4576, www.

Three Rivers

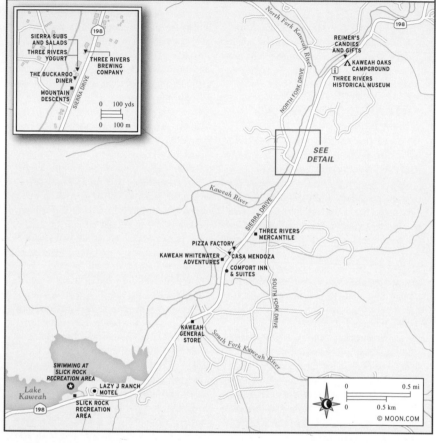

SIERRA SUBS
AND SALADS
THREE RIVERS
YOGURT
THREE RIVERS
BREWING
THE BUCKAROO COMPANY
DINER
MOUNTAIN
DESCENTS

198

SIERRA DRIVE

0   100 yds
0   100 m

North Fork Kaweah River

NORTH FORK DRIVE

198

REIMER'S
CANDIES
AND GIFTS
KAWEAH OAKS
CAMPGROUND
THREE RIVERS
HISTORICAL MUSEUM

SEE
DETAIL

Kaweah River

SIERRA DRIVE

THREE RIVERS
MERCANTILE

PIZZA FACTORY
KAWEAH WHITEWATER   CASA MENDOZA
ADVENTURES
COMFORT INN
& SUITES

SOUTH FORK DRIVE

KAWEAH
GENERAL
STORE

South Fork Kaweah River

SWIMMING AT
SLICK ROCK
RECREATION AREA
LAZY J RANCH
MOTEL
Lake
Kaweah
SLICK ROCK
RECREATION
AREA

198

0   0.5 mi
0   0.5 km
© MOON.COM

reimerscandies.com, 10am-6pm daily, $6) channels a fairy tale vibe in their little red gingerbread house. This shop offers something for every kind of sweet tooth, and some good souvenirs to boot. They make everything in-house, including fudge, nut brittles, and delightful waffle cones with the just-right level of sweetness. Ice creams are made with local fruit like blackberries and peaches. They take cash only in the ice cream shop.

Get a low-fat dessert option at **Three Rivers Yogurt** (41727 Sierra Dr., 559/690-1286, noon-4pm daily Oct.-Apr., noon-7:30pm daily May-Sept.). This immaculate fro-yo shop has a backyard overlooking the Kaweah River and offers a rotation of flavors named for regional highlights, such as Highway 198 Strawberry Stand and the vegan Alta Peak Almond. You can sample flavors before you build your own dessert, adding toppings from wall-hung cylinders. You'll weigh your creation and pay by the ounce. The shop is next door to Sierra Subs and Salads.

Exeter

Off of Highway 198 near Exeter and Lemon Cove, there are several farm stands selling local produce. **Sequoia Produce & Flowers** (20940 Ave. 296, 559/592-0022, 9am-5pm daily) is a fancy take on a fruit stand. Outside you'll find unusual citrus like oro bianco and cara cara oranges, fresh peaches and lemons, and a funky patio that houses a replica Statue of Liberty. Inside the highly decorated space, you can sample locally made toffees and pick up gourmet avocado-blossom honey, barbecue sauces, and olive oils.

Visalia

Before everyone had a brewery in their garage, **Brewbakers** (219 E. Main St., 559/627-2739, http://brewbakersbrewingco.com, 11:30am-10pm Mon.-Thurs., 11am-10pm Fri.-Sun., $10-20) was cooking up some solid beers in downtown Visalia. Since 1999, they've kept Visalia happy with Central Valley hops poured into a delicate IPA. To accompany your beer, order some of their hot, tasty food or a creative sandwich.

Accommodations

The closest hotels inside the park are in Lodgepole. Many people spend a night in the Foothills before or after their time in Lodgepole and Giant Forest. If your goal is to stay out of the snow in the winter, it's best to stay in Three Rivers, which is at a lower elevation than Lodgepole. Visalia is the closest large town. A shuttle runs in the summer from Visalia, via Three Rivers, to Giant Forest.

OUTSIDE THE PARK
Three Rivers

Classic, clean, and convenient, **Comfort Inn & Suites Sequoia Kings Canyon** (40820 Sierra Dr., 866/892-7671, www.choicehotels.com, $175-300) has 26 modern and spacious suites that include a dining area and sleeper sofa, coffee table, and large bathroom. The standard rooms are basic but very clean. A simple continental breakfast with bottomless coffee is included in the rate. Amenities include a pool, spa, and workout machines. It's just 5 miles (8 km) from the park.

A number of motels and hotels dot the highway leading into the park, including the riverside **Lazy J Ranch Motel** (39625 Sierra Dr., 559/561-4449, www.lazyjranchmotel.com, $100-200), which offers motel rooms and cozy cottages that sleep up to six people. Amenities include free breakfast and a playground.

Visalia

Many chain hotels are located along Highway 198 in Visalia, approximately a 30-minute drive from the Ash Mountain Entrance Station. **Visalia Marriott at the Convention Center** (300 S. Court St., 559/636-1111, www.marriott.com, $150-250) has a modern décor and an outdoor pool, 24-hour gym, and meeting space if you need to sneak in a little work while on vacation. Choose from a standard queen or king room, or opt for one of the executive rooms or suites. Located on higher floors of the hotel, the executive rooms offer pleasant views of the distant mountains. The shuttle to Sequoia stops here.

With 72 rooms, free parking, and an included hot breakfast, the **Comfort Suites Visalia Convention Center** (210 Acequia Ave., 559/738-1700, www.choicehotels.com, $90-200) is a convenient home base for trips to Sequoia. Even better, the Sequoia Shuttle picks up right here. All of the rooms are suites, with separate bedrooms and sofa bed-equipped living rooms. Call ahead to reserve an ADA-compliant room with roll-in shower.

The **Lamp Liter Inn** (3300 W. Mineral King Ave., 559/732-4511, www.lampliter.net, $80-160) is a popular, casual, and economical motel with 100 rooms and a conference center. The rooms are basic but clean. The motel's outdoor corridors surround a pool and garden. Also available are cottages with two queen beds, a wet bar, and a patio overlooking the garden. The ADA-compliant rooms have two different types of showers, so call ahead to ensure you get the type you need. The motel's on-site, diner-style restaurant is open all day and offers simple fare. They have a happy hour Monday through Saturday. Conveniently, the shuttle to Sequoia stops here.

Camping

INSIDE THE PARK

Conditions for camping in the Foothills region are ideal thanks to the mild weather—even in the summer, as the nights usually cool off. There are no group campsites in this part of the park.

The **Potwisha Campground** (www.recreation.gov, year-round, $22) is right on the Marble Fork of the Kaweah River and close to the confluence with the Middle Fork, offering the peaceful sounds of the river, a cool, down-canyon breeze, and a grove of trees. The 48 sites here are generally only available with an advance reservation; in winter, 38 of the sites are first-come, first-served. This is the only campground in the Foothills that's open year-round and offers services. It's also the closest to the Ash Mountain entrance. This is an ideal spot for hikers, fishers, and swimmers, thanks to features like food storage, flush toilets, a pay phone, and multiple nearby trailheads. Campsites 16, 18, 20 are the most beautiful and spacious, though some smaller tent sites on the upper loop are nice, too. There are pull-through sites for RVs, but no dump station. Ranger programs are offered here from July to September. The campground is about 4 miles (6 km) northeast of the Ash Mountain entrance, just off the Generals Highway.

Leave behind bustling Hospital Rock and turn down a narrow, curvy road for a riverside abode at **Buckeye Flat Campground** (www.recreation.gov, Mar.-Oct., $22). Of the campground's 28 tent-only sites, only one (site 20) is suitable for wheelchairs. Riverside sites are 13, 14, and 16-19. The best overall sites are 11 and 12. Picnic tables, fire rings, food storage, flush toilets, and drinking water are available. There's no electricity. Day trippers and additional vehicles must park approximately a mile

Potwisha Campground

up the road. Peak season is April-September. All sites are available by reservation only.

If you're looking for solitude—or if the other Foothills campgrounds are full, stay at **South Fork Campground** (year-round, no reservations, $6), a primitive campground with 10 tent-only, first-come, first-served sites. South Fork is a great base camp for hiking or backpacking the Ladybug Trail or along the South Fork of the Kaweah River. There's no running water here, so bring your own. There are vault toilets. It's a 13-mile (21-km) drive from Three Rivers via South Fork Drive. The road is rough and not recommended for low-clearance vehicles.

OUTSIDE THE PARK

On the shore of Lake Kaweah reservoir, **Horse Creek Campground** (37843 Sierra Dr., Lemon Cove, 559/597-2301, www.recreation.gov, $20-40) provides boaters and fishers access to amenities like flush toilets, showers, and a dump station, but little shade or protection from scorching temperatures (100°F/38°C and above) and winds. Though tent camping is possible here, those in RVs will have more company and protection from the elements. The campground has 80 sites, available by reservation only, most of which have fire pits. Horse Creek is a 20-minute drive from the Ash Mountain entrance.

A grove of oaks hides the privately owned **Kaweah Oaks Campground** (42362 Sierra Dr., Three Rivers, 559/561-3602, http://kaweahoakscampground.com, $20) from the busy road. Book online to reserve one of the campground's 13 walk-in, tent-only sites. Each site has a dirt pad and picnic table. No pets are allowed. There is a pit toilet, a shower, and electricity in the common area. Kaweah Oaks is about 5 miles (8 km) from the Ash Mountain entrance.

Transportation and Services

DRIVING AND PARKING

Road construction is a constant in Sequoia, thanks to the mountainous terrain, erosion, and rockslides. Every traveler on the Generals Highway, including bicyclists, will be impacted by road construction. Roads are often limited to one lane and delays can be up to two hours. To reduce your time in the car, leave early; traveling before 7am limits delays to 20 minutes. Alternately, leave late; traveling after 7pm also limit delays to 20 minutes. Check with the Foothills Visitor Center or the Ash Mountain Entrance Station for the latest construction schedule. No vehicles over 22 feet (7 m) are allowed between Hospital Rock and Giant Forest.

Lines at the Ash Mountain entrance can back up for about 20 minutes at peak visitation times (9am-3pm on summer weekends). Arrive early to avoid the rush. If you purchase your park pass online, you'll be waved around the long line of cars into an express lane on summer weekends.

Parking in the Foothills is typically a simpler affair than in other parts of the park. The parking lot at **Hospital Rock** generally has spots for passenger vehicles, but is a little tight for RVs. The dirt parking lot at **Potwisha Campground** is accessible to most vehicles. The **Foothills Visitor Center** has overflow parking.

SHUTTLES

The free Lodgepole and Giant Forest shuttles do not service the Foothills area. Instead, a fee-based service offered by **Sequoia Shuttle** (877/287-4453, www.sequoiashuttle.com, May-Sept., $20 round-trip) ferries passengers from Visalia, Three Rivers, and other nearby towns into the park. The shuttle makes multiple trips daily, picking up at hotels in Visalia, Exeter, Lemon Cove, and Three Rivers for drop-off at the Foothills Visitor Center and the Giant Forest Museum. Advance reservations are required. The shuttle has bike racks, luggage storage, and is wheelchair accessible. The travel time is 1.5-2.5 hours. Rates include the park entrance fee.

SERVICES

It's best to fuel up before entering the park in **Three Rivers**. Otherwise, you'll need to head north of Lodgepole, if you're running low on gas. About 12 miles (19 km) north of the Lodgepole Visitor Center, **Stony Creek Lodge** (65569 Generals Hwy., 559/565-3909) has 24-hour credit card gas pumps in the summer.

In Three Rivers, **Totem Market and Gifts** (45186 Sierra Dr., 559/561-4463, 7am-7pm daily) has plenty of picnic supplies, with fancy cheeses, assorted beverages, and a full deli.

Jerky This! (42362 Sierra Dr., 559/561-3602, http://jerkythis.com) carries bison, beef, and fish jerkies great for high-protein hiking.

At the Shell station, **Three Rivers Market** (41729 Sierra Dr., 559/561-4113, 6am-10pm daily) carries beer, wine, liquor, and snack foods.

Visalia is the largest nearby town. Its quaint downtown features eclectic dining options, curious shops, a historic theater, and a cute brick pathway. Visalia is also where you'll find major grocery stores, including **Walmart** (1819 E. Noble Ave., 559/636-2302, www.walmart.com), **Costco** (1405 W. Cameron Ave., 559/735-2400, www.costco.com) and **Save Mart** (1591 E. Noble Ave., 559/636-8405, www.savemart.com). Specialty markets in Visalia include **Watson's Health Foods** (617 W. Main St., 559/732-3866, www.watsonshealthfoods.com, 9am-6pm Mon.-Fri.), a veggie lover's treat, and a great place for sandwiches at the in-store deli.

If you need camping or backpacking gear while in Visalia, stop into **Dick's Sporting Goods** (3637 S. Mooney Blvd., 559/636-0633, www.dickssportinggoods.com, 9am-9:30pm daily) or **Big 5 Sporting Goods** (1430 S. Mooney Blvd., 559/625-5934, www.big-5sportinggoods.com, 10am-9pm daily). The stores are within a mile of each other and close to the highway.

Giant Forest and Lodgepole

If you only have one day in Sequoia National Park, Giant Forest is your stop. After realizing no two sequoias are the same, you'll return again and again, to meet them all.

Why not start with the largest living thing on earth, the General Sherman Tree? From there, take a short trip along the Congress Trail to meet more forest denizens (noisy chickaree squirrels and a variety of woodpeckers), not to mention clusters of sequoias. This special forest is open all year, for hiking in the warmer months and snowshoeing in winter, and there are plenty of paved, flat trail options too. Follow the road out to Crescent Meadow to climb Moro Rock for great views or visit the "tree you can drive through." To really understand the foundation of the park, take a guided tour into

Highlights

Look for ★ to find recommended sights, activities, dining, and lodging.

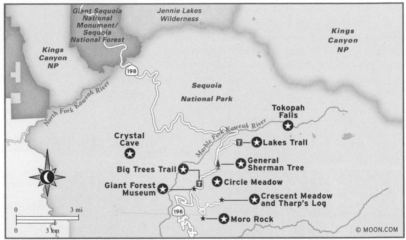

Giant Sequoia National Monument/ Sequoia National Forest

Jennie Lakes Wilderness

Kings Canyon NP

Kings Canyon NP

198

Sequoia National Park

North Fork Kaweah River

Tokopah Falls ★

Marble Fork Kaweah River

Crystal Cave ★

★ Lakes Trail

Big Trees Trail ★

★ General Sherman Tree

Giant Forest Museum ★

★ Circle Meadow

★ Crescent Meadow and Tharp's Log

0   3 mi

0   3 km

198

★ Moro Rock

© MOON.COM

★ **Explore the Giant Forest Museum:** This beautiful museum features informative exhibits about the surrounding giants. It's also a good spot to visit with a park ranger (page 69).

★ **Look up at General Sherman Tree:** Join hundreds of revelers to gawk at the largest living tree on earth (page 72).

★ **Ascend Moro Rock:** Climb 400 stone stairs to reach exhilarating views of the High Sierra and San Joaquin Valley (page 72).

★ **Go Underground at Crystal Cave:** Take a guided tour to see this cave's unique marble formations for yourself (page 74).

★ **Hike to Tokopah Falls:** It's a fairly flat hike to this ripping waterfall, where you might hear pikas chirping (page 77).

★ **Follow the Lakes Trail:** It's a rare opportunity to be able to hike to an alpine lake not far from a major road; this trail gives you the chance to stop at four different ones (page 78).

★ **Walk the Big Trees Trail:** Follow this paved loop that circles Round Meadow to enjoy the sights of sequoias, wildflowers, and wildlife (page 79).

★ **Hike around Circle Meadow:** The Congress Trail circles this less-visited meadow, showing off a quieter side of Giant Forest (page 81).

★ **See Crescent Meadow and Tharp's Log:** This dazzling alpine meadow hike gets you up close and personal with a fallen sequoia that was converted into a home in the 1860s (page 81).

Giant Forest and Lodgepole

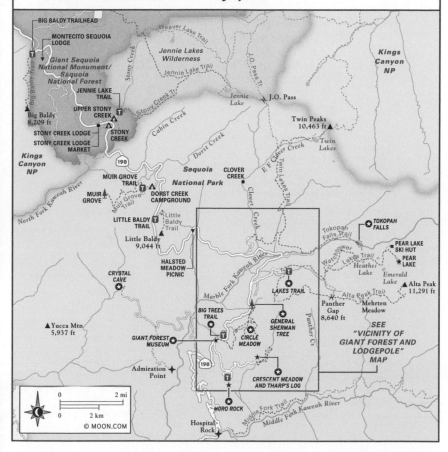

Crystal Cave, a miraculous vein of limestone transformed into stunning underground rock formations.

The larger Lodgepole area offers hikers a surplus of beauty, from Tokopah Falls to high meadows, lakes, and granite domes. Many people pass through Lodgepole, gazing at the big trees from their car on the way to somewhere else—but this is a mistake. Stop and give yourself time to truly admire the natural wonders before you. These trees have been stretching to the sky for thousands of years. And, believe it or not, the trees aren't the oldest natural marvels you'll encounter. Older still is the granite carved by glaciers. You could spend an entire lifetime admiring the magnificent landscape. After a full day, the perfect way to relax is a nice meal at the Peaks in Wuksachi Lodge or a barbecue at Wolverton Picnic Area. For those on a budget, set up your tent at Lodgepole Campground. The sites next to the Marble Fork of the

Previous: hiking through the Giant Forest; visitors demonstrating the width of the General Sherman Tree; Tharp's Log.

Where Can I Find...?

- **Accessible campgrounds:** The **Lodgepole** and **Dorst Creek Campgrounds** have accessible sites, but have varying degrees of level ground. Book an RV site for the most level options.

- **Accessible trails and attractions:** The trail leading to the **General Sherman Tree** from the accessible parking lot is paved and avoids steep climbs and stairs. The **Big Trees Trail** is a combination of pavement and boardwalk and is flat.

- **ATM:** There are ATMs at **Lodgepole Market** and **Wuksachi Lodge. Stony Creek Lodge** on Highway 198 has an ATM in the market. Most places will accept major credit cards.

- **Electric vehicle charging stations:** There's a wall outlet available at **Wuksachi Lodge.**

- **Gas:** There are no gas stations inside the park. Fill up before entering in **Three Rivers, Dunlap,** or **Squaw Valley.** The nearest gas is at **Stony Creek Lodge,** 12 miles (19 km) north of Lodgepole on the Generals Highway.

- **Showers:** The only place to shower in the park is **Lodgepole Market.** Shower hours run from 7am-1pm and 3pm-6pm daily.

- **Shuttle:** The park's hybrid buses travel several convenient routes through the area every 15 minutes. The main stops are at Dorst and Lodgepole Campgrounds, Lodgepole Market and Visitor Center, Giant Forest Museum, and the General Sherman Tree. Some routes go to Wolverton and Moro Rock/Crescent Meadows. The shuttles run all summer, 8am-6pm daily, and are free.

- **Supplies:** Find camping and hiking gear, as well as snowshoe rentals at **Lodgepole Market.** Snowshoes can also be rented from **Wuksachi Lodge.**

- **Telephones:** Depending on your carrier, very spotty cell phone service can be found along the **Generals Highway,** as well as at **Beetle Rock** and between **Dorst Creek Campground** and **Little Baldy.** Sometimes text messaging works at **Wuksachi Lodge. Lodgepole Market, Wuksachi Lodge,** both **campgrounds,** and **Wolverton Picnic Area** have **pay phones.** There's also a pay phone outside of the market at **Stony Creek Lodge.**

- **Wi-Fi:** You can connect to the internet in the lobby of the **Wuksachi Lodge.** If you're a guest of **Montecito Sequoia Lodge,** you may use their internet, available in the restaurant.

Kaweah River are so peaceful that the rangers live here, too.

PLANNING YOUR TIME

The landscape consists of many little enclaves here: the sunny slopes surrounding **Dorst Creek** and **Wuksachi Lodge,** the nestled canyon of **Lodgepole,** and the expansive circle of big trees in **Giant Forest.** Luckily, everything is within 40 minutes of each other, thanks to the area's shuttle system.

With a **full day** in Giant Forest and Lodgepole, you can easily hit most of the

area's highlights. Start the day with a visit to the **General Sherman tree** then take the shuttle to the **Big Trees Trail** or meander along **Congress Trail.** If you're hungry for some background on the park, pop by the **Giant Forest Museum.** In the afternoon, pack a picnic and head to **Beetle Rock** for a late lunch with a view of Lodgepole. Time permitting, you could tack on **Tokopah Falls** in early summer.

To tour **Crystal Cave,** you'll need to budget at least half a day. The temperature of the cave is a cool 50°F (10°C), unaffected by the external weather. Pack layers, even in the summer.

Over a **weekend,** you can split your time between Giant Forest on your first day and around Lodgepole on the second. Traveling between the two areas is easy on the shuttle, but it's not always the most efficient mode of transportation. Though weekends are crowded on **Moro Rock,** the view from the top is worth it. If you'd like fewer stairs and people but equal vistas, try **Beetle Rock** or a bigger hike to **Little Baldy.** For more views after a challenging climb, opt for **Alta Peak.** With a **week,** you will have the freedom to explore, try something new, and enjoy everything this area has to offer—all without feeling rushed.

Most park visitors come in the **summer,** but Lodgepole has enough room for everyone. Between Memorial Day and August, every campground and trail fills with people. Late August is when the crowds begin to thin. This is a great time to visit, as the weather is excellent through October. **Autumn** (Sept.-Oct.) brings brisk, starry nights and even fewer crowds, but most waterfalls dry up and trails can be quite dusty. **Winter** (Nov.-Feb.) is a quiet time, when you can admire the snowy landscape. You'll need to brave the bitter cold and icy driving conditions, though. In **spring** (Mar.-May), the snow melts and wildflowers and dogwoods bloom. This is an ideal time for photographers to visit, as there will be few other visitors in the park.

Exploring Giant Forest and Lodgepole

VISITORS CENTERS
Lodgepole Visitor Center

Stop by the **Lodgepole Visitor Center** (63100 Lodgepole Rd., 559/565-4436, www.nps.gov/seki, 7am-5pm daily May-Nov.) for informative videos, planning information, and helpful tips from local guides and rangers. The theater shows a 20-minute video that offers information on the area's history. The **wilderness desk** can advise on the best day hikes, set you up with an overnight backcountry permit, rent out a bear canister, or discuss trail conditions. Also at the visitors center is a bookstore run by the Sequoia Parks Conservancy, selling souvenirs, books, and stuffed animals. The visitors center is conveniently located at the first turnoff for Lodgepole, next to the market and less than half a mile from the campground. It's a great place to park your car and hop on the shuttle to the more crowded Giant Forest trailheads.

Wheelchairs can be rented for free from the visitors center (and the Giant Forest Museum) and can be used anywhere in the parks. You

will need to provide your name and phone number and return the wheelchair at the end of the day.

★ Giant Forest Museum

The **Giant Forest Museum** (Hwy. 198, 16 mi/26 km north of Ash Mountain entrance, 559/565-4480, www.nps.gov/seki, 9am-6pm daily mid-May-mid-Nov., 9am-4:30pm daily mid-Nov.-mid-May) offers visitors a chance to get to know the largest trees in the world through interesting exhibits on size comparisons, fire ecology, and history. Visit with rangers stationed at the front desk or participate in a ranger program in front of the Sentinel Tree. Stop in the small bookstore, which features books of all kinds, jewelry, hand-thrown pottery mugs, stuffed animals, and coloring books.

The museum's central location makes it a great jumping off point for hikes. Here you'll also find water fountains and restrooms. There's an accessible parking lot just west of the museum. Across the street you can get beautiful sunset views from Beetle Rock. The only thing missing here is food.

Vicinity of Giant Forest and Lodgepole

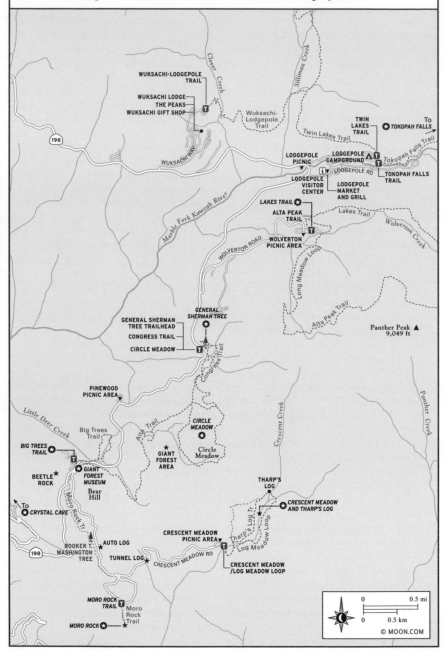

ENTRANCE STATIONS

The vehicle entrance fee is $35 for Sequoia and Kings Canyon National Parks. Giant Forest and Lodgepole are accessible from the Ash Mountain entrance in the Foothills region or by driving south along the Generals Highway from the Big Stump entrance at Grant Grove.

TOURS

Take a guided day trip of Giant Forest with **Sequoia Sightseeing Tours** (559/561-4189, www.sequoiatours.com, $99 children, $149 adults, cost covers park entrance fee). Offering an insider's experience of this part of Sequoia National Park throughout the year, the tour also includes a picnic lunch. Tours depart from Three Rivers. Another tour option visits Kings Canyon.

SCENIC DRIVES

The **Generals Highway** (Hwy. 198) stretches from Grant Grove in the north to the Foothills in the south, but this 19-mile (31-km) scenic drive covers just the greatest hits of the Lodgepole and Giant Forest sections, spanning from Dorst Creek Campground to Crescent Meadow. Traffic permitting, it can take as little as an hour to drive this section, but if you stop at all the sights along the way, budget up to four hours so you're not rushing. (For more details on the northern portion of the drive, see the *Grant Grove* chapter. To continue south, see the *Foothills* chapter.)

Start your drive at **Dorst Creek Campground.** Turn onto Dorst Creek Road and park along the side of the road after about 0.2 mile (0.3 km). Hop out of the car and look to the east to check out beautiful **Dorst Creek Meadow,** speckled with wildflowers in spring. At the end of the campground road, you can hike the **Muir Grove Trail** to better explore this area.

Exit the campground and turn right to head south on the Generals Highway for 5 miles (8 km). On the right is a pullout marking the **Halstead Meadow Picnic Area.** It's worth a stop, especially in the early spring,

to look for resident black bears foraging for grasses.

Continue heading southeast along the Generals Highway and enjoy the next 2 miles (3 km) of rolling, beautiful road. As your car dashes between the slanting light of this open forest, look for signs of past forest fires. Turn left onto Wuksachi Way and drive for about half a mile to reach **Wuksachi Lodge.** The road climbs above a granite ridge and reveals the peaks of the Silliman Crest and the upper watershed of the Marble Fork of the Kaweah River. The Wuksachi people once lived in this canyon; one of the last fluent speakers of the Wuksachi language, Eddie Sartuche, helped name the lodge. Stop at the lodge to visit its gift shop, or enjoy a bite at the elegant restaurant, **The Peaks.**

Head back the way you came on Wuksachi Way, then turn left to get back on the Generals Highway heading east. Continue another 2.3 miles (3.5 km) and turn left to reach the **Lodgepole** section of the park. Friendly rangers are on staff at the **Lodgepole Visitor Center,** ready to answer questions. If you're interested in adding a hike to your stop, you can access the trail to **Tokopah Falls** from this area. If you need a snack, stop into the **Lodgepole Market Center.**

Now it's time to make your way into the Giant Forest. From Lodgepole, turn left to head south again on the Generals Highway. In 1.5 miles (2.5 km), turn left onto Wolverton Road. Continue along the road for another 0.5 mile (0.8 km), then turn right, following signs for the General Sherman Tree. It's another 0.7 mile (1.1 km) on this road to reach the parking lot. Hop out of the car to pay a visit to the **General Sherman Tree,** the largest living tree on the planet. After you've craned your neck to admire General Sherman's beauty from all possible angles, you may want to check out the nearby **Congress Trail** to get a feel for this part of the forest.

Return to your car and exit the parking lot. Turn left onto Wolverton Road, then left again to get back on the Generals Highway heading south. This part of the road winds through the dappled shadow and sunlight of the Giant Forest. The sequoias loom above. The temptation to reach out and touch them is great. Drive slowly, windows open or top down. After 2.7 miles, you'll reach the **Giant Forest Museum,** a grand modern tribute to the trees. On the left of the museum is a beautiful lookout spot called **Beetle Rock.**

If Crescent Meadow Road is open, take the left turn after the Giant Forest Museum. (The road is closed to vehicles on summer weekends and holidays. During this time, you must take a shuttle to get to any of the sites along the road.) This 1.8-mile (3-km) spur road offers amazing views as it skirts the southern end of Giant Forest, ending at **Crescent Meadow.** Sights along the way include **Moro Rock, Tunnel Log,** and several named sequoias like the **Colonel Young Tree,** the **Booker T. Washington Tree,** and the **Roosevelt Tree.** From Crescent Meadow, you can walk along the flat path to **Tharp's Log.**

Sights

★ GENERAL SHERMAN TREE

At the windy northern edge of a sunny, open part of the forest, the **General Sherman Tree** is a magnificent natural wonder. It's the largest living tree on the planet—275 feet tall, over 36 feet wide at its base, and weighing an estimated 2.5 million pounds. About the size of the Statue of Liberty, this tree is estimated to be 2,300-2,700 years old. You can easily visit the tree in 15-30 minutes, but you'll likely want more time to spend gazing in awe.

As many as 500 people will visit the tree within an hour during high season, so be prepared to wait for your photo op—or simply go to the back side of the tree. General Sherman is distinguishable from the other trees by its sheer size, so you won't need to see the name plate on the front.

The park service has made visiting the tree easy for everyone. The main parking lot is off Wolverton Road. It opens onto a 0.5-mile (0.8-km) path to the tree; it's paved, but has a few stairs along it. There's also a parking lot designated for visitors with disability placards. From this lot, there's a wheelchair-accessible path to the tree. The shuttles stop at this accessible lot as well as the main lot.

★ MORO ROCK

The granite dome known as **Moro Rock** protrudes over a mile above sea level and thousands of feet above the surrounding landscape. You can climb to the top of this rounded bulb to gain panoramic views from the Sierra Nevada peaks to the Central Valley below. This is a strenuous, short climb: 400 granite stairs ascending 300 feet (90 m) in a very short distance. It takes about 20 minutes to complete, but the views along the way and at the top are so grand you will want to allow for at least an hour for your trek.

Moro Rock is conveniently located near Giant Forest Museum. **Shuttles** (Gray Route, 8am-6pm daily summer, free) depart from the Giant Forest Museum every 20 minutes for the half-hour trip. The road to Moro Rock, Crescent Meadow Road, is closed to vehicles summer weekends and holidays from 8am-7pm. During this time, shuttles are the only way to get beyond the Giant Forest Museum to Moro Rock. In the shoulder seasons and on summer weekdays you may drive the road and try to find a spot in the small parking lot.

In the summer, you can meet a ranger at the top of Moro Rock (10am daily). Rangers

1: General Sherman Tree **2:** view from Moro Rock **3:** entrance to Crystal Cave **4:** Tunnel Log

will answer questions and provide information about the geology of the Sierra Nevada. Kids and adults alike enjoy the opportunity to hear more about the area. Note that this is an especially crowded time of day to visit Moro Rock. For the best experience, go at dawn or dusk to avoid the crowds—and to get better photos.

TUNNEL LOG

Many motorists are interested in the "tree you can drive though," more officially known as **Tunnel Log.** In 1937 this mighty sequoia fell on the road, blocking passage to the area. Rather than removing the log outright, a tunnel was carved through it. Driving through it has been a popular tourist experience ever since.

Crescent Meadow Road, which leads to Moro Rock from the Giant Forest Museum provides access to Tunnel Log, as well as **Auto Log,** another fallen tree that visitors were once able to drive on top of. Although you can no longer drive on Auto Log, you can still pay it a visit. Note that Crescent Meadow Road is closed to vehicles on summer weekends and holidays. Hop on a shuttle to reach Tunnel or Auto Logs during these periods.

TOP EXPERIENCE

★ CRYSTAL CAVE

Sequoia and Kings Canyon National Parks are home to more than 200 caves, including the state's longest cave. One of just two caverns in the parks that are open to the public, **Crystal Cave** is a marble cavern that was discovered in 1918. (The other cave accessible to the public is Boyden Cavern.) Touring this cave is an unforgettable experience, where you can take in stunning and strange formations, refreshingly cool air, and pure silence and darkness.

Tours

Access to Crystal Cave is provided via **guided tours** (www.recreation.gov, late May-Sept., prices vary by tour type) run by the Sequoia Parks Conservancy. The cave tour season

typically begins in mid- or late May and continues through September, but it can vary from year to year. Crystal Cave may not be a good option for you if you have claustrophobia or respiratory issues. Any time of day is interesting inside the cave, but summer afternoons are best spent in the subterranean coolness here.

The **Standard Tour** ($16 adults, $5 children) is 50 minutes long, with a maximum of 50 participants. The tour route is paved and well-lit. Along it you will see rare cave formations, including cones and shields (where calcite is forced through a crack in the ceiling and forms a large fan), and more common stalagmites. In one room of the cave, you'll experience total darkness, and your other senses will take over—listen for the sounds of water everywhere around you. Participants should be able to walk 1.5 miles (2.5 km). Bring a jacket, as it is typically 50°F (10°C) inside the cave.

For the more adventurous, there are the **Discovery Tour** (1.5 hours, $25 pp, max. 18 participants, under age 13 not permitted) and **Wild Cave Tour** (4-6 hours, $140 pp, max. 6 participants, under age 16 not permitted). Both of these tours require comfort with confined spaces and the ability to walk long distances. On the Discovery Tour, you will take a deeper dive on the cave's geology and ecosystem, all by flashlight (provided). The Wild Cave Tour is a spelunker's dream: You'll crawl through tight spaces and travel along 3 miles (5 km) of the cave. You will be covered in mud and water by the end, so wear clothes that can get dirty. Note that if your chest or hip circumference is greater than 50 inches, you will not fit through the passageways of the Wild Cave Tour.

Tickets

Tour tickets must be purchased in advance. Purchase tickets online at www.recreation. gov at least two days in advance. Slots open in the winter for the following summer season.

To try for same-day tickets, go to either the **Foothills Visitor Center** (Generals Hwy., 559/565-4212, 8am-4:30pm daily Apr.-Nov.)

Named Sequoias

The naming of a sequoia is an honor bestowed on prominent members of society. Several of these giant trees are named for people who played a role in their early conservation—and their destruction. Many of Giant Forest's named trees are political in nature: The **Franklin, Hamilton,** and **Washington Trees** are named after three of the United States' founding fathers. (The Washington Tree was once the second largest tree in the world, but was struck by lightning in 2003.) Some of the other trees named for U.S. presidents include **Lincoln, Monroe, John Adams,** and **Cleveland.** The **House,** the **Senate,** and the **President Trees** are named after U.S. political bodies and positions.

remains of the Washington Tree, once the second largest tree in the world

There are also trees named for other remarkable humans who left their mark upon the world. Next to the President Tree is the **Chief Sequoyah Tree,** named after Sequoyah, a prominent member of the Cherokee Nation who is credited with inventing the written form of the Cherokee language.

The **Clara Barton Tree,** one of the few trees named for a woman, honors the humanitarian founder of the American Red Cross. The **Susan B. Anthony Tree** was named for the champion of women's suffrage, who not only fought for women's right to vote, but also the abolition of slavery and an egalitarian society. Visit this tree just past the Clara Barton Tree, on the way to Round Meadow.

When Colonel Charles Young, the first acting superintendent of Sequoia National Park and leader of the Buffalo Soldiers, was offered a namesake tree in the early 1900s, he suggested it honor his contemporary instead, Booker T. Washington. Washington was born into slavery, but eventually attended a university, then went on to help found Tuskegee University. He also served on the boards of Fisk and Howard Universities and was an adviser to several U.S. presidents. In 2003, 100 years after Colonel Young's service to Sequoia National Park, a tree near the Booker T. Washington Tree was dedicated to him. Both the **Booker T. Washington Tree** and the **Colonel Young Tree** can be found near the Auto Log.

SIGHTS

GIANT FOREST AND LODGEPOLE

or the **Lodgepole Visitor Center** (47050 Generals Hwy., 559/565-3341, 7am-5pm daily Apr.-Nov.). Note that tickets are *not* sold at the cave entrance.

Getting There

The turnoff for Crystal Cave is 2 miles (3 km) south from the Giant Forest Museum. From the Generals Highway, the road to Crystal Cave is a very curvy 7 miles (11 km) that takes 45 minutes to drive. Drive time could increase if there's road construction. Vehicles longer than 22 feet (7 m) or with trailers are not allowed on this road.

From the parking lot, a 0.5-mile (0.8-km) path descends to the cave entrance, marked by a famous gate—a large metal spiderweb built in the 1940s to protect the cave from vandalism.

Be sure to account for the drive time and the time it takes to walk to the cave entrance, so that you don't miss your tour departure time. Plan to arrive 15 minutes before your tour starts.

Giant Forest and Lodgepole Hikes

Trail	Effort	Distance	Duration
Muir Grove Trail	moderate	4.2 mi (6.8 km) rt	2 hr
Little Baldy	moderate	3.5 mi (5.5 km) rt	2 hr
Wuksachi Trail to Lodgepole Campground	easy	3.1 mi (5 km) one-way	1.5 hr
Tokopah Falls	easy	3.4 mi (5.5 km) rt	2 hr
Lakes Trail	strenuous	11.5-12 mi (18.5-19 km) rt	5-7 hr
Alta Peak	strenuous	13.8 mi (22 km) rt	8-9 hr
Big Trees Trail	easy	1-mi (1.5-km) loop	30 min
Congress Trail	easy	2 mi (3 km) rt	1 hr
Circle Meadow	moderate	6.3 mi (10 km) one-way	3 hr
Crescent Meadow and Tharp's Log	moderate	2.2 mi (3.5 km) rt	1 hr

Recreation

DAY HIKES

Lodgepole and Giant Forest are a hiker's paradise. All of the trailheads are accessible by shuttle.

Muir Grove Trail

Distance: 4.2 miles (6.8 km) round-trip
Duration: 2 hours
Elevation Change: 500 feet (150 m)
Effort: Moderate
Trailhead: Muir Grove/Dorst Creek Campground
Directions: From Lodgepole Village, drive 8.2 miles (13 km) west and north on the Generals Highway toward Grant Grove. Turn left onto Dorst Creek Road and continue through the campground for 0.9 mile (1.5 km). From the group campsites, turn left and park in the hiking parking lot. Via the Lodgepole/Wuksachi shuttle (purple route 3), get off at the third campground shuttle stop, walk west to the trailhead parking lot, and turn north. Enter the group site area on the left and turn right to head toward site B. The trailhead is just across the road from site B.

A short trail with great views brings you to the rarely visited **Muir Grove.** This is a great

mellow morning hike if you're staying at Dorst Creek Campground. The light filtering through the giants makes this a one-of-a-kind sequoia experience, especially in fall when the azaleas and dogwoods deliver colorful accompaniment to the sequoias' red bark.

From the trailhead, follow a small dirt path north for a short distance. Do not cross the bridge, which will have you continuing on the Dorst-Lost Grove Trail. Instead, turn left onto Muir Grove Trail and head west. Stay on the south side of the creek as you follow it downhill among the firs and ferns. As the forest opens up, you will see Big Baldy rising above. As you ascend to a ridgeline, the visible crowns of sequoias draw closer. Continue along the granite ridgeline until the trail crosses a small creek. Here you'll enter a section of burned sequoias, then you'll find yourself surrounded by the sequoias of Muir Grove. Return the way you came to get back to the trailhead.

Dorst Creek Road, the road to the campground, is open June through September. If you're here outside that period, you can get to the trailhead by hiking along the road, which adds another 1.8 miles (3 km) to the total distance of this hike.

Little Baldy

Distance: 3.5 miles (5.5 km) round-trip
Duration: 2 hours
Elevation Change: 750 feet (230 m)
Effort: Moderate
Trailhead: Little Baldy
Directions: From the Lodgepole Village, drive 6.6 miles (11 km) west and north on the Generals Highway. At the top of a hill is a turnout signed for Little Baldy where you can park. The trailhead is on the eastern side of the turnout.

The views on this hike are unparalleled, offering memorable sunrises, stargazing, and everything in between. In the spring, there is snow on the peaks to the east; this is also usually when the air is clearest. In fall, you'll have Little Baldy to yourself. Go in the mornings for clearer air, before the haze rolls up the mountain.

This out-and-back trail is easy to follow. Start on the first few stone steps and climb, following the sweet smells of Jeffrey pines in the sunshine. There are just two long switchbacks on this hike; you'll climb parallel to a steep hillside and come around the back of Little Baldy, the granite dome perched well above the forest. The last 0.25 mile (0.4 km) is flat. Look for Mineral King Valley to the southeast. Nowhere else in the front country will you have such expansive views. Return the way you came.

Lodgepole

The glacier-hewn granite canyons of Lodgepole are ideal for hikers looking to access the high country with relatively little effort.

WUKSACHI TRAIL TO LODGEPOLE CAMPGROUND

Distance: 3.1 miles (5 km) one-way
Duration: 1.5 hours
Elevation Change: 480 feet (150 m)
Effort: Easy
Trailhead: Wuksachi Lodge upper parking area
Directions: From Lodgepole Village, turn right and head northwest on the Generals Highway for 1.6 miles (2.5 km). Turn right onto Wuksachi Way and follow this for 0.6 mile (1 km) to the lodge.

Named for the Wuksachi people who once inhabited the area, this easy dirt trail offers a pleasant walk through the forest well above the road, but with little elevation gain. Few people walk this trail, so you're nearly guaranteed solitude. The pines and riparian areas along each creek are not only visually stunning, they also offer amazing smells and sounds—especially in early summer when hermit thrushes can be heard harmonizing.

From the end of the road by the Wuksachi Lodge, start your hike on the Wuksachi Trail. Trek along a few short switchbacks to cross Clover Creek. The trail slides around the nose of a hillside and leads you to Silliman Creek and other streambeds (which may be dry). At the junction with Twin Lakes Trail, turn right and head south on the Twin Lakes Trail. Continue your hike on the rock-lined path, which parallels the Marble Fork of the Kaweah River, until you reach Lodgepole Campground. You can return the way you came or, if it's summer, hop on a shuttle from Lodgepole Campground to return to the Wuksachi Lodge.

★ TOKOPAH FALLS

Distance: 3.4 miles (5.5 km) round-trip
Duration: 2 hours
Elevation Change: 500 feet (150 m)
Effort: Easy
Trailhead: Tokopah Falls/Lodgepole Campground
Directions: From Lodgepole Visitor Center, drive east on Lodgepole Road for 0.5 mile (0.8 km). Veer left to enter the campground.

A trip to the elegant Tokopah Falls is always memorable: towering monoliths, beautiful granite slabs and scree fields, and the wildflower-lined Marble Fork of the Kaweah River.

The path to Tokopah Falls starts from the end of Lodgepole Campground's upper loop,

Lakes Trail

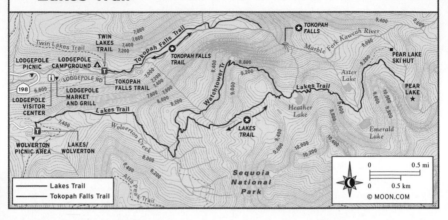

on the north side of the river. It's a straight shot and a steady grade through the sunny forest on a sandy path. The best part is the last 0.25 mile (0.4 km)—a tumble of pure white boulders where pika and marmot can be heard chirping. At the end of the trail, gaze upon the calming cascade of Tokopah Falls, whose water streams down in several strands and jumps over cracks in the granite. Stay on the trail as the rocks are slippery. Return the way you came.

★ LAKES TRAIL

Distance: 11.5-12 miles (18.5-19 km) round-trip
Duration: 5-7 hours
Elevation Change: 2,300 feet (700 m)
Effort: Strenuous
Trailhead: Lakes/Wolverton
Directions: From Lodgepole Village, turn left onto the Generals Highway, heading southwest, and drive 1.5 miles (2.5 km). Turn left onto Wolverton Road and continue to the end of the road, another 1.5 miles (2.5 km). The Lakes Trail is the main trailhead among a distraction of signs. The Wolverton shuttle (orange route 4) stops here.

This out-and-back trek offers a plethora of lakes. This is a very popular trail with plenty of wildflowers and scenery for all. A series of lakes is evidence of a valley glacier that repeatedly traveled this trail eons ago. The glacier

carved a u-shape valley, pausing intermittently before continuing its erosive steps down. Some of the lakes you'll see along this trail include **Heather Lake,** named for the favorite flower of John Muir that grows on its shores; **Aster Lake,** which appears to have just emerged from the cracks in the rock; and **Emerald Lake,** which is secluded but easy to reach.

There are two options for hiking part of this trail. About 2 miles (3 km) in, you'll choose between the **Watchtower route** and the **Hump route.** The Watchtower route includes a steep overlook and is a bit more gradual. The Marble Fork of the Kaweah River rips and turns through the canyon 2,000 feet (610 m) below. The Hump route is the only option for winter travel. It's better for hikers who don't like heights or exposure, but it's a steeper trail. In total, the Hump Route is shorter by 0.5 mile (0.8 km), but has more elevation gain.

From the Lakes trailhead, follow the wide, well-traveled dirt path eastward for the first couple miles. At the north end of Britten Meadow, at the junction with Panther Gap Trail, turn sharply left (north) to stay on the Lakes Trail. After 0.25 mile (0.4 km), the trail will fork for the Watchtower or the Hump. They diverge for about 1.5 miles (2.5 km) before rejoining just above Heather Lake. Here, the peaks of the Great Western Divide and Silliman Crest perch above the canyon.

Continue directly up the rocky and sandy trail. Eventually, the trail passes between Aster and Emerald Lakes. Pass a junction for the ranger station (open in winter to skiers) and continue to **Pear Lake**. Once you've had your fill of this glacier-carved lake, go back the way you came.

ALTA PEAK

Distance: 13.8 miles (22 km) round-trip

Duration: 8-9 hours

Elevation Change: 4,000 feet (1,220 m)

Effort: Strenuous

Trailhead: Lakes/Wolverton

Directions: From Lodgepole Village, turn left onto the Generals Highway, heading southwest, and drive 1.5 miles (2.5 km). Turn left onto Wolverton Road and continue to the end of the road, another 1.5 miles (2.5 km). The Lakes Trail is the main trailhead among a distraction of signs. You can also take the Wolverton shuttle (orange route 4) to this trailhead.

This trail offers incredible views. Nowhere else in the front country can you get such vistas within a day's walk. Spending the whole day ascending this mountain, at 11,204 feet (3,410 m) above sea level, will definitely have you huffing and puffing, but the trail meanders among some of the most scenic parts of Lodgepole. This trail is awesome from spring, when the snows have melted out, through the first big storm, usually in October.

From the north end of the parking lot, take the Lakes Trail for the first 1.8 miles (3 km). Stay to the right to join the Alta Trail, which meanders and climbs through the Giant Forest. Continue along the Alta Trail, passing Panther Peak to the south. The trail takes you to **Mehrten Meadow,** with wildflowers and a small cascade. Take a break here if you need to.

Continue on Alta Trail for another easy mile until you reach the tough, steep climb to the peak. At the junction with Alta Meadow Trail, stay left to continue on Alta Trail to the peak. Along the way, try and spot rare foxtail pines, which are only found in California. When you reach the peak, take in the gorgeous

views. The glaciated ridges along the Great Western Divide show the path of ice rivers, steeply descending over thousands of years. When you're ready, head back down and return the way you came.

Giant Forest

There are almost 40 miles (64 km) of trail within the Giant Forest and each one is unique. Climb a granite dome for spectacular views at Moro Rock or visit Crescent, Circle or Round Meadows for wildflowers. The trails described here are ordered from north to south on the Generals Highway.

★ BIG TREES TRAIL

Distance: 1-mile (1.5-km) loop

Duration: 30 minutes

Elevation Change: Negligible

Effort: Easy

Trailhead: Big Trees

Directions: Park in the lot for the Giant Forest Museum or take the Giant Forest shuttle (green route 1). There's a paved, accessible path that leads to the trailhead from the museum. Visitors with disability placards can park at the small lot at the Big Trees trailhead.

This easy, fully accessible, paved trail encircles **Round Meadow** and is surrounded by sequoias. Rangers lead hikes on this popular trail daily, but you can learn on your own thanks to interpretive signs. There are several unique trees—a pair that has grown together named **Ed by Ned,** which start the hike, and several fire scarred trees, including one you can walk through. It doesn't matter which direction you take the loop.

Despite its popularity, Round Meadow often boasts wildlife sightings: chickaree squirrels, Steller's jays, garter snakes, and bears can be spotted across the meadow and along the hillsides. Giant wildflowers like corn lily, ranger's buttons, and cow parsnip grow over three feet in height and fill the meadow, blooming through September. Sunrise and sunset here are especially nice, but Round Meadow is a treasure no matter the time of day.

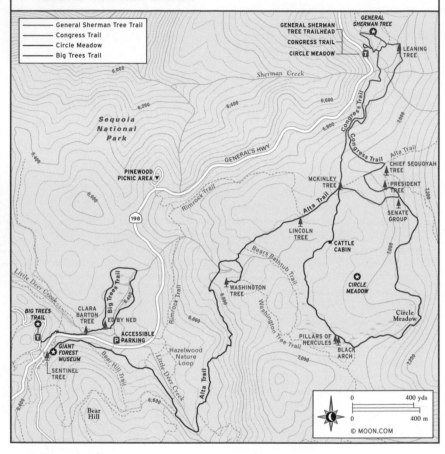

Giant Forest Trails

- General Sherman Tree Trail
- Congress Trail
- Circle Meadow
- Big Trees Trail

CONGRESS TRAIL

Distance: 2 miles (3 km) round-trip

Duration: 1 hour

Elevation Change: Less than 500 feet (150 m)

Effort: Easy

Trailhead: General Sherman Tree

Directions: From Lodgepole Village, turn left onto the Generals Highway and drive southwest for 1.5 miles (2.5 km). Turn left onto Wolverton Road. After 0.6 miles (1 km), turn right. Follow this road for 0.7 miles (1.1 km) to reach the General Sherman Tree parking lot.

This paved loop hike takes you from the great General Sherman Tree to several other impressive sequoias nearby. From the parking lot, walk south on the paved trail to reach the General Sherman Tree. Near General Sherman, at the Leaning Tree (marked with a kiosk and bench), turn left onto the Congress Trail; you'll be hiking this loop clockwise.

When the trail forks, take a right over a small bridge. This 0.8-mile (1.2-km) section of trail is crowded, but there are several amazing trees along the way. When the Congress Trail dead-ends into the Alta Trail, take a sharp right and, 100 yards later, at a small meadow, take a left on a spur trail. Admire the tremendous **President Tree,** which is the third largest sequoia in the world—topped only by

General Grant and General Sherman. Nearby is the **Chief Sequoyah Tree,** a short walk off trail. Retrace your steps and get back on the paved trail, toward the **Senate Group,** an unmistakable cluster of sequoias, then continue your walk, following signs for Congress Trail heading northwest.

As you return north toward the parking lot, the trail brings you to the massive **McKinley Tree,** named for President William McKinley. Continue along this leg of the Congress Trail until you reach the General Sherman Tree once more.

★ **CIRCLE MEADOW**

Distance: 6.3 miles (10 km) one-way
Duration: 3 hours
Elevation Change: 500 feet (150 m)
Effort: Moderate
Trailhead: General Sherman Tree
Directions: From Lodgepole Village, turn left onto the Generals Highway and drive southwest for 1.5 miles (2.5 km). Turn left onto Wolverton Road. After 0.6 miles (1 km), turn right. Follow this road for 0.7 miles (1.1 km) to reach the General Sherman Tree parking lot.

This hike is a way to get off the beaten path and experience the bliss of seemingly endless meadows, carpets of indigo lupine, and some of the most wonderful giant sequoias that the park has to offer. Wildlife like pine marten and black bears are also more likely in these parts of the sunny forest. You'll venture along seven different trails on this hike.

From the parking lot, go south on the paved trail. Turn left to join the Congress Trail and follow it to Alta Trail. Turn right and follow Alta Trail for 100 yards. At a small meadow, turn left onto a spur trail to reach the **President Tree,** and, just off the trail, the **Chief Sequoyah Tree.**

From the President Tree, follow the path to the **Senate Group,** a stand of six giant sequoias. On the south side of the Senate Group, follow the unnamed trail. The forest floor here is blanketed by green and purple lupine. Innumerable giant sequoias offer shade. Enjoy this ethereal section of the trail as you head south for 1 mile (1.5 km).

Continue slightly uphill and into the **Circle Meadow Basin.** You'll enter the meadow by curving around its easternmost edge. The trail wraps around some fallen giants. Admire the meadow's many flowers and grasses. At the edges, get a fleeting whiff of the Sierra rein orchid—30 tiny blossoms line a 16-inch-tall stem; each flower is hardly bigger than the mosquitoes and moths that pollinate them.

Cross the bridge at the southern end of the meadow to pass a couple of cool trees: **Black Arch,** a living tree you can walk through, and **Pillars of Hercules.** Past the trees, you'll arrive at the **Cattle Cabin,** a one-room structure built a century ago. People lived here until 1916 when the cabin was purchased by the National Park Service. From Cattle Cabin northward, you are reentering a busier part of the forest, but you will still have plenty to enjoy.

Visit the beautifully symmetrical **McKinley Tree** before backtracking to take the trail to the west along a recently burned area and to the **Lincoln Tree,** the fourth largest tree alive today.

Next, take the Alta Trail southwest along a ridge. There is a left turn to a dirt path turnoff that leads to the **Washington Tree.** Once the world's second largest tree, lighting struck this massive being in 2003, burning the inside and blasting limbs and bark some 30 feet outward.

From the Washington Tree, return north, retracing your path to get back to the Alta Trail. Continue southwest into a glen of dogwoods. As you cross Little Deer Creek along the Alta Trail, you'll travel downhill to the Hazelwood Nature Trail, where yet another small meadow boasts bright yellow flowers. Turn left to reach the closest shuttle stop at the Giant Forest Museum and the Sentinel Tree. Hop on the shuttle to get back to your car at the General Sherman Tree parking lot.

★ **CRESCENT MEADOW AND THARP'S LOG**

Distance: 2.2 miles (3.5 km) round-trip
Duration: 1 hour
Elevation Change: Less than 500 feet (150 m)

Effort: Moderate

Trailhead: Crescent Meadow

Directions: From the Giant Forest Museum, take the shuttle or drive the road to Moro Rock (Crescent Meadow Rd.) to the end, where there's a parking lot. The trailhead is at the east end of the parking lot.

Most tourists come to this part of Sequoia to hike Moro Rock or go through Tunnel Log. But at the end of the road to Moro Rock is a network of trails surrounding Crescent and Log Meadows, strung together by Crescent Creek. This loop trail takes you to the top sights, including sequoia couples and triplets, as well as burnt, dead, and hollowed-out varieties. You can tack on other trails here if you have time and energy to spare for some rolling hills; most of the trails lead back to the parking lot. The signage can be confusing, so pick up a detailed map at the Giant Forest Museum. Deer and black bear are not uncommon in this part of the Giant Forest.

From the trailhead, follow signs for Crescent Meadow/High Sierra Trail heading east. The trail immediately crosses a little creek. When the High Sierra Trail veers right, stay to the left on Crescent Meadow Trail, which hugs the south end of **Crescent Meadow.** In just 0.2 mile (0.3 km), you will be taking the next right onto Log Meadow Trail, after the creek.

After a short uphill hike, you'll overlook **Log Meadow** to the east, named for the extraordinary number of logs within. As you descend to meadow level, you will reach **Dead Giant.** Get up close and personal with the sheer magnitude of this recently fallen sequoia. (Note: This portion of the hike is rolling, but the trail flattens out as you cross two small and flower-filled creek beds.)

Continue along the trail to reach **Tharp's Log.** This fallen sequoia once housed a man named Hale Tharp. He was one of the first non-Native American people to visit Giant Forest, led by two Yokuts guides in 1858. He lived in this hollowed-out tree each summer from 1861-1890, raising cattle in the meadow. His fireplace, kitchen, and living quarters remain well-preserved in the dark log. (You'll need to use the flash if you'd like a photograph.)

From Tharp's Log, a paved path leads south and west back to Crescent Meadow and the parking lot.

BACKPACKING

Lodgepole's easy-to-follow trails are ideal for backpacking novices—they lead to unique scenery with moderate elevation gain, there are relatively few creepy crawlies or scary animals, and the night skies are spectacular.

Twin Lakes

This strenuous 13.6-mile (22-km) out-and-back trek can be an ambitious day hike, but it's best done as a backpacking trip, which will allow you to relax and delight in the shores of the Twin Lakes. The Twin Lakes Trail follows water for almost the whole way and arrives at two lakes, which are more like fraternal twins than identical. A stunning meadow and views of the massive peaks of the Kings-Kaweah Divide, all over 10,000 feet (3,000 m), including Mount Silliman at 11,188 feet (3,410 m), are your rewards for the steep climb. This trip will appeal to fishers, swimmers, and wildflower lovers alike.

At the designated campsites at Twin Lakes, you'll find fire rings, bear lockers, and a pit toilet. The best sites are on the shores of the larger lake, overlooking the talus slope and sheltered by trees. There are also passable campsites at Cahoon Meadow and the JO Pass junction, if you want to stop earlier. Even though this trail doesn't always hit capacity, you'll want to book your wilderness permit early.

Starting from Lodgepole Campground, follow the bridge across the Marble Fork of the Kaweah to the Tokopah Falls Trail. Almost immediately, take a left at the Twin Lakes trailhead. Walk along the trail through the forest into Tokopah Valley, where the path starts climbing.

1: Watchtower route on the Lakes Trail 2: Round Meadow 3: Cattle Cabin 4: Big Trees Trail

Crescent Meadow and Tharp's Log

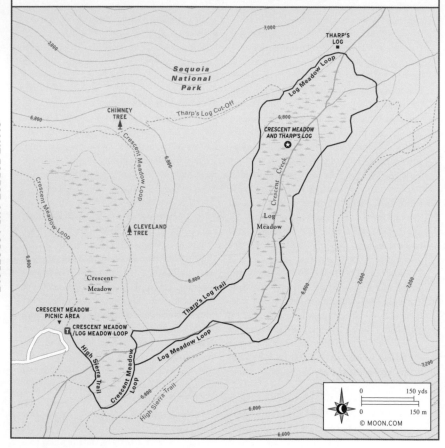

After about a mile, the trail levels out and the forest closes in, changing to shade-loving firs. Follow the trail over windy Silliman Creek; you'll cross twice in this section of trail. Continue to **Cahoon Creek** and **Cahoon Meadow.** These creek beds and meadows burst with wildflowers, attracting local birds.

Continue along the trail, steadily climbing up to **Cahoon Gap,** nearly 8,700 feet (2,650 m) in elevation. From Cahoon Gap, descend toward the junction that leads to JO Pass, where you will find a few campsites.

Stay right at the junction to continue east

on Twin Lakes Trail, climbing along the trail until you arrive at **Twin Lakes,** signaled by an informational sign. The southern lake is larger and more exposed with reflections of Twin Peaks to the north. The northern lake is smaller and more forested.

High Sierra Trail to Bearpaw High Sierra Camp

Because of the scenery, accessibility, and relative ease, this 11.5-mile (18.5-km) trip on the High Sierra Trail to Bearpaw High Sierra Camp is extremely popular. Staying at Bearpaw is a backpacker's dream: You don't need to pack meals or bedding, because the camp provides all that for you. If you're new to backpacking, or just looking to hike with a light pack, this trip is a great option.

You'll want to snag your Bearpaw reservation the day that they are made available for your desired date—366 days in advance. It costs around $200 per person per night (includes all meals), and spots go quickly. Reserve online (www.visitsequoia.com) or via phone (877/436-9726). Meals at Bearpaw are served up family style, with a vegetarian option at every meal. Beer and wine are available for purchase.

Wilderness permits are also required, but they're free for confirmed Bearpaw guests. If you have a reservation at Bearpaw, you don't need to reserve your wilderness permit in advance. Pick up your permit the day your hike begins at the Lodgepole Visitor Center's **wilderness desk** (559/565-3766, 7am-11am and noon-3:30pm daily).

The High Sierra Trail is a gentle ribbon of rock, spanning from the sequoias to Mount Whitney, the highest peak in the continental United States. If you love the High Sierra but your knees or lungs can't take the steepness of Cedar Grove or Twin Lakes, this is the hike for you. Starting at 6,800 feet (2,070 m) elevation,

this hike ends just 1,000 feet (300 m) higher. If this is your first backpacking trip, the high mileage makes it a strenuous effort; it's closer to moderate for those with more experience. The last mile is a real butt-kicker, going up several steep switchbacks. But, oh, the reward: vistas in every direction. Along the way you will pass several meadows and water features.

The trail begins at the Crescent Meadow picnic area, cutting east from the restrooms. After 0.5 mile (0.8 km), the trail departs Crescent Meadow and the sequoias. About 1 mile (1.5 km) in, after meandering through the eastern edge of the Giant Forest, you will reach **Eagle's View,** an overlook where you can see into a 7,000-foot-deep (2,130-m) canyon—it's deeper than the Grand Canyon.

Continue along the trail and you'll reach **Mehrten Creek,** where a natural waterslide cascades over granite that's speckled with wildflowers. Walk farther along the trail and you'll reach the **Buck Creek Bridge.** From here, you have a strenuous 600-foot (180-m) climb over a mile of switchbacks before reaching **Bearpaw High Sierra Camp.** Just south of the camp is Bearpaw Meadow. If you were to venture some 60 miles (97 km) farther on the High Sierra Trail, you would reach **Mount Whitney**—the highest point in the Lower 48.

High Sierra Trail

Summiting Mount Whitney

Positioned at the eastern edge of the Sierra Nevada, Mount Whitney is the highest point in the continental United States, at an elevation of 14,505 feet (4,420 m) above sea level. Thousands of people hike to the top each summer.

There are several options for approaching this glorious mountain. The most popular option is to start from the town of Lone Pine and do the 22-mile (35-km) hike in one day, starting and leaving from the trailhead at Whitney Portal, just west of Lone Pine. This same trip can also be done as an overnight backpacking trip.

hiking Mount Whitney

PLANNING TIPS

Plan for at least three days for your Whitney trip: one day for your arrival and getting your permit, one day for the hike, and one day (or more) for the recovery and return home.

If you can, budget extra time in the Sierra for acclimating to the high elevation. Know the symptoms of altitude sickness: headache, nausea, and feeling loopy, lightheaded, or tired.

Start training early. Do practice hikes of at least 16 miles and with 5,000 feet (1,520 m) or more elevation change. Practice using your trekking poles in preparation for the long, steep downhill return.

Here are some helpful items to pack that you might not normally carry on a day hike:

· headlamp and extra batteries for the pre-dawn start

· ibuprofen or Tylenol to help with minor symptoms of altitude sickness

· water filter or sterilization system to keep your pack weight down

· salty snacks, electrolyte powder or tablets

PERMITS AND RESERVATIONS

Wilderness permits (www.recreation.gov, $6 per permit, $15 recreation fee per person) are required year-round for day trips in the Mount Whitney Zone and overnight trips in wilderness areas. Permits are issued via a lottery system on Recreation.gov in early March.

To enter the permit lottery, have the following information on hand: method of travel, planned route, and the names of the primary and alternate trip planners. Permits must be picked up by noon the day before your scheduled departure.

THE HIKE

The route from Whitney Portal is 22 miles (35 km), with over 5,000 feet (1,520 m) of elevation gain. Start by 5am to avoid afternoon thunderstorms at the summit. The major sights and stops along the trail include Lone Pine Lake, Outpost Camp, Mirror Lake, and Trail Camp. Just before you reach the summit is the Smithsonian Hut, a stone cabin that was constructed in 1909. Be sure to sign the log inside to prove you made it. Continue a bit farther and you've made it to the top of Mount Whitney. Take in the panoramic views for as long as you can.

Head back the way you came for 11 miles (18 km) to reach the trailhead at Whitney Portal. Be sure to take extra care on the descent, when exhaustion can take a toll on your knees and your balance.

To get to the trailhead at Crescent Meadow from the Lodgepole Visitor Center, drive south on the Generals Highway for 4.3 miles (7 km). Turn left onto Crescent Meadow Road (immediately after the Giant Forest Museum) and continue 2.6 miles (4.2 km) to its eastern terminus. On summer weekends, Crescent Meadow Road is closed. You'll need to leave your car in the parking lot of the Giant Forest Museum and take the Moro Rock shuttle (gray route 2) to Crescent Meadow.

WINTER RECREATION
Snowplay
There is a designated snowplay area at **Wolverton Picnic Area** (eastern end of Wolverton Rd.). This open grassland area has two hills with few trees and sits at 7,250 feet (2,210 m) elevation, prime for the perfect amount of snow. Bring your sled, toboggan, and winter gear and head out on plowed Wolverton Road, located between Giant Forest and Lodgepole.

TOP EXPERIENCE

Snowshoeing and Cross-Country Skiing
No winter trip to Sequoia is complete without a snowy trek through the Giant Forest. Many trail options are detailed in the cross-country skiing pamphlet available at the Giant Forest Museum.

Beginners should opt for a shorter hike with less elevation gain, like Crescent Meadow Road. Seasoned and advanced skiers will be delighted by challenging climbs into the wilderness, and might want to spend a day on the Alta Trail or a night at the Pear Lake Ski Hut.

You can rent snowshoes from Wuksachi Lodge or Lodgepole Market. Rangers lead free two-hour **guided snowshoe walks.** The walks occur on weekends and holidays, weather permitting. Call the Giant Forest Museum (559/565-4480) for departure times and to reserve a spot. Snowshoes are provided for free for these walks.

CRESCENT MEADOW ROAD AND BEAR HILL
From the Giant Forest Museum, follow the wide, relatively flat Crescent Meadow Road for an easy snowshoeing trip. The road is not marked with blazes, but is easily followed due to its width. It is 2.5 miles (4 km) from Giant Forest Museum to **Crescent Meadow,** where the road ends.

When you're ready to head back, return the way you came. After about 1.4 miles (2.3 km), you can depart Crescent Meadow Road to take the route to **Bear Hill,** which will add 1 mile (1.5 km) to the trip. Turn right onto Bear Hill Trail and follow the trail blaze, a yellow triangle with a bear on it. After you've climbed Bear Hill, turn left onto the Alta Trail and return to the museum.

OLD LODGEPOLE ROAD/ CONGRESS TRAIL
This 1.2-mile (2-km) out-and-back trek along Old Lodgepole Road (also signed as the Congress Trail) passes by some of the largest living trees on earth. Start from the wheelchair-accessible parking lot for the General Sherman Tree, on the Generals Highway. (It's open to all in the winter.) From the parking lot, join the path (usually cleared of snow) and head north on the General Sherman Tree trail. Keep left at each T intersection and you will arrive at the General Sherman Tree after 0.2 mile (0.3 km). Unlike in summer, you may have a chance of solitude with the world's largest living tree. Consider the awe-inspiring fact that this tree has survived over 2,000 winters.

When you're ready, return the way you came until you meet up with the yellow triangle signs marked with an L, indicating the old Lodgepole Road, or signs for the Congress Trail. About 100 yards from the parking lot, take the fork to the left, heading south. This is a good time to put on your snowshoes.

Continue south along the old Lodgepole Road and admire some of the largest trees in all of California's groves, including the

Ski-In to the Pear Lake Winter Hut

Few activities are more spectacular than cross-country skiing in a national park. It feels as if the park belongs just to you. Make the experience even more memorable by spending the night in a cozy cabin in the backcountry.

It's a 6-mile (10-km) trek to the **Pear Lake Winter Hut** (www.sequoiaparksconservancy. org, mid-Dec.-mid-Apr., $50 pp/night). You'll gain 2,000 feet (610 m) of elevation along the way. This trip is only for advanced skiers and snowshoers who are skilled at navigating the backcountry in winter conditions.

The hut sleeps 10 people and comes equipped with mattresses, a stove, cooking utensils, and a composting toilet. You'll need to bring your own sleeping bag (rated for 32°F/0°C or colder), propane, water purification equipment, and food.

To reserve the hut, enter the lottery on the website for the Sequoia Parks Conservancy before the November assignments (usually the first week of the month). Both reservations and a wilderness permit are required.

McKinley and **Lincoln Trees,** which are close to each other. Turn around at the Lincoln Tree to return to the parking lot.

WUKSACHI TRAIL TO SILLIMAN CREEK

Starting from Wuksachi Lodge, this moderate out-and-back trek (3.8 mi/6 km round-trip) to two creeks will have you feeling lucky to be here. Wuksachi Trail, marked by a four-leafed clover blaze, is for intermediate skiers and snowshoers.

From the lodge's upper parking lot, the trail heads northeast. Trek along a few switchbacks before coming to the **Clover Creek Bridge.** Continue through the red fir forest for 0.8 mile (1.3 km) until you come to **Silliman Creek.** The swift creek leads your eye up to the great, beautiful **Mount Silliman.** Both creek and mountain were named for the Yale University chemistry professor Benjamin Silliman, who trained the leader of the first California state geologic agency, William Brewer. Cross the creek and continue another 0.2 mile (0.3 km) to the Twin Lakes Trail junction. Turn around when you get to a sharp right turn. Admire the scenery and then return the way you came.

Entertainment and Shopping

RANGER PROGRAMS

Lodgepole and Giant Forest are the heart of Sequoia summertime storytelling. There are more rangers and programs here than anywhere else in the park. To see what unique programs are happening during your visit, check the kiosk at either of the campgrounds or stop by the visitors center.

Many programs are offered at the same time daily, including ones about bears at Lodgepole Visitor Center, guided walks along the Big Trees Trail, and campfire programs at Lodgepole and Dorst Creek Campgrounds.

Rangers are positioned at the base of the General Sherman Tree and on top of Moro Rock, and can also be found wandering Giant Forest and cruising Tokopah Falls Trail. Or you can stop into the Giant Forest Museum or Lodgepole Visitor Center for help on finding the perfect hike for you, tips on how to find a pika or identify a flower, or descriptions of a bear's amazing birth.

There are a couple of great programs that the Sequoia Parks Conservancy sponsors at Wuksachi Lodge. Each morning you can attend **Coffee with a Ranger** and get a free

Charles Young and the Buffalo Soldiers

You may be familiar with musician Bob Marley's tribute to the Buffalo Soldiers, who in the final verse are described as "trodding through San Juan in the arms of America." What you may not know is that since the Civil War, African American troops have been crucial in defending the United States and its natural resources. The song's reference to the Spanish American War in 1898, where brave African American troops and cavalry fought up the slope of San Juan Hill in Cuba, is only one component of their legacy: The Buffalo Soldiers were also some of the first guardians of Sequoia National Park.

The national park service was not established until 1916, but the big trees were so wonderful—and so imperiled—that they needed immediate protection. In 1903, six days after they escorted President Theodore Roosevelt around San Francisco, the Buffalo Soldiers were dispatched from the Presidio to Sequoia National Park. The M and I troops of the 24th Infantry and the 9th Cavalry journeyed over 300 miles (480 km) across California to reach Sequoia.

a Buffalo Soldier reenactor

Under the direction of Captain Charles Young, one of the few African American officers in the segregated military, the troops established fire watches, surveyed a path to Mount Whitney, ran off loggers, prevented herders from letting their sheep graze the meadows, and protected other park resources. Young was born to parents who were enslaved and became the third African American graduate of the United State Military Academy. During his tenure as acting superintendent of Sequoia, he put his education in engineering to work by leading the construction of new roads and the maintenance of old ones.

When offered a named tree in his honor during this period, Young instead dedicated it to Booker T. Washington. A century later, in 2004, another tree was named in Young's honor. Today, you can visit the **Colonel Young Tree** and the **Booker T. Washington Tree** on Crescent Meadow Road, which Young helped design.

cup of joe while you chat about the park. On select evenings there are **living history performances,** which tell of the hardships and successes of early park denizens.

EVENTS

Some of first defenders of Sequoia National Park were the Buffalo Soldiers—African American calvary and infantry units sent from the U.S. Army to protect the fledgling national park. Each year, **Buffalo Soldier Day** celebrates their legacy, as well as showcasing the group's engineering feats in developing the road to the park. Events include guided walks at Giant Forest Museum, a special horse-led trip to the Colonel Young

Tree, named for the first African American superintendent of a national park, and a living history reenactment of the daily life of the regiment. The event usually occurs in August; check the park website for the exact dates.

SHOPPING

For any camping gear, food, clothes, maps, and books, visit the **Lodgepole Market Center** (63204 Lodgepole Rd., 559/565-3301, www.visitsequoia.com, 7am-9pm daily summer, winter hours are reduced). They have long hours, a nice selection of beverages and hiking snacks, along with almost anything you might need (and may have forgotten) for your stay in the campground, such as rain gear. The market also carries fresh and refrigerated foods.

Your best bet for cool books is the **Lodgepole Visitor Center** (63100 Lodgepole Rd., 559/565-4436, www.nps.gov/seki, 7am-5pm daily May-Nov.) or the **Giant Forest Museum** (Hwy. 198, 16 mi/26 km north of Ash Mountain entrance, 559/565-4480, www.nps.gov/seki, 9am-6pm daily May-Nov., 9am-4:30pm daily Dec.-Apr.). Both are run by the Sequoia Parks Conservancy which means every purchase helps support programs in the park. They have many publications that were created exclusively for the conservancy, on topics including Crystal Cave, sequoias, and John Muir. They also carry neat hats, shirts, mugs, water bottles, stuffed animals, and games.

Visit the lobby of the Wuksachi Lodge, where the small **Wuksachi Gift Shop** (64740 Wuksachi Way, no phone, 8am-9pm daily summer) carries local goods like honey, geological treasures, postcards, shirts, and jewelry. You can also find some interesting art to bring home so you will always remember your Sequoia adventure.

Food

INSIDE THE PARK

Lodgepole Café (63204 Lodgepole Rd., 559/565-3301, www.visitsequoia.com, 7am-9pm daily summer, winter hours are reduced), inside the Lodgepole Market Center, is a great option for on-the-go meals to take on the trails. In the morning, order grab-and-go breakfast sandwiches or burritos. In the afternoon, get made-to-order burgers or a chicken sandwich.

If you're looking for table service, metal utensils, and views of 11,000-foot (3,350-m) peaks, then head to **The Peaks** (Wuksachi Dr., 559/625-7700 ext. 7608, www.visitsequoia.com, 7am-10am, 11:30am-3pm, and 5pm-10pm daily, lounge and bar with limited menu 2:30pm-5pm daily and full menu 5pm-9pm daily, $20-25). There are delicious options for everyone, including vegans, gluten-free folks, and kids. Enjoy some creative entrées, like mouthwatering burgers composed of short rib and brisket meat, as well as fresh salads, including a delightful shrimp and melon combination. The wine selection is basic (and expensive), but there are draft beers from local breweries for $8.50 per pint, as well as a full bar. It is highly recommended that you make a reservation for dinner (up to 30 days in advance). On Sunday mornings, the breakfast buffet has many options and a mimosa bar to boot. Whatever your order, a meal at the Peaks will be a memorable part of your vacation.

OUTSIDE THE PARK

If you're tired of roasting marshmallows at Dorst Creek Campground, enjoy some creature comforts in the form of fresh pizza at **Stony Creek Lodge** (65569 Generals Hwy., 559/565-3909 or 877/828-1440, www.mslodge.com/stonycreeklodge, 4pm-7:30pm daily May-Oct., $10-20), just 5 miles (8 km) north on the Generals Highway. The lodge's restaurant offers a casual buffet dining option with pizza, wine, and beer on a simple patio.

The sister of Stony Creek Lodge, the **Montecito Sequoia Lodge** (63410 Generals Hwy., 559/565-3388, www.mslodge.com, 7:30am-9am, noon-1:30pm and 5:30pm-7pm daily summer, noon-1pm and 6pm-7:30pm daily off-season, breakfast $9, lunch $10, dinner $20-30) provides home-cooked, casual buffet dining perfectly positioned on a lake on the Generals Highway. In addition to the views, you can fill up on hot buffet choices, with two kinds of meat, special breads, and pastries. Vegetarian options are available daily. If you have allergies or other dietary restrictions, call ahead. Come at the beginning of the buffet hours for the best options.

Best Picnic Spots

view from Beetle Rock

One of the best ways to enjoy the scenery is sharing a snack with family and friends in the company of trees. Many of these picnic areas are temperate and available in the middle of the day, and hardly anyone stops by in the morning or evening. There may be fire restrictions in place, so check ahead if you want to grill.

Halstead Meadow Picnic Area is just the place to make a cup of coffee and wait for whatever may saunter into the peridot pasture. At 21 acres, the montane meadow is one of the park's largest. Don't miss the wildflowers in the summer. Halstead Meadow is 4 miles (6 km) west of the Lodgepole Visitor Center on the Generals Highway.

Away from the crowds, campground, and store, the **Lodgepole Picnic Area** gives visitors a taste of idyllic life, where you can swim in the Marble Fork of the Kaweah River and have dinner on a granite boulder. A loop parking lot, picnic tables, vault toilets, and water spigots mark this simple picnic area. You can walk down along the river until you reach the foothills; if you continue a bit farther, you'll get your own private riverfront picnic spot. (Be careful walking along the river in springtime—the water is swifter, deeper, and colder than it appears and can be deadly if you fall in.) The picnic area is less than half a mile north of the Lodgepole Visitor Center, accessible from the Generals Highway.

Tucked away between Lodgepole and Giant Forest is a little valley and meadow with a quaint picnic spot overlooking the meadow at **Wolverton Picnic Area.** Barbecues and water are available. Heading south from Lodgepole Visitor Center on the Generals Highway, turn left onto Wolverton Road and continue to the end of the road.

After a hike in Giant Forest, replenish your energy by relaxing on a forested ridge. **Pinewood Picnic Area** features water, restrooms, and grills. Though not exactly a suppertime serenade, ravens and chickarees will add to the ambience, and the vanilla smell of Jeffrey pines will encourage dessert. Pinewood is near Round Meadow, on the north side of the road. Heading south on the Generals Highway from the General Sherman Tree, take the first right after about 1 mile (1.5 km).

Crescent Meadow Picnic Area does not have grills, but it has sequoias and sometimes deer and bears. After a hike through the Giant Forest, you can end your adventures with a picnic and take the shuttle back to your campground. The picnic area is at the eastern end of Crescent Meadow Road.

Though not an official picnic area, **Beetle Rock** has great views, access to restrooms by the Giant Forest Museum, and is near the museum's parking lot. On a clear day, visibility extends to the bottom of the Central Valley, a mile below. On a hazy day, the sunset will be all the more vibrant. To access Beetle Rock, drive or take the shuttle to the Giant Forest Museum. In the parking lot across the street, walk to the right of the entrance. A short distance down a dirt path is a picnic table and an open rocky area, shaped like the domed back of a ladybug beetle.

Accommodations

INSIDE THE PARK
Wuksachi Lodge

If you didn't already know about **Wuksachi Lodge** (64740 Wuksachi Way, 866/807-3598, www.visitsequoia.com, from $140 winter, from $260 summer), you would never realize that a highly rated and popular hotel is tucked away on the ridgetop forest. With 102 rooms, the lodge is an ideal home base for visitors with a loose definition of "roughing it." It affords stunning vistas, luxe amenities, and the ability to meet other like-minded nature lovers. Located 2 miles (3 km) north of Lodgepole and 6 miles (10 km) north of Giant Forest, the lodge's discrete log-cabin buildings are mostly hidden, except for the main lodge, which houses a full-service restaurant, cocktail lounge and bar, gift shop, conference center amenities, and a deck with a window-service food spot.

Guest rooms are set back in quiet nooks a couple hundred yards away from the lodge. Each room has a mini-fridge, television, and coffee maker. There are three room options: Standard rooms accommodate four people but do not have the sofa. Deluxe rooms have more space and can include a crib or rollaway bed for a maximum of five people, as well as a sofa or table and chairs. The Superior room can accommodate six people and has an alcove for seating or sleeping. There is Wi-Fi, but it's best for social media and email access, not for streaming videos. Guests can order box lunches ($10-14) ahead of time to take on the trail the following day. The boxes include a sandwich (veggie or meat), chips, fruit, and a drink.

The lodge has services to help guests with luggage; there are no elevators. They also have rooms with mobility and hearing accessibility, including roll-in showers and visual alarms. Views are best from the Stewart Building. Pets are allowed for an additional fee of $25.

The lodge is open all year, but you might need chains to get here in the winter. Call and make your dinner reservation at the lodge's on-site restaurant, The Peaks, up to 30 days before your stay.

OUTSIDE THE PARK

For family fun, stay at the all-inclusive **Montecito Sequoia Lodge** (63410 Generals Hwy., 559/565-3388 or 800/227-9900, www.mslodge.com, from $180 winter, from $250 summer). Surrounded by beautiful views and on the edge of a lake, this secluded resort has been helping families unplug and enjoy the peace of the mountains since the 1970s. Instead of televisions, guests enjoy swimming and boating in the lake, horseback riding, tennis, beach volleyball, and archery. Book a room in the lodge or a standalone cabin. Some of the cabins have a separate, shared bath. The lodge has Wi-Fi, accessible from its restaurant. Rates include buffet meals, snacks, and drinks, activities, and kids' programs.

The halfway point between Lodgepole and Grant Grove is **Stony Creek Lodge** (65569 Generals Hwy., Sequoia National Forest, 559/565-3909 or 877/828-1440, www.mslodge.com/stonycreeklodge, May-Oct., $170-230), the sister property of the Montecito Sequoia Lodge. This rustic 12-room hotel, seemingly hewn from the mountains around it, lies near the border of Sequoia National Park. Breakfast is included in the rate.

Camping

INSIDE THE PARK

Within view of the granite mountains above, **Lodgepole Campground** (Apr.-Nov., $22) provides the closest access to excellent hiking and creature comforts. With all 203 sites within earshot of the Marble Fork of the Kaweah River, the campground provides rest and relaxation with a perfect soundtrack. Conveniently, several trails leave right from this area: Tokopah Falls, Twin Lakes, and Wuksachi Trail. It's also walking distance to Lodgepole's market, restaurant, laundry, showers, and shuttle. The campground has a dump station, flush toilets, and a pay phone. Be sure to store everything that smells in a bear locker and stay within arm's distance of your food: Bears are very active in this area. For backpackers starting or ending trips, there are some walk-up sites available. Make a reservation early (starting in November of the previous year) because this campground is very popular.

Despite some tight quarters, uneven ground, disruptions by bears, early risers, and late night singers, **Dorst Creek Campground** (June-Sept., $22) is perfectly located for family or solo trips. Located 9 miles (14 km) from Lodgepole and 18 miles (29 km) from Grant Grove, the 212 sites of this midway point campground are often full because of its combination of landscape and amenities, which include flush toilets, water, fire pits, picnic tables, dump station, and a pay phone. Sometimes last-minute reservations can be found, and walk up sites are available on weekdays. The campground offers group sites for 15-50 people ($50-70) and wheelchair-accessible sites. It also provides access to Muir Grove and Dorst Creek Trails.

OUTSIDE THE PARK

Two campgrounds on national forest land offer over 70 sites and access to Lodgepole and Giant Forest, Grant Grove, and Hume Lake, all within 20 miles (32 km). Perhaps because of their proximity to good mountain biking, Big Baldy, and Jennie Lakes Wilderness, as well as easy access to the amenities at Stony Creek Lodge, both campgrounds are popular. Located half a mile east of Stony Creek Lodge on the Generals Highway, both campgrounds are open from late May through late September or early October, depending on weather. You may need a permit for your campfire or stove, so check fire restrictions before you arrive. **Stony Creek Campground** (Sequoia National Forest, 877/444-6777, www.recreation.gov, late May-mid-Sept., $27, $7 for extra vehicle) has 50 sites with flush toilets and an amphitheater. Across the highway, a more rustic **Upper Stony Creek Campground** (Sequoia National Forest, 877/444-6777, www.recreation.gov, late May-mid-Sept., $18, $5 for extra vehicle) has vault toilets and 23 RV and tent sites.

Unlike in the national park, which only allows camping in the backcountry or in campgrounds, **dispersed camping** is an option in the national forest. If you plan to have a fire, pick up a free permit at the visitors center in Grant Grove, at Hume Lake Ranger Station, or online at www.fs.usda.gov/sequoia. You'll need to bring your own water and manage your waste properly.

Transportation and Services

DRIVING AND PARKING

The Generals Highway cuts through steep mountainsides, which means that rockslides and other hazards are common. The park service is constantly working to keep it drivable for visitors—and safe for wildlife, too. Ongoing road-widening projects can cause delays of up to an hour.

You can attempt to avoid delays by planning to your trip around construction hours, especially between Hospital Rock and Beetle Rock, and between Grant Grove and Lodgepole. The parks' entrance stations provide clear schedules so that you can plan accordingly. Another alternative is to make your accommodations in Lodgepole or at the Wuksachi Lodge, Stony Creek Lodge, or Montecito Sequoia Lodge, which are all within shuttle or walking distance of area attractions.

In the summer, the roads are more crowded with visitors. Get ready for bear jams—when people spontaneously stop or abandon their cars to snap a photo of a bear somewhere close to the road—and try to be patient. Fall and winter see fewer crowds, Crescent Meadow Road is fully open to vehicles, and visitors can park in the wheelchair-accessible lot for the General Sherman Tree (in the summer, this lot is open only to vehicles with disability placards). While some areas may be closed due to snow, plows work quickly to open up Wolverton Road.

There are several parking options in the area. Across the street from the Giant Forest Museum is a large lot for both RVs and personal vehicles. The main parking lot for the General Sherman Tree is off Wolverton Road. Lastly, just beyond the Lodgepole Market and just after entering the campground, there is a huge parking area that will provide access to the Tokopah Falls Trail. All of these areas are frequently serviced by shuttles, allowing you to park your car for the day while you explore the area.

SHUTTLES

The free shuttles in Sequoia offer convenient routes, spanning from Dorst Creek Campground and Wuksachi Lodge to the Giant Forest, Moro Rock, and Crescent Meadow. The longest trip is about an hour, but most stops are within 20 minutes of each other and can make one-way hikes more convenient. The shuttles run every day in the summer from 8am to 6pm. In the winter, shuttles run every 30 minutes on **weekends only.** For more information on the different routes, visit www.nps.gov/seki.

SERVICES

It's best to fuel up before entering the park, in Three Rivers, Squaw Valley, or Dunlap. There is one **gas station** not too far from Lodgepole, if you're running low. About 13 miles (21 km) north of the Lodgepole Visitor Center, **Stony Creek Lodge** (65569 Generals Hwy., 559/565-3909) has 24-hour credit card gas pumps in the summer. Electric cars can use the local plugs at Wuksachi Lodge, but they may not be suitable for your vehicle.

Grant Grove

Grant Grove is a perfect introduction to the big trees, with sequoias in every state of being, from birth to death, and everything in between—including thousand-year old giants. Grant Grove was a standalone park before the establishment of Kings Canyon in 1940. It's home to abundant trees, waterfalls, canyons, and epic views. Here, sequoias stand amid meadows and alongside creeks, their brilliant red bark stretching far up into the forest canopy. White dogwood blossoms abound in spring, and as summer arrives, peridot-colored sequoia cones appear in the treetops. A visit here allows you to surround yourself with the greatest trees in the world and to better understand your place in the universe.

There is so much history in Grant Grove. People have lived in this

Highlights

Look for ★ to find recommended sights, activities, dining, and lodging.

★ **Drive to Junction View:** Take a trip along the peaceful Highway 180 to Junction View for vistas of one of the deepest canyons in the country (page 99).

★ **Stand atop Big Stump:** Get an up-close sense of just how big giant sequoias truly are on this appropriately named tree stump (page 102).

★ **Look up at General Grant Tree:** See the world's second largest tree from multiple angles on a short paved path (page 102).

★ **Head to Panoramic Point:** Take in awe-inspiring views from this spot that's accessible via a short walk (page 104).

★ **Follow North Grove Loop:** Descend into this peaceful area for a hike among sequoias at all stages of life (page 106).

★ **Wander along Sunset Loop:** This flat hike offers the greatest hits of Grant Grove, including giant sequoias, waterfalls, and early summer azalea blooms (page 107).

★ **Explore Redwood Mountain Sequoia Grove:** You will have the trails to yourself as you hike through the largest standing sequoia grove, full of young trees and ancient giants deep in a shaded canyon (page 109).

★ **Hike along Big Baldy Ridge:** This straightforward hike takes you to the highest point in Grant Grove—the top of a granite dome known as Big Baldy. The payoff is an excellent vista of Redwood Canyon and the Great Western Divide (page 112).

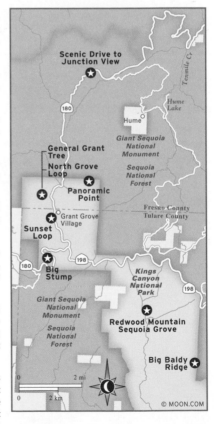

Grant Grove

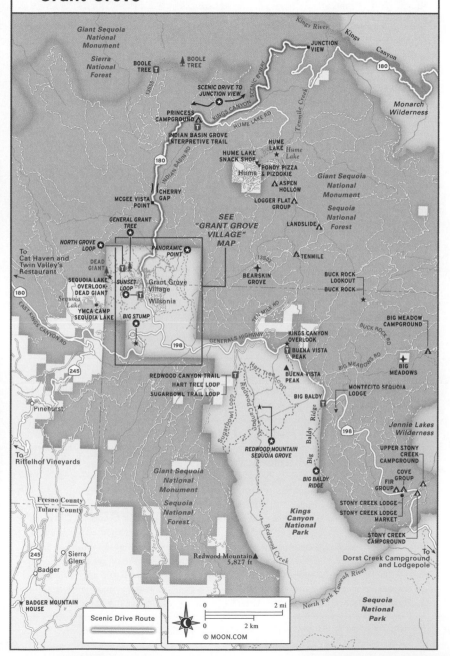

Giant Sequoia National Monument

Sierra National Forest

Kings River

Kings Canyon

180

Monarch Wilderness

JUNCTION VIEW

BOOLE TREE

BOOLE TREE 13560

SCENIC DRIVE TO JUNCTION VIEW

PRINCESS CAMPGROUND

INDIAN BASIN GROVE INTERPRETIVE TRAIL

KINGS CANYON SCENIC BYWAY

HUME LAKE RD

Tenmile Creek

HUME LAKE SNACK SHOP

HUME LAKE

Hume Lake

180

CHERRY GAP

Hume

PONDY PIZZA & PIZOOKIE

ASPEN HOLLOW

Giant Sequoia National Monument

MCGEE VISTA POINT

INDIAN BASIN RD

LOGGER FLAT GROUP

Sequoia National Forest

GENERAL GRANT TREE

SEE "GRANT GROVE VILLAGE" MAP

LANDSLIDE

NORTH GROVE LOOP

PANORAMIC POINT

13560

TENMILE

To Cat Haven and Twin Valley's Restaurant

DEAD GIANT

BEARSKIN GROVE

BUCK ROCK LOOKOUT

BUCK ROCK

SEQUOIA LAKE OVERLOOK- DEAD GIANT

SUNSET LOOP

Grant Grove Village

Wilsonia

180

EAST KINGS CANYON RD

Sequoia Lake

YMCA CAMP SEQUOIA LAKE

BIG STUMP

TEN MILE RD

BUCK ROCK RD

BIG MEADOW CAMPGROUND

198

GENERALS HIGHWAY

KINGS CANYON OVERLOOK

BUENA VISTA PEAK

BIG MEADOWS RD

BIG MEADOWS

Pinehurst

REDWOOD CANYON TRAIL

HART TREE LOOP

SUGARBOWL TRAIL LOOP

Hart Tree Loop

BUENA VISTA PEAK

MONTECITO SEQUOIA LODGE

BIG BALDY

198

Jennie Lakes Wilderness

245

To Riffelhof Vineyards

Sugarbowl Loop

Redwood Canyon

Big Baldy Ridge

UPPER STONY CREEK CAMPGROUND

COVE GROUP

FIR GROUP

REDWOOD MOUNTAIN SEQUOIA GROVE

BIG BALDY RIDGE

Big Baldy

STONY CREEK LODGE

STONY CREEK LODGE MARKET

Giant Sequoia National Monument

Sequoia National Forest

Kings Canyon National Park

STONY CREEK CAMPGROUND

Fresno County
Tulare County

245

Sierra Glen

Badger

Redwood Mountain 5,827 ft

Redwood Creek

To Dorst Creek Campground and Lodgepole

BADGER MOUNTAIN HOUSE

North Fork Kaweah River

Sequoia National Park

Scenic Drive Route

0   2 mi
0   2 km

© MOON.COM

Where Can I Find...?

- **Accessible campgrounds:** The **Azalea, Sunset,** and **Crystal Springs Campgrounds** have accessible sites. Crystal Springs is probably the best due to ease of parking and proximity to Grant Grove Village.

- **Accessible trails and attractions:** There's a paved trail at the **General Grant Tree.** It's uneven and not fully level, but is generally accessible for wheelchair users and others with mobility issues. In summer, you can drive the road to **Panoramic Point.** Take in the views from the road, or follow the paved (though somewhat steep) path for a short distance to an **overlook.**

- **ATM: Grant Grove Market** has an ATM just inside the entrance. **Stony Creek Lodge** on Highway 198 toward Lodgepole has one in the market. Most places will accept major credit cards.

- **Electric vehicle charging stations:** There's a wall outlet available at **Grant Grove Market.**

- **Gas:** There is no gas inside the park, so fill up in **Squaw Valley** or **Dunlap.** You can get fuel at **Hume Lake** (hours vary) and **Stony Creek Lodge,** but you'll pay a premium price and pump hours are limited.

- **Showers:** There are no showers in Grant Grove; the nearest ones are in Cedar Grove and Lodgepole.

- **Supplies: Grant Grove Market** has a wide beverage selection, food, souvenirs, and some camping gear like tent stakes and propane. The **Grant Grove Gift Shop** has similar gear and clothing items like t-shirts and fleeces.

- **Telephones:** Cell service is spotty. **Pay phones** are available at the **Kings Canyon Visitor Center** and the **Grant Grove Market.**

- **Wi-Fi:** You can connect to Wi-Fi in the lobby of the **John Muir Lodge.** If you're a guest of **Montecito Sequoia Lodge,** you may use their internet, available in the main restaurant.

GRANT GROVE

area for millennia. Grinding mortars, cabins built in fallen logs, and other evidence of human habitation across countless years abound. Also evident are the remains of a once-thriving logging industry. Human-made dams and lakes that once funneled felled trees are now spots for swimming and fishing. Giant stumps in barren meadows serve as reminders of the massive trees that once stood in their place.

This small area has something for every visitor, running the gamut from accessible sights, like the famous General Grant Tree, all the way up to strenuous hikes and backpacking trips through sequoia groves. Despite

being a prime location, Grant Grove feels like a throwback to quieter days, when it was easy to find solitude in a national park. Even when you're alone, though, you'll still have company: The calls of chickadees, the chatter of squirrels, and the drum of woodpeckers fill the air with nature's conversation.

PLANNING YOUR TIME

Grant Grove is easy to get to, just one hour from Fresno. From Fresno, you can easily take a **day trip** here or spend **one night** for a quick getaway. If you only have a **few hours** in Grant Grove, make your first stop the **General Grant Tree** and its 30-minute

---

Previous: walking in North Grove; Big Stump; entrance to Kings Canyon National Park.

loop. Pause at the **Kings Canyon Visitor Center,** then get a view into Kings Canyon from the **Junction Overlook.**

To truly experience the best of Grant Grove, **three days** is optimal. On your first day, enter via the Big Stump entrance and stop to see the **Big Stump.** Continue just past Grant Grove Village, and start with the **General Grant Loop.** Settle in at your campsite, cabin, or your room at the John Muir Lodge, and have a nice meal at the restaurant. Conclude the evening with a **campfire ranger talk** or a sunset drive to **Panoramic Point** (summer only). The next day, take on a long hike, like the Park Ridge Trail or Big Baldy. If you're craving a treat after, head to **Hume Lake** for a milkshake and a swim. On your last day in the area, visit one of the logged areas like **Indian Basin** or **Converse Basin,** and take a short drive to **Junction Overlook** for a peak into Kings Canyon.

If you are interested in exploring Kings Canyon as a day trip, staying in Grant Grove is a must. Plan on 2-3 hours of driving into and back out of the canyon, best accomplished in daylight as the road is dangerous, steep, narrow and curvy.

Grant Grove is accessible almost **year-round** and every season is stunning. In the **winter** (Dec.-Feb.), you'll have the park to yourself. In **summer** (May-Sept.), it never gets too hot, with highs around 75°F (24°C). Camping is chilly in the winter and **spring** (Feb.-May), with lows around freezing. In summer, overnight lows are around 45°F (7°C). Be prepared for cool weather and pack layers.

Exploring Grant Grove

VISITORS CENTERS

Only 4 miles (6 km) from the Big Stump entrance and the first building in Grant Grove, the **Kings Canyon Visitor Center** (83918 Hwy. 180, 559/565-3341 ext. 0, 8am-5pm daily late May-early Sept., 9am-4pm daily late Sept.-Dec. and early Mar.-May, 10am-3pm daily Jan.-early Mar.) is where you can enrich your experience of the park. Spend half an hour looking at interactive exhibits and bronze animal statues, chatting with a ranger, and watching an introductory film. The visitors center is home to three large murals that depict the area's trees, the canyon, and the high country. This is where you can sign up for ranger-led hikes. Pick up a souvenir like a ranger hat, puppets and toys, maps, books, or hand-thrown pottery. Clean restrooms and a water-bottle filling station are just outside the wheelchair-accessible entrance. For winter wilderness travel, a self-serve permit is available. Exhibits are in English and Spanish.

ENTRANCE STATIONS

The **Big Stump Entrance Station** (Hwy. 180, open year-round, $35 vehicles, $30 motorcycles, $20 on foot or bike) is located on Highway 180 and provides access to Grant Grove, Hume Lake, Cedar Grove, and Sequoia National Monument as well as the Generals Highway, which leads to Lodgepole. On busy summer days, expect a 30-minute wait and have your parks pass ready. You will receive a map and newspaper about seasonal park programs upon entrance.

As you continue up Highway 180, stay straight for Grant Grove, Cedar Grove, and Hume Lake. After 3 miles (5 km) you will be in Grant Grove Village, where lodging, camping, food, and the amazing sequoias await.

SCENIC DRIVES
★ Grant Grove to Junction View

This 21-mile (34-km) out-and-back drive takes a little under an hour and offers a

Grant Grove Village

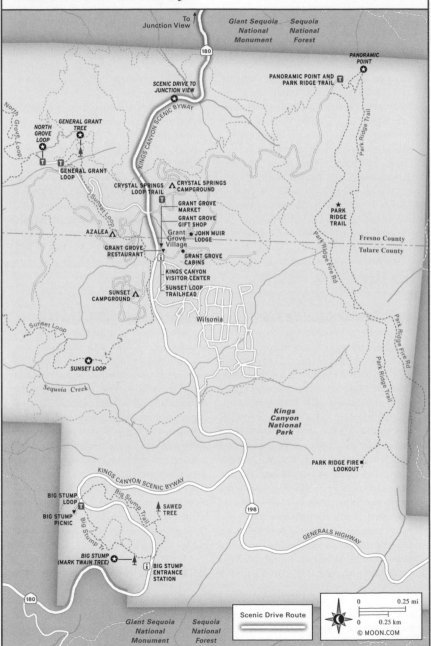

To Junction View

Giant Sequoia National Monument

Sequoia National Forest

180

PANORAMIC POINT

PANORAMIC POINT AND PARK RIDGE TRAIL

SCENIC DRIVE TO JUNCTION VIEW

KINGS CANYON SCENIC BYWAY

North Grove Loop

NORTH GROVE LOOP

GENERAL GRANT TREE

Park Ridge Trail

GENERAL GRANT LOOP

Sunset Loop

CRYSTAL SPRINGS LOOP TRAIL

CRYSTAL SPRINGS CAMPGROUND

GRANT GROVE MARKET

GRANT GROVE GIFT SHOP

PARK RIDGE TRAIL

AZALEA

JOHN MUIR LODGE

Grant Grove Village

GRANT GROVE RESTAURANT

GRANT GROVE CABINS

Fresno County

Tulare County

KINGS CANYON VISITOR CENTER

Park Ridge Fire Rd

SUNSET LOOP TRAILHEAD

SUNSET CAMPGROUND

Wilsonia

Sunset Loop

Park Ridge Fire Rd

Park Ridge Trail

SUNSET LOOP

Sequoia Creek

Kings Canyon National Park

PARK RIDGE FIRE LOOKOUT

KINGS CANYON SCENIC BYWAY

198

BIG STUMP LOOP

Big Stump Trail

SAWED TREE

BIG STUMP PICNIC

Big Stump Tr.

GENERALS HIGHWAY

BIG STUMP (MARK TWAIN TREE)

BIG STUMP ENTRANCE STATION

180

Giant Sequoia National Monument

Sequoia National Forest

Scenic Drive Route

0   0.25 mi
0   0.25 km

© MOON.COM

variety of views. This route is not fully open in the winter.

From Grant Grove Market, turn right onto **Highway 180 North.** At mile 3 (km 5), you will drive past the turnoff for what led to the conservation of this area. Once the largest sequoia grove in the world, **Converse Basin** was decimated by logging between 1891 and 1892. Only 60 large trees survive out of the thousands that once stood tall here. Use caution if you take the turn onto Forest Road 13S03; the dirt road takes you along the edge of a mountainside affected by fire in 2015.

At mile 6 (km 10), to enjoy **Indian Basin,** a recovering sequoia grove, turn right into **Princess Campground** and drive straight toward the meadow. A short, paved, and accessible interpretive trail will introduce you to the history of the basin.

After cruising past some overhanging granite boulders, you will be heading down toward Kings Canyon. There are several pullouts from which to take in the views, but the best is **Junction View,** at mile 10.5 (km 17). This is the most popular viewpoint on the highway for its breathtaking views into one of the deepest canyons of North America. Kings Canyon is 8,200 feet (2,500 m) deep; the Grand Canyon is 6,100 feet (1,860 m) deep. At the overlook, you also get a birds-eye view of the convergence of the middle and south forks of the Kings River.

From Junction View, head back the way you came. In 8 miles (13 km), you'll approach the pullout for **McGee Vista Point.** From this point, you can see the evidence of the 2015 Rough Fire, which burned over 150,000 acres. Burnt pine trees stand among the charred land. Fortunately, the underbrush is recovering, evidenced by blooming wildflowers. Continue another 2.5 miles (4 km) south on Highway 180 to return to Grant Grove Village.

Generals Highway to Dorst Creek Campground

General Sherman and General Grant are connected by the scenic **Generals Highway** **(Hwy. 198).** This road was surveyed and designed by the Buffalo Soliders, and built in 1935 with just shovels and mules. It only takes an hour to drive the 30 miles (48 km) between the two trees, but it's better to take your time to savor the beautiful views. The route described here departs from the General Grant Tree and brings you 17 miles (27 km) to the highway's midway point at Dorst Creek Campground. From the campground, you can return the way you came or continue on to the General Sherman Tree. (For more details on continuing the drive, see the *Giant Forest and Lodgepole* chapter.)

From the General Grant parking lot, turn right onto Highway 180. Head south, past the historic community of **Wilsonia.** In 3.6 miles (5.8 km), at a three-way junction, turn left onto the Generals Highway to travel southeast. Reset your odometer to follow the mile markers as described here.

At 3 miles (5 km) after the junction, on the right-hand westerly side of the road is an **unnamed viewpoint** where you can stand on top of a granite outcropping and observe the protruding crowns of sequoias below. A wayside sign describes what you're seeing.

Continue down Highway 198. In 4.5 miles (7.2 km), park in the pullout on the left-hand side of the road. Here, **Kings Canyon Overlook** offers a unique view of the High Sierra wilderness. A wayside marker indicates the peaks you can see on the other side of the Kings River. Just 100 yards south of the overlook, on the right side of the road, is the trailhead for Buena Vista Peak.

If you get peckish, there are a couple possible lunch spots on the route: 3.5 miles (5.5 km) south of the overlook is **Montecito Sequoia Lodge.** Another 4 miles (6 km) farther is **Stony Creek Lodge.**

After 17 miles (27 km) from the Highway 180/Highway 198 junction, you will arrive at **Dorst Creek Campground** on the right side of the road. Pop in to check out the wildflowers in the meadow, or take a walk in Muir Grove.

Sights

★ BIG STUMP

Just after the entrance to the park, stop to visit the **Big Stump,** originally known as the **Mark Twain Tree.** While people had lived with the sequoias for millennia, the arrival of pioneers, loggers, miners, and fortune-seekers to the Sierra Nevada changed the relationship between trees and people forever. Incredulous people who would never make the trip to California wanted a piece of the big trees. The Mark Twain Tree was felled for exhibition purposes in 1891: Two men chopped for 13 days and cut a cross-section of the tree for the American Museum of Natural History in New York and another for the British Museum in London. Today, the Big Stump is all that remains of a tree that was some 1,350 years old when it was cut down. The stump is on the edge of a lush meadow surrounded by sequoias of varying ages. Stairs lead up to the top of the stump. As you stand in the middle of the stump, which measures 16 feet across, behold its many years of growth, each marked by a ring. Notice the healed fire scars, the holes where bark curled around to protect its inner layers.

To get to the Big Stump, park on the south side of the road in a large pullout immediately after the Big Stump Entrance Station. Use the crosswalk and make your way toward a stump on the north side of the road. Follow the dirt path mostly downhill for 0.2 mile (0.3 km). It's also possible to hike a 2-mile (3-km) loop to the stump starting from the Big Stump Picnic Area.

TOP EXPERIENCE

★ GENERAL GRANT TREE

Named the Nation's Christmas Tree in 1926, the **General Grant Tree** is the second largest tree by volume in the world. (The first largest tree is of course, the General Sherman Tree, in the Giant Forest region of Sequoia National Park.) Set in a grove of its fellow sequoias, the General Grant is nearly 270 feet tall, about 100 feet around its base, and estimated to be about 1,650 years old. Around the base of this vast tree, you'll see the many notches, fire scars, and other signs of survival on this special sequoia.

An easy 0.5-mile (0.8-km) paved path runs through the grove, detailing the area's history and the unique features of the giant sequoia. Nearby General Grant is the **Gamlin Cabin,** built in 1872. It was originally owned by Israel Gamlin, a cattle rancher, but was later used as housing for the national park's first rangers. Another interesting element in the grove is a hollowed-out sequoia, known as the **Fallen Monarch.** Walk through the entirety of this fallen tree, which was once used to stable the U.S. cavalry's horses.

Despite being a popular and sometimes crowded attraction, the sounds of nearby wildlife abound in the area. Listen for the drumming of the pileated woodpecker and the ethereal double-flute tune of the robin. The hermit thrush is like a siren drawing you toward its eerie and mysterious song, but it stays hidden from view most of the time.

Go in the morning to beat the crowds. Sunset's golden hour, especially in winter and fall, is a special time. And even when the rest of the park is snowy, the park crews work hard to keep the grove's path free of ice and snow. It's possible to hike down to the General Grant Tree via the Sunset Trail, which starts across the street from the visitors center. Note that this hike is all downhill on the way out, so you'll have an uphill trek to get back to Grant Grove Village. It's also possible to connect a walk in Grant Grove with the North Grove

1: General Grant Tree 2: Big Stump 3: walking through the Fallen Monarch 4: view from Panoramic Point

Loop and Dead Giant Overlook, which allows for more solitude.

★ PANORAMIC POINT

Head up to **Panoramic Point** for expansive views overlooking the north and eastern parts of the park. In the foreground is Hume Lake; beyond it is the entire Kings Canyon. Come in the morning for the best views, when the air is clearest. From the parking lot, the overlook is 0.2 mile (0.3 km) along a path. The road up to Panoramic Point is 2.3 miles (3.7 km). It's cleared of snow in spring.

HUME LAKE

About 30 minutes from Grant Grove is **Hume Lake,** a reservoir surrounded by national forest campgrounds, casual eateries, and a private Christian camp. Hume Lake is an artifact of the logging era. It was built in the early 1900s to catch cut logs and send them down a waterway to the Central Valley for processing. The dam that created Hume Lake was the world's first reinforced concrete multiple arch dam. The lake's water was funneled into a flume that moved lumber from the active logging area to the town of Sanger, 79 miles (127 km) away. The flume was the longest one ever created, and was eventually used by thrill-seekers, who would ride down it in open-prow boats. Today, tourists find more relaxing activities like hiking around the lake, paddling, and fishing.

To get here from Grant Grove Village, take Highway 180 towards Cedar Grove, and at 6 miles (10 km), turn right onto Hume Lake Road. Stay on the paved road as you wind around to the far end of the lake, and after 4.5 miles (7 km) the boat house will be on the left.

CAT HAVEN

Outside of the park and 14 miles (23 km) from Grant Grove towards Fresno on Highway 180, **Cat Haven** (38257 E. Kings Canyon Rd., Dunlap, 559/338-3216, 10am-5pm Mon.-Sat., 10am-3pm Sun., $15 adults, $10 children 8-12) is a tourist attraction where you can see big felines from around the world in captivity. On the 45-minute tour of this educational nonprofit, you can watch tigers swim, jaguars skulk, snow leopards lounge, and bobcats waggle their short tails. This is not an animal rescue or sanctuary, but 20 percent of proceeds do go to conservation projects in the wild. Expect to wait for a tour for 15-30 minutes; a typical visit lasts 1-1.5 hours. There's a gift shop, and beverages and snacks are for sale.

Hume Lake

Grant Grove Hikes

Trail	Effort	Distance	Duration
Big Stump Loop	easy	2-mi (3-km) loop	45 min-1 hr
North Grove Loop	moderate	2-mi (3-km) loop	1 hr
Sunset Loop	strenuous	6-mi (10-km) loop	3-4 hr
Park Ridge Trail	moderate	5.5-mi (9-km) loop	2.5-3 hr
Hart Tree Loop	strenuous	7.3-mi (11.8-km) loop	3 hr
Sugarbowl Loop	moderate	6.8-mi (11-km) loop	3-4 hr
Buena Vista Peak	moderate	2 mi (3 km) rt	45 min-1 hr
Big Baldy Ridge	moderate	4.2 mi (6.8 km) rt	2 hr
Boole Tree Loop	moderate	2.5-mi (4-km) loop	1.5 hr
Indian Basin Grove Interpretive Trail	easy	1-mi (1.5-km) loop	30-45 min

Recreation

Adventures of all kinds await in Grant Grove and the surrounding wilderness, where you can find solitude, big trees, and waterfalls. Winter snowshoeing and cross-country skiing make Grant Grove a year-round destination.

DAY HIKES

Big Stump Loop

Distance: 2-mile (3-km) loop
Duration: 45 minutes-1 hour
Elevation change: 250 feet (75 m)
Effort: Easy
Trailhead: Big Stump
Directions: From the Big Stump Entrance Station, after 0.8 mile (1.3 km) take a left into the Big Stump Picnic Area, a parking lot with full-service restrooms and picnic tables. The trailhead is by the restrooms.

On this hike, you can get a sense of what the park might have looked like if it hadn't been protected. Today, this former logging area is home to sequoias of all ages, as well as fallen trees and massive stumps, markers of the loggers that once worked here. Though you are often within earshot of the road, this trail is rather meditative. Follow the trail back behind the restrooms, heading southeast. You'll be doing this loop counterclockwise.

The trail begins with a short, evenly graded descent into a lush meadow surrounded by sequoias of all ages and full of fallen giants. As you round the path, notice sequoia cones (slightly larger than golf balls) littering the path. A sign marks this area as the site of the **Smith Comstock Mill,** the company that once logged and processed the trees here.

The trail continues, opening on another meadow. The remains of the **Mark Twain Tree,** now better known as the **Big Stump,** stands 10 feet high and 14 feet across. It was 1,350 years old when it was cut down. Two men chopped for 13 days, cutting one cross-section for the American Museum of Natural History in New York and another for the British Museum in London. Take a moment to climb the stairs that lead up to the top of the stump and consider this great being.

Continue to road, just east of the Big Stump Entrance Station. The path heads uphill before leading you across the road. (Use caution—and the crosswalk—as you cross.) On this side

Big Stump Loop

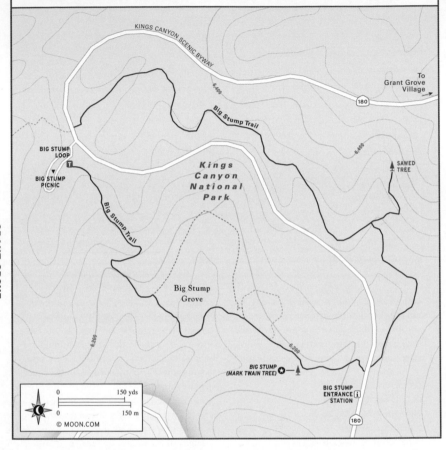

of the trail, turn right for a quick look at the ultimate survivor, **Sawed Tree.** As its name implies, this tree was once sawed partway through—but the job was never completed, and the tree, amazingly, carried on living.

The rest of the trail has dogwoods and forest views. You will drop down to the highway just north of the Big Stump parking lot. The trail doesn't loop directly back to the trailhead, so you can head directly to your car from here.

In the winter, you can snowshoe and play in the snow in this area, but the trail is more interesting when you can see the meadow. The best times to hike this sunny slope are in the spring and fall or on summer mornings.

★ North Grove Loop

Distance: 2-mile (3-km) loop
Duration: 1 hour
Elevation change: 500 feet (150 m)
Effort: Moderate
Trailhead: North Grove/Sunset
Directions: From the General Grant parking lot, continue to the area where RVs and buses park. Turn left and go downhill to the western-most paved parking area. The trailhead is at the gate at the western end of the parking lot.

This moderate trail gives you the chance to view the sequoia's full life cycle. From birth to adolescence, adulthood, then death, thousands of years of forest time are on display here. Sequoias surround you at every step, their cones littering the ground.

From the trailhead, follow the fire road downhill into the North Grove. There will be a junction at 0.25 mile (0.4 km); continue straight downhill, staying to the left. (You will return via that turnoff to complete the loop.) At 0.75 mile (1.2 km), you will come to a junction and take the fork to the right. If you continued to the left, you would add the **Dead Giant and Sequoia Lake Overlook Loop,** which encircles a meadow. Sequoia Lake was part of the old logging infrastructure from the turn of the 20th century and is now privately operated. At one point the Kings River Lumber Company sent 19 million board feet through this lake. Along the way, you'll also see the Dead Giant, a fully dead sequoia that has been standing for many years. With this additional loop, the distance of the hike extends to 3.25 miles (5 km).

After turning right, the trail gradually climbs. You'll begin to notice recent fire scars, some charred pines, and evidence of recovery. The sequoia's oat-sized seeds sprout only after a fire. From the bare soil, spiky buds break through the surface and race toward the sunlight. Though this area was burned during the 2015 Rough Fire, new life abounds. Sequoias can add a foot of growth per year.

The loop ends as you reenter the intact forest. Notice the comparative coolness of this ecosystem and listen for the chickadees calling to one another. Return back up the last hill to the parking area.

★ Sunset Loop

Distance: 6-mile (10-km) loop
Duration: 3-4 hours
Elevation change: 2,000 feet (610 m)
Effort: Strenuous
Trailhead: Kings Canyon Visitor Center
Directions: From the Big Stump Entrance Station, follow Highway 180 for 3.1 miles (5 km). Turn right to enter Grant Grove Village. The visitors center is the first building on the right.

The Sunset Loop offers the greatest hits of Grant Grove: a beautiful forest, the General Grant Tree, the North Grove, and waterfalls, among other breathtaking sights. Cross Highway 180 from the Kings Canyon Visitor Center to a dirt path. Take the first right and walk downhill into Azalea Campground. You'll pop out on the other side of the

North Grove Loop

Sunset Loop Trails

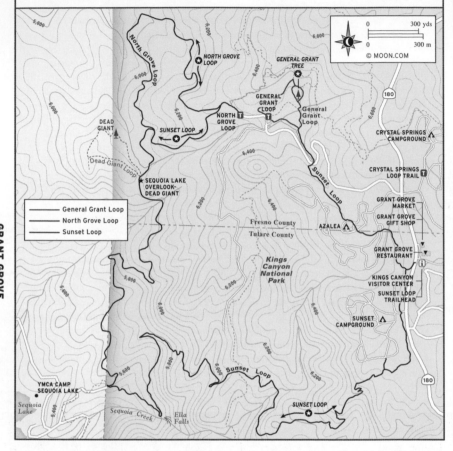

campground and pass between the Columbine picnic area on the right and the Grant Tree road on the left.

Following a small meadow, the faint path departs the picnic area and meets the Grant Tree road near a crosswalk. As you pass beneath some stick-straight sequoias, you'll arrive at the edge of the General Grant Tree parking lot.

Head left and downhill toward the RV parking area. At the end of the lot is a metal gate where you'll join the North Grove Loop Trail. Traipse down an old fire road, following a creek to Lion Meadow. After the meadow,

the trail is more open. Views of the valley and Sequoia Lake give you a sense of height: You are at almost 6,000 feet (1,830 m) elevation for this entire trip.

At the end of the fire road, there's a T-junction. Turn uphill and east, following Sequoia Creek, up some mini-switchbacks to **Ella Falls**—a verdant and lovely little waterfall in the spring, and a cool geologic feature in the summer.

A long switchback takes you away from the falls and to a four-way junction. Get a look at **Viola Falls** by turning right at the junction and following a spur trail for 0.4 mile (0.6

km). Here you'll see an overflow of ferns and fairy-like flowers. When you return to the junction from Viola Falls, turn right to get back onto the main trail, which leads to Sunset Campground. Complete the loop by walking between the road and the campground back to Grant Grove Village.

For a shorter option that's ideal in the spring when the falls are running, start from site 118 of Sunset Campground. Head downhill for 1.2 miles (2 km) to the four-way junction and take a left to see Viola Falls. Return the way you came for a total of 3.2 miles (5 km). A map is helpful to explore the many side loops and spurs of this trail.

Park Ridge Trail

Distance: 5.5-mile (9-km) loop
Duration: 2.5-3 hours
Elevation change: 1,500 feet (460 m)
Effort: Moderate
Trailhead: Panoramic Point
Directions: Drive past Bradley Meadow toward the John Muir Lodge. When the road forks, follow it to the right to get on Panoramic Point Road. Drive 2.3 miles (3.5 km) to the end of the road.

This hike, which starts at Panoramic Point, traces a ridge to reach a fire lookout tower, where you'll get breath-taking views. Follow the paved trail to Panoramic Point. From here, look for the Park Ridge trailhead to the right of a gnarled fir leaning against an improbably balanced boulder.

As its name indicates, the trail is atop a ridge. After 1.4 miles (2.3 km), the undulating trail crosses a service road. This area of the forest is full of wildlife: Keep your ears open to hear squirrels chatter and birds sing. After another mile and some climbing, you'll end up at a fire lookout tower, set at 7,700 feet (2,350 m) elevation. Here, you can see many of the highest peaks in the Sierra Nevada. To the north, you'll see the remote peaks above the Kings River, all part of the San Joaquin Valley.

Return the way you came. Alternately, you can turn right onto a fire road at the intersection 250 yards from the lookout tower and follow it back to the trailhead. This option

won't save you any mileage, but it is a bit quicker thanks to the road being smoother and graded. The fire road also has some spots with clear views. Look for birds in the recovering logged area.

★ Redwood Mountain Sequoia Grove

Redwood Mountain is the largest grove of sequoias in the world today. Over 2,000 big trees, wider than 10 feet in diameter, thrive in this shady canyon, a haven for hikers. Fewer visitors make the trip to this area than to the rest of Grant Grove. Three main trails are worth exploring throughout the year: Hart Tree Loop and Sugarbowl Loop are good day hikes; the longer Redwood Canyon Trail is best done as a backpacking trip.

The road to the grove is only open in the summer and fall (Memorial Day-early Nov.). Though the unpaved road is rough, a four-wheel-drive vehicle is not required. It can be a challenge if you encounter a car coming from the opposite direction; one vehicle may need to reverse to a place where both cars can safely pass.

HART TREE LOOP

Distance: 7.3-mile (11.8-km) loop
Duration: 3 hours
Elevation change: 1,000 feet (300 m)
Effort: Strenuous
Trailhead: Redwood Canyon
Directions: From Grant Grove Village, drive 5.5 miles (9 km) south on Generals Highway and turn right onto Redwood Mountain Saddle, directly across from the Hume Lake turnoff. Continue approximately 2 miles (3 km, 20 minutes) to the bottom of the narrow road. Use the bear boxes to lock up food or anything else in your car that might attract a bear.

This trail has a smorgasbord of scenery, interesting sequoias, and views of Buena Vista Peak. Start on the Redwood Canyon Trail, where you'll descend through a group of sequoias for 0.5 mile (0.8 km). Continue among ferns and wild strawberries, before staying to the left on **Hart Tree Trail,** taking the loop in a clockwise direction.

Redwood Mountain Sequoia Grove Trails

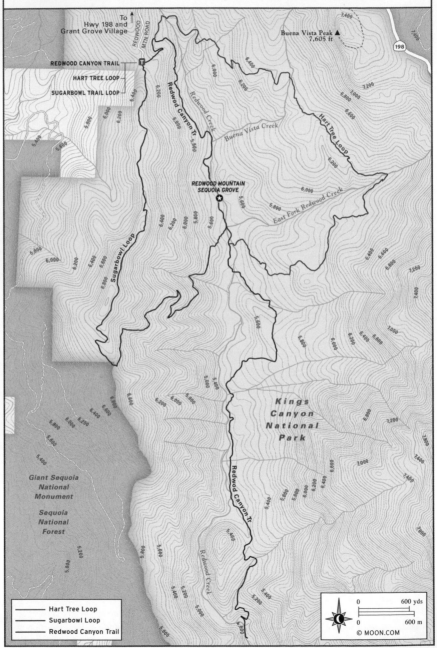

To Hwy 198 and Grant Grove Village

Buena Vista Peak ▲ 7,605 ft

REDWOOD CANYON TRAIL

HART TREE LOOP

SUGARBOWL TRAIL LOOP

REDWOOD MTN ROAD

Redwood Canyon Tr.

Redwood Creek

Buena Vista Creek

Hart Tree Loop

REDWOOD MOUNTAIN SEQUOIA GROVE

East Fork Redwood Creek

Sugarbowl Loop

Redwood Canyon Tr.

Kings Canyon National Park

Giant Sequoia National Monument

Sequoia National Forest

Redwood Creek

Hart Tree Loop
Sugarbowl Loop
Redwood Canyon Trail

0   600 yds
0   600 m

© MOON.COM

Loggers once tried to make a living here. You can see some evidence of their work about a mile in. Look for the ruins of a cabin set in a fallen tree, a sequoia stump with notches sawn into its side, and a sequoia with the beginnings of an undercut in its trunk.

Next are two short, steep climbs. At 1.5 miles (2.5 km), the view from a rocky knoll is the reward. At 2 miles (3 km), you arrive at **Tunnel Log,** a hollowed-out sequoia that you can walk through. After the highest point on the trail you come to **Hart Meadow.** Take a 100-yard spur trail to the left to reach the signed **Hart Tree,** the 24th largest sequoia in the world: 277 feet tall and 21.3 feet wide. On the tree's eastern side, you can see its splayed-out roots and a huge fire scar. Uphill, 120 feet away, the base of the **Roosevelt Tree** is relatively straight compared to the buttressed Hart Tree.

After 5 miles (8 km), you'll reach Redwood Creek, which parallels the trail. Head uphill to return to the junction with Redwood Canyon Trail. Turn left onto Redwood Canyon and continue for 0.5 mile (0.8 km) to the trailhead.

SUGARBOWL LOOP
Distance: 6.8-mile (11-km) loop
Duration: 3-4 hours
Elevation change: 2,150 feet (660 m)
Effort: Moderate
Trailhead: Redwood Canyon
Directions: From Grant Grove Village, drive 5.5 miles (9 km) south on Generals Highway and turn right onto Redwood Mountain Saddle, directly across from the Hume Lake turnoff. Continue approximately 2 miles (3 km, 20 minutes) to the bottom of the narrow road. Use the bear boxes to lock up food or anything else in your car that might attract a bear.

On this hike, which takes you deep into the Redwood Mountain Grove, you'll likely be alone—aside from black bears, which thrive among the manzanita and bear clover on the sunny hillslope.

President Franklin Roosevelt added Redwood Mountain Grove to what was then called General Grant Grove National Park in 1940. As you start from the south end of the parking lot, you will see stumps along the trail, evidence that federal protections could not have come soon enough.

After 1 mile (1.5 km), you will get great views of Big Baldy and Buena Vista Peak above and the Central Valley below. After 2 miles (3 km), you descend into the **Sugarbowl,** named for a group of sequoias within the grove.

A dense collection of young sequoias ushers you to Redwood Creek. Here, turn left at the junction to join with the central trail, Redwood Canyon. You'll head upstream and climb up and out of the canyon. In June, dogwoods blossom and sword ferns unfurl, lending a primordial feel to this already sacred-seeming place. When you reach a T-junction, turn left again. In 0.5 mile (0.8 km) you'll return to the trailhead and close the loop.

Buena Vista Peak
Distance: 2 miles (3 km) round-trip
Duration: 45 minutes-1 hour
Elevation change: 200 feet (60 m)
Effort: Moderate
Trailhead: Buena Vista Peak
Directions: From the junction of Highway 180 and Highway 198, drive 5 miles (8 km) southeast on Highway 198. Just past Kings Canyon Overlook, a sign marks the trailhead. Park in the small dirt lot on the right side of the road.

This out-and-back hike takes you up to the top of Buena Vista Peak, actually a granite dome. Bring a picnic lunch to best enjoy the views from the top. The trail begins with some switchbacks, climbing to a lunar landscape of huge, rounded boulders. The size of buses, these unusual-looking rocks balance on thin stems, a result of erosion.

Several granite domes exist between the High Sierra and the Central Valley. Erosion over millennia has sloughed off layers of rock, resulting in a rounded appearance. These are known as **exfoliation domes.** You'll be able to see for yourself as you climb up steps of layered granite before reaching a large dome; this is Buena Vista Peak. For an easier approach, follow the switchbacks on the back of the dome. Your reward will be miles of views, including Redwood Mountain Grove, where sequoia crowns stand high above the rest of the forest. After enjoying lunch on the top of the dome, return the way you came.

It's easy to lose this trail when there's snow on the ground. There are no trail blazes on the trees to guide your way. Do this hike in May or June when the trail is clear.

★ Big Baldy Ridge

Distance: 4.2 miles (6.8 km) round trip
Duration: 2 hours
Elevation change: 650 feet (200 m)
Effort: Moderate
Trailhead: Big Baldy
Directions: From the junction of Highway 180 and Highway 198 (or 2 mi/3 km west of Grant Grove Village), head 6.6 miles (11 km) south on the Generals Highway (Hwy. 198). A turnout large enough for ten cars is on the west side (right side) of the road. If you get to the turn for Montecito Sequoia Lodge, you have gone too far. The trailhead is marked with a large brown sign.

The journey is as wonderful as the destination on this hike, which flits through sunny forest and along hillslopes covered in fragrant wild mint. The gradual climb to **Big Baldy,** an exposed granite dome, takes you along a ridge, with just one short steep section at the last 0.2 mile (0.3 km). From Big Baldy, the San Joaquin Valley is in full view: the peaks above Kings Canyon, the High Sierra, and redwood forests. As you go back the way you came, listen for mountain chickadees and red-breasted nuthatches.

Bring a hat, sunscreen, and water. Go in the morning, before the valley haze rises with the heat. In the winter, this trail is a popular snowshoe hike. Keep your eyes peeled for climbers; several routes ascend Big Baldy's face.

Boole Tree Loop

Distance: 2.5-mile (4-km) loop
Duration: 1.5 hours
Elevation change: None
Effort: Moderate
Trailhead: Boole Tree Loop
Directions: From Grant Grove Village, drive 4.4 miles (7 km) on Highway 180 and take a left on the road marked with a sign for Converse Basin, Stump Meadow, and Boole Tree Trail. In 2 miles (3 km), turn right. Shortly after the turn, Stump Meadow is worthy of a pause. The road cuts across this logged meadow that once housed giants. Continue on the road 1.4 miles (2.3 km) to the end of the road, where you'll find the trailhead.

Converse Basin, where the Boole Tree is

located, is one of the reasons that Sequoia and Kings Canyon National Parks exist today. In the 1890s, activists spread word of the existence of giant sequoias and the damage that logging was inflicting on these majestic trees. Sadly, the axe was faster than the pen; conservation laws could not save what was once the largest grove in the Sierra Nevada. Today, only 60 large trees survive out of the thousands that once stood here.

This hike takes you counter-clockwise along the trail, but you can follow it in either direction. From the trailhead, follow the creek to the **Boole Tree.** Measuring 25.5 feet in diameter, it was once thought to be the world's largest tree. In truth, it's the sixth largest giant sequoia in the world. Continue on the trail for views into Kings Canyon.

Due to the presence of mountain lions, it is not recommended to hike alone in this area. This hike is best done after the snow clears, from June to November.

Indian Basin Grove Interpretive Trail

Distance: 1-mile (1.5-km) loop
Duration: 30-45 minutes
Elevation change: None
Effort: Easy
Trailhead: Princess Campground
Directions: From Grant Grove Village, drive 6.2 miles (10 km) north on Highway 180. Turn right into Princess Campground. As you enter the campground, stay straight, near the camp host site, or park on the highway outside the campground.

This trail is easy, partially accessible and paved, and perfect for seeing new sequoias growing in the space of their logged counterparts in a lush meadow. Almost all the trees in this grove were removed in the 1800s by loggers, but some are returning. Signs along the interpretive trail tell the story of this sequoia grove and the history of conservation in the area. It's accessible for most mobilities.

BACKPACKING

All backpacking in the national park requires a permit. If you only stay in the national forest, no wilderness permit is needed. Carry plenty of water and a map. Camp only in established campsites with fire rings. Be sure to communicate your location and expected return to a friend before venturing out.

Redwood Canyon Trail

Redwood Canyon Trail is the perfect overnight backpacking trip, full of solitude and sequoias. This 10-mile (16-km) trek combines two loops, the Hart Tree Loop and the Sugarbowl Loop into one big one. It also has as an out-and-back section to Big Springs, a stream that emerges from a series of caves.

Starting from the Redwood Canyon trailhead, go south on Redwood Canyon Trail, which parallels Redwood Creek. The first spot to camp is 1 mile (1.5 km) in. There's another spot just 0.5 mile (0.8 km) farther along, with views of Buena Vista Peak.

Campers are limited to a maximum of two nights in Redwood Canyon; your group size cannot exceed 10 people. Pack plenty of water as by mid-summer the creeks are mostly dry.

Jennie Lakes Wilderness

Accessible from Grant Grove, **Jennie Lakes Wilderness** in **Sequoia National Forest** (559/338-2251, www.fs.usda.gov) has many different trails that allow you to craft a backpacking trip of nearly any distance. Start from **Big Meadows** (12 mi/19 km east of Grant Grove Village) or **Rowell Meadow** (19 mi/31 km east of Grant Grove Village), two popular trailheads. Some of the more interesting places to visit include an old **snow survey cabin** at Rowell Meadow, **Weaver Lake,** and **Jennie Lake.** Deeper into the wilderness area, **Belle Canyon Trail** and **Sugarloaf Trail** offer spectacular vistas of gleaming granite.

To get to Big Meadows or Rowell Meadow trailheads from Grant Grove Village, go south on Highway 180 to Highway 198. Turn left onto Highway 198 and continue southeast for 7 miles (11 km), then turn left onto Forest Road 14S11. It's 4 miles (6 km) from here to Big Meadows and 11 miles (18 km) to Rowell Meadow.

HORSEBACK RIDING

Saddle up at the **Grant Grove Stables** (559/335-9292, 9am-4pm daily May-Sept., $50 for one-hour ride, $90 for two-hour ride) for a guided trip through the forest. Routes include North Grove, Lion Meadow, and Dead Giant Loop. The stables are not run by rangers and rides are dependent on weather conditions. Reservations are recommended. The stables are located near the General Grant Tree.

FISHING

If you would like to catch the biggest and best, visit **Hume Lake** (Sequoia National Forest, 559/338-2251) on fishing season's opening weekend in April. Monster rainbow trout are stocked in spring and summer; resident bluegill, small- and large-mouth bass, crappie, and catfish also reside in this mountain reservoir. For best results, ply the water with powerbait from a boat in the morning.

To access the lake, you can rent a boat at the boat launch, walk along the shores from Hume Lake Campground or launch your own boat (electric motors only). Before flipping your reel, purchase a California fishing license for all people 16 years of age and older. Licenses are available at the **Hume Lake General Store** (64144 Hume Lake Rd., Hume, 559/305-7770, www.hume.org) or at sporting goods stores in Fresno. California residents can purchase a license online.

WINTER RECREATION
Snowplay

There are two designated snow-play areas in the park. **Big Stump Picnic Area,** less than a mile from the Big Stump Entrance Station, has nice accessible slopes for your snowball fight and sledding. The area also has flush toilets, shelters to protect you from the weather, and grills. Many people use these outdoor grills in the 30-40 degree temperatures while their kids play in the snow. **Columbine Picnic Area,** on the same road as the General Grant Tree, is the other snow-play area. Here you'll find a running-water restroom, picnic tables, and grills. Snow play is not permitted elsewhere in Grant Grove inside of the park, especially near the Grant Tree.

In the national forest lands nearby, **Big Meadows, Quail Flat,** and **Cherry Gap** areas are recommended for snowplay. These areas are accessible from Highway 198.

Snowshoeing and Cross-Country Skiing

Whether this is your first time trying snowshoes or you are seasoned cross-country skier, there is a trail for you in Grant Grove. If you do not own your own equipment, you can rent cross country skis and snowshoes at the Grant Grove Gift Shop or at the market. An inexpensive paper map and guide depicting winter trails is available at the Kings Canyon Visitor Center.

NORTH GROVE LOOP

North Grove Loop (2 mi/3 km) is marked with red blazes on the trees. This is a great walk for people new to snowshoes or those with kids. From the trailhead, follow the service road down a gully to travel counter clockwise around the loop, avoiding some tighter downhill turns for skiers. About 1 mile (1.5 km) in, you will see a large standing dead tree, called the **Dead Giant,** where you will begin your return loop. This tree is unusual because it is was killed by fire, but it is still standing. The trailhead is accessible from the overflow parking lot for the General Grant Tree.

CRYSTAL SPRINGS LOOP TRAIL

For just a short spin on your snowshoes, opt for the **Crystal Springs Loop Trail** (1.3 mi/2.1 km), with little elevation change. Get a different view of the Crystal Springs campground (closed for winter) and its nearby meadow. Follow the blue trail blazes from Grant Grove Village along Bradley Meadow through Crystal Springs Campground. Look

1: sequoia grove in winter 2: ranger-led snowshoe hike

for sugar pines as you go: An easy way to identify the tree is by its great height, droopy branches, and long, large pinecones.

PANORAMIC POINT AND THE PARK RIDGE FIRE LOOKOUT

For a big adventure and a long day, make the popular climb up to **Panoramic Point** (2.5 mi/4 km) following Panoramic Point Road (closed to vehicles in winter). Look for the yellow blazes on the trees. You can continue for another 2.5 miles (4 km) and go out to the **Park Ridge Fire Lookout,** following the ridge and gaining 1,000 feet (300 m) in elevation. The full round-trip distance is 10 miles (16 km). If you are not staying at the John Muir Lodge or Grant Grove cabins, park in the village and walk towards the lodge to start up Panoramic Point Road. You will pass through beautiful Round Meadow, an open and serene clearing, on your way up to 7,520 feet (2,290 m) and epic 360-degree views. Continue beyond Panoramic Point, up and over a little knoll, and up to the fire lookout, which is active in the summer. The only thing that might disturb the peace on this long and remote walk is the hammering of a pileated woodpecker or the chatter of a chickaree. Otherwise, you will feel like you are the only person around. Due to the remoteness of this trek, it's a good idea to go with at least one other person.

BIG BALDY'S BASE

A steady gradual climb to the base of the **Big Baldy dome** (5.2 mi/8.4 km) rewards winter revelers with crystalline blue skies and views for miles. Follow trees marked with red blazes and the number "10" on this out-and-back trail, which takes 4-5 hours. The snow-capped Great Western Divide and views into Redwood Canyon will be your well-deserved reward.

Entertainment and Shopping

RANGER PROGRAMS

Check the bulletin boards at Grant Grove's campgrounds and the Kings Canyon Visitor Center for listings for ranger walks and talks. Listings are also posted on the park website (www.nps.gov/seki) and the website for the **Sequoia Parks Conservancy** (www.sequoiaparksconservancy.org), whose naturalists also offer programs at the park. Options include guided snowshoe walks, interpretive talks held at the General Grant Tree, and some campfire programs. At the John Muir Lodge in the summer, you can take in an entertaining and enlightening living history program, usually on Saturdays. Programs offered by the Sequoia Parks Conservancy sometimes cost $10-15, but some programs are free.

The **guided snowshoe walks** last two hours, departing on weekend mornings for the North Grove. Snowshoes are provided for free. A moderate level of fitness is recommended, but no snowshoeing experience is required. Ranger-led **full-moon snowshoe walks** are offered once a month and run from November through March, snow permitting.

Kids can stop in at the Kings Canyon Visitor Center to become a **Junior Ranger.** Pick up a complimentary booklet and complete the activities—like picking up litter or identifying animals—to earn your Junior Ranger badge. **Junior Ranger Day** is one of the last Saturdays in April, a day for free entrance and special activities for kids.

SHOPPING

The **Grant Grove Market** (86728 Hwy. 180, 866/807-3598, www.visitsequoia.com, 7am-9pm daily spring-fall, 9am-6pm daily winter) has just about everything you could need in a small space, including camping gear, coffee, and pre-made sandwiches and salads, as well as souvenirs to bring home. There are some well-designed stainless steel water bottles with sequoias printed on them.

There is a wide assortment of wine and you can even build your own six-pack of beer, including local craft beers. Restrooms are just outside.

Help remember your adventures with a keepsake from the **Grant Grove Gift Shop** (86728 Hwy. 180, 866/807-3598, www.visitsequoia.com, 8am-9pm daily spring-fall, 8am-6pm daily winter), next to Grant Grove Market. It carries clothing, camping gear, postcards, jewelry, and even sequoia saplings. In the winter, you can rent snowshoes here.

Food

INSIDE THE PARK

For a hearty meal or snack, head to the only restaurant in Grant Grove. Set in a stately modern log cabin, **Grant Grove Restaurant** (Grant Grove Village, 559/335-5500 ext. 305, www.visitsequoia.com, 7am-10pm, 11:30am-3:30pm, and 5pm-8pm daily, $10-25) serves local, sustainable, and organic comfort food, including perfectly prepared omelets, burgers, pork chops, and fancy pastas. On tap are local beers and California wines. The dining room offers views of Bradley Meadow. For a quicker snack, a walk-up window operates during summer, offering coffee, pizza, sandwiches, and ice cream. Dinner reservations are recommended in the summer. The restaurant is across from the visitors center.

OUTSIDE THE PARK

A throwback to the 1950s family-style buffet dining, the **Montecito Sequoia Lodge** (63410 Generals Hwy., 559/565-3388, www.mslodge.com, 7:30am-9am, noon-1:30pm, and 5:30pm-7pm daily late May-early Sept., 7:30am-9am, noon-1pm, and 6pm-7:30pm daily mid-Sept.-Apr., $9 breakfast, $10 lunch, $20 dinner) offers hotel guests a unique buffet experience in stunning surroundings. For breakfast, enjoy freshly made funnel cakes with powdered sugar, fruit salad, egg dishes, pancakes, coffee and tea. Hike Big Baldy in the morning and come in for a hearty lunch at the make-your-own sandwich bar with soup or salad. Rich cheeses, fruit, and nuts start off dinner, then a course of barbecued meats. It will be hard to leave room for the decadent desserts. There are always

vegetarian, gluten-free, or dairy-free options, and the staff are very accommodating. People who are not staying at the hotel can come for a meal September-May, and it is best to call ahead.

Near Montecito Sequoia Lodge is their sister bed-and-breakfast site: **Stony Creek Lodge** (65569 Generals Hwy., 559/565-3909 or 877/828-1440, 4pm-7:30pm daily May-Oct., $10-20) serves fresh pizza where you can eat on a simple outdoor dining patio. Also here are a market and gift shop and a gas station.

A 30-minute drive from Grant Grove, **Twin Valley's Restaurant** (39216 Dunlap Rd., Dunlap, 559/338-0160, breakfast, lunch and dinner, hours vary by season, $10-30) specializes in barbecue steak, potatoes, and pie. Their version of poutine, called Viking fries, are a decadent treat for at least two people. Or just come for some mile-high chocolate pie.

The **Badger Mountain House** (48711 Hwy. 245, Badger, 559/337-2321, 8am-7pm daily, $10-15) is a saloon and grill with a small separate area for dining with kids. Sit outside on the back patio for sunset while you enjoy a brew. The restaurant is about 45 minutes outside of Grant Grove, and is a convenient stop if you're traveling between the parks when the Generals Highway is closed.

For a fast food fix that's a 30-minute drive from Grant Grove, stop by **Hume Lake Snack Shop** (64144 Hume Lake Rd., Hume, 559/305-7770, hours vary Mon.-Sat.). The snack shop primarily serves guests of the Hume Lake Christian Camp, but anyone can visit this scenic spot for the best milkshakes in 100 miles. The shop also offers hot meals

GRANT GROVE
FOOD

like fish and chips, chili cheese fries, burgers, and chicken strips. Avoid going during the camp's free time (1pm-5pm) when the shop sees masses of kids. Hume Lake also hosts **Pondy Pizza & Pizookie** (hours vary Mon.-Sat.). Order at the window to get pizzas whole or by the slice, as well as sweets like pizookies (oversized pan-baked cookies topped with ice cream), shaved ice, ice cream, and churros.

Accommodations

INSIDE THE PARK

The **John Muir Lodge** (Grant Grove Village, 866/807-3598, www.visitsequoia.com, from $200 winter, from $250 summer) is a massive log cabin atop a hill surrounded by granite boulders and pine forest. You will enjoy warmth and comfort in the basic rooms of this hotel, remodeled in 2014. The shaded back porches on each floor have swings and lounge chairs from which to watch the sunset. Historical photos adorn the hallways, and local art hangs above the log bedframes in each room. There are minifridges, coffee pots, and flat screen TVs in each room. A standard room is a double queen; the deluxe rooms have a king and a sofa bed. A fireplace warms the lodge's common room, inviting you to unplug and play a board game. Wi-Fi is only available in the lobby and common room. Check in promptly in order to avoid a long wait for your room. In the winter, request an even-numbered room for views overlooking Panoramic Point Road. The lodge's rooms populate two floors, but there's no elevator. A wheelchair ramp is hidden in the back of the entrance; access is especially challenging in the snow. For $25 extra, you can bring your dog, but note that dogs aren't allowed in the national park's groves. To get to the lodge, follow the road from the visitors center for about 0.5 mile (0.8 km).

The rustic wooden **Grant Grove Cabins** (Grant Grove Village, 866/807-3598, www.visitsequoia.com, $40-150) provide comfort at an economical price point. Overlooking Bradley Meadow, the cluster of hard-sided **Camp Cabins** (open year-round) have electricity, heat, a wood stove, and a porch. The hard-sided cabins are decorated with regional art and quilts and contain a wooden table and two or three double beds. Note that you have to walk to the shared bathroom and showers. If you would prefer a private bath, go for the popular duplex cabin (but you'll need to book about a year in advance). The **Tent Cabins** (open late spring-early fall) have canvas siding and a battery-powered lamp. There's no heat or electricity. Campers have access to a shared bathroom. Pack your headlamps and extra blankets. Options for rooms include two doubles or two doubles and one twin. Check-in for the cabins is at the John Muir Lodge.

OUTSIDE THE PARK

For family fun, stay at the all-inclusive **Montecito Sequoia Lodge & Summer Family Camp** (63410 Generals Hwy., 559/565-3388 or 800-227-9900, www.mslodge.com, from $180 winter, from $250 summer). Surrounded by beautiful views and on the edge of a lake, this secluded resort has been helping families unplug and enjoy the peace of the mountains since the 1970s. Instead of televisions, guests enjoy swimming and boating in the lake, horseback riding, tennis, beach volleyball, and archery. Book a room in the lodge or a standalone cabin. Some of the cabins have a separate, shared bath. Rates include buffet meals, snacks, drinks, activities, and kids' programs.

At the halfway point between Grant Grove and Lodgepole is **Stony Creek Lodge** (65569

1: John Muir Lodge 2: one of the Grant Grove Cabins

Generals Hwy., 559/565-3909 or 877/828-1440, www.mslodge.com/stonycreeklodge, May-Oct., $170-230), the sister property of the Montecito Sequoia Lodge. This rustic 12-room hotel, seemingly hewn from the mountains around it, lies near the border of Sequoia National Park. Breakfast is included in the rate.

Camping

Each standard campsite comes equipped with a grill over the fire ring and a picnic table with two benches. Usually there is a tent pad large enough for two tents and parking for one vehicle. RV sites are larger, but there are no electric or water hookups in the park. Dump stations are in Dorst Campground near Lodgepole or Princess Campground on the way to Hume Lake. Reservations are recommended via www.recreation.gov, especially on summer weekends and holidays. Some walk-up sites are available at Landslide, Azalea, Crystal Springs, and Princess. The best time to nab a spot is in the morning, ideally Monday through early Friday, before the majority of the crowds appear on Friday afternoons and Saturday mornings. Most campgrounds have bear boxes; store everything with a scent in these lockers. The bear boxes are big enough for a cooler, cooking gear, and snacks. Only burn dead and down wood for fires; do not bring in firewood from another place.

National park campsites have more amenities and generally are reservable online. Typically, national forest campsites require packing in toilet paper, sometimes water, and most cannot be reserved in advance. National forest sites sometimes provide an overflow option.

INSIDE THE PARK

In the heart of Grant Grove Village is the bustling but beautiful **Crystal Springs Campground** (mid-May-early Sept., $18), with 36 tent and RV sites. There are also 14 group sites (for 7-15 people, by reservation only, $40). Since the campground is conveniently close to the market and restaurant, you can pack light with just a tent and sleeping bag. Some of the sites offer more privacy than others. In summer, the sugar pines offer shade. It gets chilly in May and September. Group site F is wheelchair-accessible. Bear boxes, a fire ring, picnic tables, and potable water are available. Ranger programs are offered most summer evenings. There's no dump station for RVs. Individual sites are first-come, first-served.

Azalea Campground (year-round, $18) is aptly named for the fragrant azaleas that bloom in summer. Best of all, this campground offers access to the General Grant Tree via a short trail. There are 110 first-come, first-served sites for tents and RVs. Sites along the western edge have the best views (60, 64, 65, 67, and 92). Site 30 is wheelchair-accessible. The campground has flush toilets and bear boxes. This is the only campground in the park that's open during winter. Pets are allowed, but must be leashed.

Busy **Sunset Campground** (mid-May-early Sept., $22) is directly across from Kings Canyon Visitor Center, offering 157 tent and RV sites. This is a walkable campground, but not a peaceful one: Generators can be heard right up until quiet hours. Sites along the western edge of the campground (including 54, 80, 81, and 100) have the best views. A couple hike-in sites make for a more private experience. Sites 26 and 116 are wheelchair-accessible. Two large group sites (15-30 people, by reservation only, $50) are on a separate stem of the campground. There are flush toilets but no showers. Ranger programs are offered here during the summer.

360-Degree Sunsets

sunset at Grant Grove

Grant Grove may be known for its big trees, but it also offers epic sunsets. The valley burns like an ember; on clear days, the Great Western Divide is lit with alpenglow for what seems like hours as orange fades to indigo. Bring your tripod or selfie stick, and pack a headlamp or flashlight for the return trip. Below are some of the best spots in Grant Grove to catch sunset.

- **Big Baldy and Buena Vista Peak:** These short hikes take you up and away from the road. Wait for the sun to make a golden lining around the crowns of Redwood Canyon's sequoias below.

- **Kings Canyon Overlook:** There's no need to go far from the road if you're seeking sunset. From this overlook on the Generals Highway, watch the granite change color as the sun dips below the horizon.

- **Panoramic Point:** It should come as no surprise that an overlook with a name like Panoramic Point offers amazing sunset views. This spot is easily reached by car from Grant Grove Village.

- **Buck Rock Lookout:** At this fire lookout station set at 8,500 feet (2,590 m), few obstacles stand in the way of your views from the Coast Range to the Sierra, making for a memorable sunset. From the junction of Highways 198 and 180, drive 8 miles (13 km) down Generals Highway, turn left on Forest Road 14S11 for 3 miles (5 km) to Horse Camp Campground. Turn left on Forest Road 13S04, down a narrow dirt road for 2.5 miles (4 km), and hike up to Buck Rock fire lookout station and imagine what it would be like to live here.

OUTSIDE THE PARK

Princess Campground (Sequoia National Forest, 877/444-6777, www.recreation.gov, late May-early Sept., $27) offers 88 shaded spots, 19 of which are tent-only. Just off of Highway 180, near the junction of Hume Lake Road, this Forest Service campground makes up for the sounds of passing cars and lack of privacy with its location—nestled into a small pine grove beside a lush Sierra meadow. The sites on Shining Cloud Loop are the farthest from the road and have the least traffic noise. The campground has an amphitheater that hosts weekend campfire ranger talks. It also offers access to the Indian Basin interpretive trail and the Indian Basin Grove of giant sequoias. Drinking water and vault toilets are available. Princess also has a dump station for RVs ($7 usage fee). Most of the sites are only available with advance reservations. To get here from Grant Grove Village, drive 5.9 miles (9.5 km) on Highway 180 towards Hume Lake, then take a right into Princess Campground. If you get to the turn for Hume Lake you have gone too far.

Across the highway from Princess Campground is the biggest group site in Sequoia National Forest. **Logger Flat Group Campground** (Sequoia National Forest, 877/444-6777, www.recreation.gov, mid-May-mid-Sept., $193) can accommodate 50 campers and 30 vehicles, including up to 10 RVs. There is drinking water and vault toilets, but no electric hookups.

At the national forest's **Stony Creek Campground** (Sequoia National Forest, 877/444-6777, www.recreation.gov, late May-mid-Sept., $27, $7 for extra vehicle) and **Upper Stony Creek Campground** (Sequoia National Forest, 877/444-6777, www.recreation.gov, late May-mid-Sept., $18, $5 for extra vehicle), set along Stony Creek, there are firs and pines to hang your hammock on as you escape the heat of the Central Valley. The downsides are there's some mosquitoes and not much privacy. Stony Creek offers 48 sites and flush toilets. (Sites 17-21 are the farthest from the road.) Upper Stony Creek has 18 sites and vault toilets. Amenities are available at nearby Stony Creek Lodge, including food and beverages. A day-use picnic area, nearby trails, and healthy forests full of twittering birds make these campsites perfect for nature lovers.

With 43 sites (15 of which are tent-only), the peaceful **Big Meadow Campground** (Sequoia National Forest, 877/444-6777, www.recreation.gov, late May-late Sept., $23) is a jumping off point for exploring the Jennie Lakes Wilderness. There is ample shade, a picnic table, and a fire pit and ring at each site.

The campground has vault toilets. Be sure to arrive while it's still light out, as the sites are spread along Forest Road 14S11 and can be hard to find in the dark. If you need help, check in with the camp host at site 7. Bring your own water. To get here from the junction of Highways 180 and 198, take the Generals Highway for 6.9 miles (11 km), past Big Baldy trailhead, and turn left on Big Meadow Road or Forest Road 14S11 and continue for 2.8 miles (4.5 km).

Hume Lake Campground (Sequoia National Forest, 877/444-6777, www.recreation.gov, late May-mid-Sept., $27-29) is within walking distance of the water and is one of just three campgrounds near Hume Lake. Sites 22-29 have lake views. The 64-site campground has drinking water, flush toilets, and a pay phone. There are laundry services and a gas station nearby.

On Forest Road 13S09, which connects Hume Lake to the Generals Highway, are two quaint campgrounds. The 11-site **Tenmile Campground** (Sequoia National Forest, 877/444-6777, www.recreation.gov, late May-mid-Sept., $23) is small, quiet, and a 15-minute drive upstream and uphill from Hume Lake. Even smaller than Tenmile is the nine-site **Landslide Campground** (Sequoia National Forest, no reservations, late May-mid-Sept., $23). Landslide is about a mile northeast of Tenmile, along Forest Road 13S09. Bring your own water. Forest Road 13S09 can close due to weather conditions from late fall to early spring.

Dispersed camping is permitted in Sequoia National Forest (unless posted otherwise), but you will need a permit for any fire, open flame, or stove. Otherwise, you can nab a spot at one of the national forest campgrounds near Grant Grove, just miles from the park boundary. Heading towards Lodgepole on the Generals Highway (Hwy. 198), there are several campgrounds. This area is close to Big Baldy and Redwood Canyon.

Transportation and Services

DRIVING AND PARKING

Parking is limited in Grant Grove. At the General Grant Tree, there is **overflow parking** down to the left near the North Grove. In Grant Grove Village, there is a narrow lot in front of the market and post office. Continue past the Visitor's Center to a wider lot with more parking next to Bradley Meadow. Once you have reached your cabin, campsite, or the lodge, it's easy to travel by foot or bicycle around the village and to the General Grant Tree.

SHUTTLES

There are no park shuttles in Grant Grove. Most of the attractions and trailheads are within a mile or two of the visitors center, but the roads are not particularly bike and pedestrian friendly—please be careful as you drive and walk.

SERVICES

It's best to fuel up before entering the park, in Squaw Valley or Dunlap. There are two **gas stations** near Grant Grove, though, if you're running low. About 13 miles (21 km) past the Big Stump entrance, **Stony Creek Lodge** (65569 Generals Hwy., 559/565-3909) has 24-hour credit card gas pumps in the summer. Hume Lake's pumps are open when the store is, but hours vary based on when camps are in session. Electric cars can use the local plugs at Grant Grove Market, but they may not be suitable for your vehicle.

Kings Canyon and Cedar Grove

Spending time in this part of the park is a bit of a paradox: Though time seems to slow down in this special canyon, you'll always want more of it. The road descending into Kings Canyon, carved by the erosive might of the Sierra snowmelt, is lined with yucca, white blooms over eight feet tall, and marbling bands of metamorphic rock. Once you've entered the canyon and reached the river, chevron folds of yellow and black rock show the true history of the Sierra Nevada: folding, faulting, and immense pressure revealed by the Kings River.

Though the daring can have the bicycle trip of a lifetime here, traveling thousands of feet down to the river, most of us arrive by vehicle.

Highlights

Look for ★ to find recommended sights, activities, dining, and lodging.

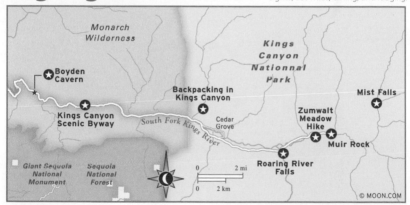

© MOON.COM

★ **Drive Kings Canyon Scenic Byway:** Every turn of this road through Kings Canyon reveals breathtaking views of mountain peaks, waterfalls, and the Kings River (page 130).

★ **Go Underground at Boyden Cavern:** On a tour of this limestone cave, you can see the brain-bending rock formations that have formed over eons (page 132).

★ **Feel the Spray from Roaring River Falls:** It's just a short paved walk to these booming waterfalls that flow into an emerald pool (page 132).

★ **Relax on Muir Rock:** Lounge on this flat boulder that's perched above the Kings River (page 134).

★ **Walk around Zumwalt Meadow:** On this loop trail, you'll have your eyes full no matter what direction you look: looming granite faces above, a green river below, and wildflowers all around (page 137).

★ **Hike to Mist Falls:** After the hot hike to this popular waterfall, you're rewarded with the refreshing snowmelt spray. This is the best day hike in Cedar Grove (page 139).

★ **Go Backpacking in Kings Canyon:** This is the ideal place for a backpacking trip, thanks to the stunning scenery and solitude accessible just a few miles from the road (page 140).

Kings Canyon and Cedar Grove

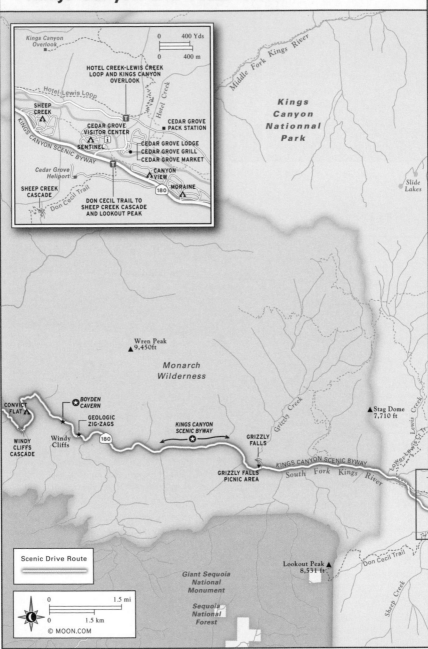

Kings Canyon Overlook

HOTEL CREEK-LEWIS CREEK LOOP AND KINGS CANYON OVERLOOK

Hotel-Lewis Loop

Hotel Creek

Middle Fork Kings River

Kings Canyon National Park

SHEEP CREEK

CEDAR GROVE PACK STATION

CEDAR GROVE VISITOR CENTER

KINGS CANYON SCENIC BYWAY

SENTINEL

CEDAR GROVE LODGE
CEDAR GROVE GRILL
CEDAR GROVE MARKET

Cedar Grove Heliport

CANYON VIEW

MORAINE

180

SHEEP CREEK CASCADE

Don Cecil Trail

DON CECIL TRAIL TO SHEEP CREEK CASCADE AND LOOKOUT PEAK

Slide Lakes

0   400 Yds
0   400 m

Wren Peak
9,450ft

Monarch Wilderness

Grizzly Creek

Stag Dome
7,710 ft

CONVICT FLAT

BOYDEN CAVERN

GEOLOGIC ZIG-ZAGS

KINGS CANYON SCENIC BYWAY

GRIZZLY FALLS

Lower Lewis Cr.

WINDY CLIFFS CASCADE

Windy Cliffs

180

GRIZZLY FALLS PICNIC AREA

KINGS CANYON SCENIC BYWAY

South Fork Kings River

Scenic Drive Route

Lookout Peak
8,531 ft

Don Cecil Trail

Giant Sequoia National Monument

Sheep Creek

0   1.5 mi
0   1.5 km

Sequoia National Forest

© MOON.COM

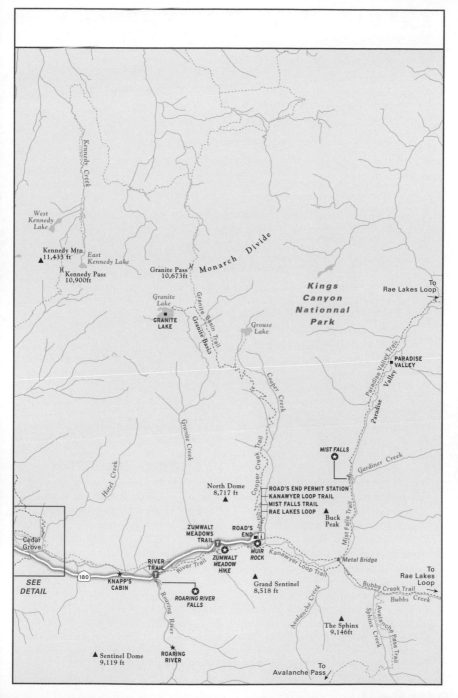

Kennedy Creek

West Kennedy Lake

Kennedy Mtn.
11,433 ft

East Kennedy Lake

Kennedy Pass
10,900ft

Granite Pass
10,673ft

Monarch Divide

Granite Lake

GRANITE LAKE

Granite Basin Trail

Granite Basin

Grouse Lake

Kings Canyon Nationnal Park

To Rae Lakes Loop

PARADISE VALLEY

Paradise Valley Trail

Paradise Valley

Cooper Creek

Hotel Creek

Granite Creek

Cooper Creek Trail

MIST FALLS

Gardiner Creek

North Dome
8,717 ft

ROAD'S END PERMIT STATION
KANAWYER LOOP TRAIL
MIST FALLS TRAIL
RAE LAKES LOOP

Buck Peak

Mist Falls Trail

ZUMWALT MEADOWS TRAIL

ROAD'S END

River Trail

ZUMWALT MEADOW HIKE

MUIR ROCK

Kanawyer Loop Trail

Metal Bridge

To Rae Lakes Loop

RIVER TRAIL

River Trail

KNAPP'S CABIN

180

SEE DETAIL

Cedar Grove

ROARING RIVER FALLS

Roaring River

Grand Sentinel
8,518 ft

Avalanche Creek

Bubbs Creek Trail

Bubbs Creek

Avalanche Pass Trail

The Sphinx
9,146 ft

Avalanche Creek

Sentinel Dome
9,119 ft

ROARING RIVER

To Avalanche Pass

KINGS CANYON AND CEDAR GROVE

Where Can I Find...?

- **Accessible campgrounds:** The **Moraine, Sentinel,** and **Canyon View Campgrounds** have accessible sites that include extended picnic tables.

- **Accessible trails and attractions:** There's a paved path to access **Roaring River Falls,** though it's steep in places.

- **ATM:** There's an ATM inside **Cedar Grove Market.**

- **Electric vehicle charging stations:** Not available in Cedar Grove.

- **Gas:** Fill up before entering the parks in **Dunlap** or **Squaw Valley.** The nearest gas is at **Hume Lake** (hours vary) off of Highway 180 on Tenmile Road, between Grant Grove Village and Junction View. The distance is only 20 miles (32 km), but it will take over 40 minutes. Gas is costly in this remote location.

- **Showers:** Showers and **laundry** are available at **Cedar Grove Lodge.** Get a shower key at the market. Laundry machines are coin-operated; the last laundry load needs to be in one hour before closing.

- **Supplies:** You'll find all the essentials at **Cedar Grove Market,** like fuel for your stove, marshmallows, beer, and wine. You can also rent a bear canister here.

- **Telephones:** Telephones are available in **Cedar Grove Lodge,** and **pay phones** can be found at the **Cedar Grove Visitor Center** and **Cedar Grove Market.** Having cell phone service in the canyon is unlikely.

- **Wi-Fi:** Not available in Cedar Grove.

- **Wilderness Permits:** For all overnight visits, a permit and a bear canister is required. Reserve your desired trail up to two weeks before your trip online or by phone starting in March of each year. In person, stop into the **Road's End Permit Station,** 6 miles (10 km) east of Cedar Grove Village. After September, you can self-register outside of the permit station.

Drive along the raging Kings River, pausing for short jaunts to waterfalls along the road.

Eventually you'll reach Cedar Grove, a meadow in the base of the canyon with plenty of campgrounds and a quaint, clean lodge. Cedar Grove is the launching points for steep but stunning hiking trails as well as a stroll through Zumwalt Meadows.

The backcountry of Kings Canyon is unparalleled in the lower 48, offering easy overnight backpacking trips up to multi-day off-trail adventures, where you'll traverse waves of rock and visit pristine lakes. Warm days and cool nights make for perfection while sleeping under the stars. Even day trippers will feel their truest selves in the wild,

drawn ever upward to the top of the mountain range.

PLANNING YOUR TIME

Access to Cedar Grove is limited to spring through fall, generally from mid-April to mid-November. Highway 180 past the Hume Lake turnoff is closed in the winter.

Cedar Grove sits at 4,610 feet (1,400 m) elevation, which lends to a temperate climate. Pack a jacket and pants because nights can be chilly and mosquitoes aggressive. The summer days reach well over 90°F (32°C), with nightly lows in the 50s (10-15°C). In spring, the temperature ranges 30-80°F (-1 to 27°C). In September and October, plan for lows in the

Previous: Kings Canyon Scenic Byway; lupine; crossing the bridge to Zumwalt Meadow.

30-40s (-1 to 4°C) and highs of 70°F (21°C). As the park's season winds down, so does visitation—the trails are all the more lovely when you have them to yourself.

In order to see the highlights of Cedar Grove and Kings Canyon, plan at least **four days** here. On the first day, visit **Grizzly Falls** on the way in and walk **Zumwalt Meadow.** Days two and three can be spent hiking to **Mist Falls** or **Kings Canyon Overlook,** then swimming at **Muir Rock.** On your last day, stop by **Boyden Cavern** on the way out.

For the best vacation possible, camp for a couple of nights or a week at one of the campgrounds and explore all that this special valley has to offer: bike paths, paved and sandy paths for easy strolls, strenuous hiking trails, a stunning trout steam for fly-fishing, and a cool marble cavern. This part of the park also offers some of the best backpacking in all of California, including easy options for beginners.

This is a driving park; most visitors will require a car. Luckily, the drive is part of the fun. You can get around Cedar Grove a bit easier thanks to the River Trail, which connects key sites like the campgrounds, Roaring River Falls, and Zumwalt Meadow.

There's no cell service or Wi-Fi in this part of the park.

Exploring Kings Canyon and Cedar Grove

VISITORS CENTERS
Cedar Grove Visitor Center
In Cedar Grove Village, visit the intimate **Cedar Grove Visitor Center** (Hwy. 180, 559/565-3793, 9am-5pm daily May-Sept.) to check out colorful interpretive programs and historical photographs, as well as to chat with dedicated rangers. The visitors center also rents out bear canisters to backpackers. A pay phone is outside the one-room center. The visitors center is 32 miles (52 km) northeast of the Big Stump entrance, a drive of about an hour.

Road's End Permit Station
The **Road's End Permit Station** (Hwy. 180, 559/565-3341, 7am-3pm daily May-Sept.) is where to pick up your wilderness permits, specifically for the nearby trailheads of Woods Creek, Bubb's Creek, Copper Creek, and Lewis Creek. This one-room wooden shack is decorated in topographic maps. A ranger who has traveled nearly all of the trails in this part of the park will be your encyclopedic resource if you can't get onto the trail you had planned. After late September,

self-register for a permit outside the station. There's a water fountain close by and access to the Kings River. The permit station is 6 miles (10 km) east of the Cedar Grove Visitor Center on Highway 180.

ENTRANCE STATIONS
The vehicle entrance fee is $35 for Sequoia and Kings Canyon National Parks. Kings Canyon and Cedar Grove are most accessible from the Big Stump entrance in Grant Grove. An alternate option is to come from the south, via the Ash Mountain entrance in the Foothills region.

TOURS
The energetic expert guides of **Sequoia Sightseeing Tours** (559/561-4189, www.sequoiatours.com, $169 adults, $119 children 12 and under) offer a full-day guided tour of Kings Canyon, stopping at Grizzly Falls, Roaring River Falls, and other park spots on the way to Road's End. Tours depart from Grant Grove and include a picnic lunch. Group size is about 10 people. You can also book a private tour ($875 for 4 people, $149

Kings Canyon Scenic Byway

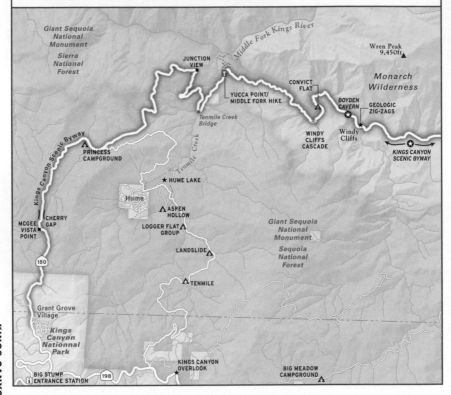

Giant Sequoia
National
Monument

Sierra
National
Forest

JUNCTION
VIEW

Middle Fork Kings River

Wren Peak
9,450ft

Monarch
Wilderness

CONVICT
FLAT

YUCCA POINT/
MIDDLE FORK HIKE

BOYDEN
CAVERN

GEOLOGIC
ZIG-ZAGS

Tenmile Creek
Bridge

Tenmile Creek

Kings Canyon Scenic Byway

PRINCESS
CAMPGROUND

WINDY
CLIFFS
CASCADE

Windy
Cliffs

KINGS CANYON
SCENIC BYWAY

HUME LAKE

Hume

ASPEN
HOLLOW

MCGEE
VISTA
POINT

CHERRY
GAP

LOGGER FLAT
GROUP

Giant Sequoia
National
Monument

180

LANDSLIDE

Sequoia
National
Forest

TENMILE

Grant Grove
Village

Kings
Canyon
Nationnal
Park

BIG STUMP
ENTRANCE STATION

198

KINGS CANYON
OVERLOOK

BIG MEADOW
CAMPGROUND

for each additional person). The company also offers guided tours of Giant Forest.

SCENIC DRIVES

TOP EXPERIENCE

★ Kings Canyon Scenic Byway

The 34-mile (55-km) drive along the **Kings Canyon Scenic Byway** allows you to explore one of North America's deepest canyons from the comfort of your own vehicle. You'll drive along a zigzagging road next to the roaring Kings River, among granite, wildlife, and wildflowers aplenty.

This drive starts at Grant Grove Village and traces Highway 180 north and east until Road's End. Drive 10.5 miles (17 km) north on Highway 180 to **Junction View,** an overlook on the left side of the road. This is a spectacular angle from which to see the depth of Kings Canyon.

Continue downhill, observing high elevation plants such as blazing stars, which trace the highway with eruptions of their spiky blooms. Twisting and turning on the two-lane road, you'll arrive at a bridge over **Tenmile Creek,** an outlet of nearby Hume Lake.

Continue down Highway 180. At 14 miles (23 km), you'll reach **Yucca Point Trail,** a good fishing spot where you can hike into the canyon and see firsthand the confluence of the Middle and South Forks of the Kings River.

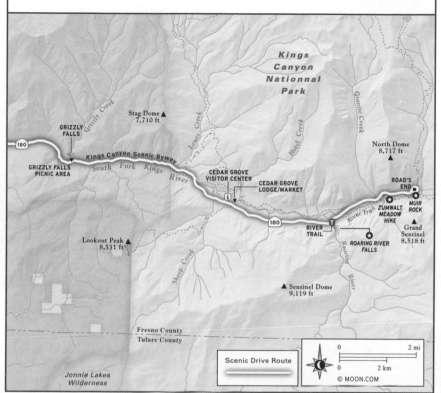

At 18 miles (29 km), you'll start the drive into the canyon itself. The road heads east and meanders along cliffsides in a series of fun zigzags above the river. Across the canyon is a sheer slate-colored face. This is home to the **Boyden Cavern.** You'll reach its parking lot at mile 19.5 (km 31). Stop for an hour and enjoy a guided tour through this unique geological underworld.

In another 5 miles (8 km), you will reach a small parking lot for **Grizzly Falls,** a lovely cascade that can be viewed from the car, a designated picnic area, or at its misty base, just a short walk from the parking lot.

Over the next 10 miles (16 km), you will experience the totality of Highway 180. Stop at **Cedar Grove Village,** taking the second left north and following the park service signs. Here you'll find a restaurant and market, as well as the **Cedar Grove Visitor Center.**

As you approach the highway's eastern terminus, you can get out of the car and explore **Roaring River Falls** and **Zumwalt Meadow,** both of which offer stunning views of the area.

The drive ends at the appropriately named **Road's End.** Here you can stand on **Muir Rock** and peer into the King River's crystalline waters, or go on one of several hikes.

Go slowly on this drive. Downshift into a lower gear (rather than ride your brakes) and use turnouts. Trailers longer than 24 feet (7 m) are not recommended on Highway 180.

Sights

These sights are ordered from west to east along Highway 180.

★ BOYDEN CAVERN

This part of the park is hot from June to September, regularly reaching over 90°F (32°C). To cool off, go underground and explore **Boyden Cavern** (19 mi/31 km northeast of Grant Grove, Hwy. 180, 888/965-8243, http://boydencavern.com, tour times vary by season, $16 adults, $8 children 5-12, $5 children 4 and under). Technically located in Sequoia National Forest, this cave is set at the base of a canyon. On a tour of this cave, led by a geology expert, you can spend a couple of hours exploring what took 100,000 years to form. You'll see how water has carved through marble to create strange formations that resemble tiny straws, shards of glass, a stack of pancakes, and a giant wedding cake. The tour covers about 750 feet (230 m) of cave in 50 minutes, and is suitable for all ages. If you are only visiting the northern half of the park, this is a wonderful alternative to Crystal Cave.

Book your tour spot online or in person. Advance reservations are not required. Budget approximately two hours for this attraction to give yourself enough time to get here, purchase tickets, and browse the souvenir shop afterward. Bring a jacket for inside the chilly cave.

To get to Boyden Cavern from Cedar Grove, it's a 10-mile (16-km) drive west on Highway 180, which takes around 15 minutes. From Grant Grove, it's a 20-mile (32-km) drive northeast on Highway 180, which takes less than an hour.

Just 0.5 mile (0.8 km) before Boyden Cavern is a turnout on the east side of the road. Park and walk upstream about 100 yards to feast your eyes on layers of **zig-zagging rock.** The folds were formed over eons as the tectonic plates underneath them shifted.

GRIZZLY FALLS

Make a quick stop to cool down in the spray from the beautiful **Grizzly Falls.** Set in a shady canyon, these cascades bounce and flutter off of dark rocks, affording waterfall lovers a quick photo op.

There's a picnic area by the road. It gets a little noisy and dirty here, but the waterfall sure is beautiful. There's a bathroom here. Dogs are permitted.

From Cedar Grove, drive 4.5 miles (7 km) west and park at the signed turnout on the north side of Highway 180. Follow the short dirt and rock path for about 0.1 mile (160 m) to reach the falls.

KNAPP'S CABIN

In the 1920s, a wealthy industrialist and philanthropist, George Knapp, built this cabin to store gear for his fishing and hunting outings. Perched on a glacial moraine above the Kings River, **Knapp's Cabin** is a humble, windowless, one-room shed, constructed of rot-resistant cedar. It's less than 200 square feet in size. The sheltered porch overlooks the river. The cabin has sat empty since the establishment of Kings Canyon National Park in 1940. It was added to the National Register of Historic Places in 1978.

From the road, it's just a 50-yard walk to reach the cabin. The best times to visit are in the morning or evening, when the light is optimal for admiring the surrounding views. To get here, look for the signed turnout on the north side of Highway 180, 2 miles (3 km) east of Cedar Grove.

★ ROARING RIVER FALLS

Refresh yourself in the snowmelt spray of **Roaring River Falls.** Here, a lush band of

---

1: Grizzly Falls **2:** Knapp's Cabin **3:** Muir Rock **4:** Roaring River Falls

Kings Canyon and Cedar Grove Hikes

Trail	Effort	Distance	Duration
Hotel Creek-Lewis Creek Loop and Cedar Grove Overlook	moderate/ strenuous	3.6 mi (5.8 km) rt/6.9-mi (11-km) loop	3 hr/5-6 hr
Don Cecil Trail to Sheep Creek Cascade and Lookout Peak	moderate/ strenuous	1.8 mi (2.9 km) rt/13 mi (21 km) rt	1 hr/5-6 hr
River Trail and Zumwalt Meadow	easy	4 mi (6 km) rt	2 hr
Zumwalt Meadow	easy	1.8-mi (2.9-km) loop	1-2 hr
Kanawyer Loop Trail	easy	4.5-mile (7.2-km) loop	2-3 hr
Mist Falls	moderate	9.1 mi (14.7 km) rt	6 hr

alders and cottonwoods wobble along the riverside. Wildflowers bloom from every cranny. The falls are appropriately named, booming as the water bounces between the canyon walls it has carved for itself. The mist is strongest from May to July, but it's a pleasant stop throughout the season.

The 0.5-mile (0.8-km) trail to the falls is paved, but steep, and may not be ideal for visitors using wheelchairs. This makes a great walk for children. Practice caution as you approach the falls: In spring, the rocks at the end of the path are very slippery. Don't get any closer; falling into the pool could prove deadly.

★ MUIR ROCK

This flat boulder bears the name of one of the Sierra's greatest travelers, John Muir. **Muir Rock,** located on the north edge of the Kings River, commemorates Muir's work to preserve what would become Sequoia National Park, among other areas. In late summer, you can jump from the rock into the river below; year-round, it's a great spot to lounge in the sun.

To reach the rock from Cedar Grove Village, drive 5.5 miles (9 km) east on Highway 180 to Road's End and park in the southern lot. The rock is on the south side of the road, and the north shore of the river.

Recreation

DAY HIKES

There are two kinds of hikes in Cedar Grove: climbing up and out of the canyon for incredible views or meandering on the canyon floor, following either side of the river. There are some opportunities to see waterfalls throughout the canyon and wildflowers are the divine gems of Cedar Grove.

Hotel Creek-Lewis Creek Loop and Cedar Grove Overlook

Distance: 3.6 miles (5.8 km) round-trip to overlook; 6.9-mile (11-km) loop
Duration: 3 hours; 5-6 hours
Elevation change: 1,200 feet (370 m); 1,500 feet (460 m)
Effort: Moderate; strenuous
Trailhead: Hotel Creek/Cedar Grove Village

Directions: From Cedar Grove Lodge, go 0.3 mile (0.5 km) north to a T-junction with Cedar Grove Road and Motor Nature Trail Road. Turn right; immediately on the left is the signed trailhead for Hotel Creek and a small parking area. If you reach the stables, you've gone too far.

This hike through shrubland and pine forest travels to a vista point above Kings Canyon. To do it, you can choose between an out-and-back or a loop route. The first 0.2 mile (0.3 km) of this hike is easy, leading east to a pack station and a horse trail. The next mile (1.5 km) is a steep and steady climb up the canyon. After the switchbacks, the trail levels out and you can cruise along a ridge with great views all along the way.

At 1.4 miles (2.3 km), you'll approach a Y-junction that can be confusing. Leave Hotel Creek Trail and take the left spur trail 0.4 mile (0.6 km) to the **Cedar Grove Overlook.** Looking upstream and across the canyon, feast your eyes on **Grand Sentinel** (8,520 ft/2,600 m), a massive tower to the east. Directly to the south, **Sheep Creek Cascade** may be running below **Sentinel Dome** (9,115 ft/ 2,780 m). Below you, watch the peridot-colored river slithering across the canyon floor. As you look west, you can spot the outline of the Monarch Divide, a mountain range just outside the boundary of the park.

Return to Hotel Creek Trail from the overlook. From here, you can return the way you came, or you can continue up Hotel Creek Trail to make a loop hike. To continue, turn left onto Hotel Creek Trail and walk northwest for 1.25 miles (2 km).

At the next junction, turn left onto Lewis Creek Trail. You'll descend out of the alpine zone fairly rapidly and into chaparral. In 2015, one of the largest and most intense wildfires in California's recent history burned from Grant Grove east to this trailhead. The Rough Fire burned 151,000 acres and required the help of almost 3,000 firefighters to contain it. In the aftermath of the fire, small wildlife has taken up residence in the area: giant carpenter bees whiz along the path, lizards angle for the prime spot on a dead log, and hummingbirds swarm this low-elevation area.

As you reach the Lewis Creek trailhead, you can cross the highway to take a pit stop at the restroom in the turnout on the south side of the road. There is some good fishing in the narrow pools below the trail near this turnout.

Get back on the trail by heading east from the Lewis Creek trailhead on a pack trail that parallels the north side of the roadway. It's a dusty, rolling 1.4 miles (2.3 km) back to the Hotel Creek trailhead and Cedar Grove via this trail.

Leave very early in the morning if you're doing this hike in the middle of summer. Wear pants rather than shorts, even when it's hot: The lower elevations are home to thorny plants as well as ticks. Practice caution when passing stock and horses—give them the right of way.

Don Cecil Trail to Sheep Creek Cascade and Lookout Peak

Distance: 1.8 miles (2.9 km) round-trip to Sheep Creek; 13 miles (21 km) round-trip to Lookout Peak

Duration: 1 hour; 5-6 hours

Elevation change: 1,200 feet (370 m); 8,450 feet (2,580 m)

Effort: Moderate; strenuous

Trailhead: Don Cecil

Directions: From Highway 180 at Cedar Grove Village, pass the turnoff for Sentinel Campground (North Side Dr.). The signed trailhead is 400 feet (120 m) farther east, on the south side of the highway.

This hike has two options: a short, shady trek to Sheep Creek Cascade or a strenuous climb to Lookout Peak. This trail has more shade and fewer hikers than others in the canyon. Sheep Creek is most lovely in June and July, when the surrounding area is brimming with deep purple delphinium, tangerine leopard lilies, crimson columbine, and sunshine-yellow asters. On a clear day at Lookout Peak, you can see across the San Joaquin Valley. The trail to Lookout Peak, though challenging, is accessible for hikers of moderate fitness levels.

Zumwalt Meadow Trails

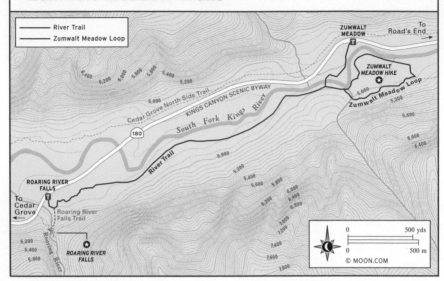

From the trailhead, the first 0.8 mile (1.3 km) of the Don Cecil Trail is straightforward, following a path southwest toward **Sheep Creek.** The trail converges with the creek as it steadily climbs. From the trail, the springtime froth of white water offers a zen-like atmosphere. Though you cannot swim here (it's the water source for Cedar Grove, including the campgrounds and hotel), you can stay awhile and take in the peaceful surroundings.

Exploring farther up the trail leads to a handful of switchbacks on an open, steep hillside. As you begin 3 miles (5 km) of uphill hiking, you'll hear the West Fork of Sheep Creek before you see it. Where the trail parallels the West Fork is a good place to look for wildlife. After the trail leaves the creek, another set of longer switchbacks brings you open vistas of the peaks to the north, Cedar Grove below, and the top of Lookout Peak.

When you reach the park boundary signs, you are nearly there. The trail becomes fainter, but keep climbing up and to the west, following the short switchbacks to the ridge, then continuing to the summit. There are several trails in this area, so the end of the hike can be confusing. If you hit a Forest Service road, the Summit Meadow trailhead, or a parking lot, turn north and scramble 0.25 mile (0.4 km) to the top, using your hands for balance. After surveying the miles of wilderness above Kings Canyon, return the way you came.

River Trail and Zumwalt Meadow

Distance: 4 miles (6 km) round-trip
Duration: 2 hours
Elevation change: 250 feet (75 m)
Effort: Easy
Trailhead: Roaring River Falls
Directions: Drive 3.2 miles (5 km) east from Cedar Grove on Highway 180 to the signed turnout and parking lot for Roaring River Falls.

Solitude is the main attraction of this quiet meander. Follow the Roaring River Falls Trail 0.2 mile (0.3 km) to the waterfall. From there, turn east to trace the River Trail on the south side of Highway 180 and the Kings River. You'll follow a simple path along the floor of the canyon. The light shifts, and your senses heighten. Listen for the song of the hermit thrush reverberating among the rocks. If you hear a sharp chirp, scan for pika (a small creature resembling a chinchilla); they can often be spotted in the jumble of boulders.

Eventually you'll meet up with a junction that leads to Zumwalt Meadow. No matter which direction you go, you'll trace a loop around the meadow. Follow the trail to the left (clockwise) to see the riverfront first. Follow it to the right (counterclockwise) to first see some rocky views: To the northeast, you can see North Dome. Once you're back on the River Trail, head west to return the way you came.

Some of the rocky boulder crossings can be challenging for people with stiff knees. This trail is not well-maintained. It's best to wait to hike it until June, when spring's high river levels have usually subsided.

★ Zumwalt Meadow

Distance: 1.8-mile (2.9-km) loop
Duration: 1-2 hours
Elevation change: 150 feet (45 m)
Effort: Easy
Trailhead: Zumwalt Meadow
Directions: From Cedar Grove, drive 5 miles (8 km) east on Highway 180. The Zumwalt Meadow trailhead is on the south side of the road.

The highlight of Cedar Grove is this easily accessible meadow hike that offers **river views** and endless **wildflowers.** If you do one walk in Cedar Grove, or if you only have one day, this is the trip to take. A boardwalk traces both river and meadow, passing beneath mature trees and granite rock faces.

Daniel Zumwalt, who once owned this meadow, pushed for the preservation of Kings Canyon in the 1890s and 1900s. He was friends with preservationists like Joseph LeConte and even guided for the Sierra Club.

From the trailhead, follow a short dirt path southwest along the Kings River, then cross the bridge that spans it. Looking upstream (north), you will see North Dome more than half a mile above the valley floor, standing at 8,715 feet (2,660 m) in elevation. This next section of trail can be soggy or overrun with rivulets of water in the spring, but you'll only

be on it for a short distance before reaching the meadow's boardwalk.

Turn left to follow the boardwalk; this is also the easier half of the path. The boardwalk parallels the river, garnished with ferns, reeds, and the brush-like plant equisetum (also known as horsetail). Green is the theme of the first mile. Pine trees are making their best effort to encroach this area, but for now, only cottonwoods, willows, and vine maples have taken hold.

The boardwalk ends after about 0.3 mile (0.5 km), but the trail continues through the forest on the marsh's edge. Departing from the river, the trail forks. Take the well-traveled path to the right (the one to the left eventually leads to Road's End on the River Trail) to begin looping back. As you round a bend to face southeast, the view changes and granite becomes the focus. This section of the trail is rocky; you'll clamber up stone steps (some of which are natural) for about 100 feet (30 m). Here you'll enjoy some great views, as light glints off the surrounding peaks. The trail continues west and skirts the southern edge of the meadow. When you get back to the first junction (where the boardwalk starts), you'll continue west along the river, then north to return to the trailhead and parking lot.

This hike is suitable for almost everyone. The rocky part of the trail can be a little tough for hikers with bothersome knees. There's a restroom available at the parking lot, but no water.

Kanawyer Loop Trail

Distance: 4.5-mile (7.2-km) loop
Duration: 2-3 hours
Elevation change: 100 feet (30 m)
Effort: Easy
Trailhead: Bubb's Creek, Road's End
Directions: Drive to Road's End in Cedar Grove, passing all of the campgrounds on the left. A couple of large parking areas hug the river and the dead-end in the road.

This loop hike parallels the Kings River past Road's End. As it goes between towering granite cliffs, it gives you an immersive

KINGS CANYON AND CEDAR GROVE
RECREATION

Wander Through Wildflowers

Redbud trees and golden poppies fill the bottom of the river canyons in the foothills, and sky pilots burst with color at the top of the highest peaks. Every elevation of Sequoia and Kings Canyon boasts blooming wildflowers from February through August. You'll be able to spot a rainbow of colors as you hike, from crimson columbine to violet lupine. Pull your car over along the Kings Canyon Scenic Byway to admire towers of yucca and blasts of blazing star blossoms. No matter where you are in the parks, there will be wildflowers, but the spots on this list are the best of the best.

blazing star flower

ZUMWALT MEADOW

In May, **Zumwalt Meadow** (page 137) is lush with green, hinting of the abundance to come. When summer fully hits, the meadow becomes striped with magenta shooting stars and golden asters. In the autumn, the foliage echoes the flowers, changing to shades of amber and garnet.

ROUND MEADOW

In **Round Meadow** (page 79), towering stalks of white wildflowers seem to mimic the surrounding sequoias. You'll spy corn lilies with their broad leaves and trident of blossoms, the bulbous finger-like tips of ranger's buttons, and a spray of cow parsnip.

EAGLE AND MOSQUITO LAKES

The richest wildflowers in Mineral King can be found near **Eagle Lake** (page 162) and the **Mosquito Lakes** (page 164). Deep purple larkspur, horsemint, and large, daisy-like asters fill the sagebrush steppe while leopard lilies and crimson columbine flowers dance delicately along the streams, blooming well into September.

MIDDLE FORK TRAIL

For early season flowers, head to the Foothills—specifically, the **Middle Fork Trail** (page 48). Along the riverside are redbud trees, buckeyes, and fiddleneck flowers are accessible from the trail via Hospital Rock or Potwisha Campground.

ALTA PEAK

Hike to **Alta Peak** (page 79) for a bird's-eye view of the Great Western Divide and a close-up look at columbines, Indian paintbrush flowers, and some of the prettiest alpine plants around.

experience of the canyon. From the trailhead, follow Bubb's Creek Trail east. The first 2 miles (3 km) of this hike take place on the area's most popular trail: It provides access to Paradise Valley, Mist Falls, and the Rae Lakes Loop.

After hiking through shady groves and over several tiny creeks, turn right at a Y-junction and go over the big metal bridge, pausing to appreciate the river's unique shade of green. After crossing the bridge, turn right again at another junction. (The option to the left is Bubb's Creek Trail, which heads southeast and up, up, up.) Going right will begin

Mist Falls

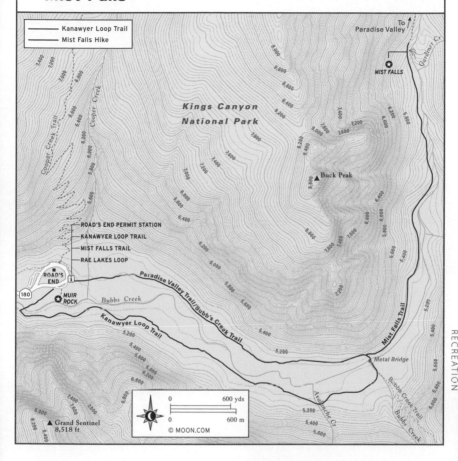

Kanawyer Loop Trail
Mist Falls Hike

Kings Canyon
National Park

7,400
7,200
7,000
6,800
6,600

Cooper Creek

Cooper Creek Trail

6,400
6,200
6,000
5,800
5,600

8,800
8,600
6,400
6,200
7,800

7,600
7,400
7,200

8,200
8,400
8,000
7,600

▲ Buck Peak
8,800

6,600
6,400
6,200
6,000
5,800
5,600
5,400
5,200

7,600
7,400
7,000
6,800
6,600
7,200
7,400

To ↑
Paradise Valley

Gardiner Cr.

✪
MIST FALLS

7,800
7,600
7,400
7,000
7,200

7,800
6,800
6,600
6,400
6,200

7,000
7,200
7,400
7,600

7,800
6,800
6,600
6,400
6,200
6,000

ROAD'S END PERMIT STATION
KANAWYER LOOP TRAIL
MIST FALLS TRAIL
RAE LAKES LOOP

ROAD'S
END

180

MUIR
ROCK

Bubbs Creek

Paradise Valley Trail/Bubb's Creek Trail

Kanawyer Loop Trail

5,200
5,400
5,600
5,800
6,000
6,800

5,650
5,600
5,800

5,400
5,200

Mist Falls Trail

5,200
5,400
5,600

Metal Bridge

Bubbs Creek Trail

Avalanche Cr.

5,200
5,400
5,600

Bubbs Creek

7,400
7,200
8,000
8,200
8,400

▲ Grand Sentinel
8,518 ft

0   600 yds
0   600 m
© MOON.COM

KINGS CANYON AND CEDAR GROVE
RECREATION

looping you back, but this time on the little-traveled Kanawyer Loop Trail on the south side of the river. You'll cross Avalanche Creek via a log bridge, passing through a conifer forest and (briefly) over a boulder field. As you continue west, you'll see Muir Rock on the north side of the river.

The River Trail picks up where this trail ends—at another bridge 100 yards past Muir Rock. Return to your car in the parking lot by crossing the bridge and following the trail northeast. The trail is mostly flat and is great for children.

★ Mist Falls

Distance: 9.1 miles (14.7 km) round-trip
Duration: 6 hours
Elevation change: 650 feet (200 m)
Effort: Moderate
Trailhead: Paradise Valley/Bubb's Creek, Road's End
Directions: Drive to Road's End Cedar Grove, passing all of the campgrounds on the left. A couple of large parking areas hug the river and the dead-end in the road.

For waterfall aficionados, this popular out-and-back trail is a rare Sierra treat. Mist Falls is so powerful that you can hear it half a mile before you see the white water blasting from the granite flume. On a hot summer afternoon, the mist is welcome. One look at the broad, Niagara-esque cascade and you'll understand why this hike is so popular.

From Road's End, start hiking directly east on Paradise Valley/Bubb's Creek Trail, paralleling the river as it heads upstream. Over the first 2 miles (3 km), you will cross several small creeks and meander through the forest on the sandy trail. After 2 miles (3 km), a bridge across the Kings River comes into view on the right side of the trail. You will stay to the left (north) and not cross the bridge, but you can still appreciate the unique view of the river.

Past the bridge, begin a gradual ascent into a narrow canyon. As you climb, the trail opens up, becoming hotter and more exposed, but you'll have better views of the surrounding granite. As you approach mile 4 (km 6) of the hike, turn around periodically for a great look at the Sphinx, a monolithic pyramid-shaped granite formation on the other side of the canyon. Soon, the roar of the falls draws you onward. Once you reach the viewing area, take some time to cool off as you appreciate its awesome power and beauty. Return the way you came.

Be careful scrambling around the rocks—they are deceptively slippery. Rattlesnakes have also been found at the base of the falls. The best time of year to visit is first thing in the summer, but the falls are still impressive with waning water in autumn.

★ BACKPACKING

Kings Canyon's astonishing backpacking is unparalleled in California, the Americas, and, dare I say, the world. One of America's finest wilderness parks, Kings Canyon boasts nearly half a million acres of roadless wilderness, surrounded by national forests that are also designated wilderness. Take a week—or a month!—and spend it in the backcountry of Kings Canyon. But if you only have a weekend, there's still plenty of opportunity to find a sense of peace.

Kings Canyon, despite its vastness and remoteness, is an excellent place to start backpacking. There are few dangerous critters; the trails described here are well-traveled; and water is frequently available. Though the climb out of the canyon can take time and the bright sun and heat saps your energy, the hardest part about backpacking is putting your camera away so you can cover some distance.

Many of the park's day hikes are popular as backpacking trips, but you'll need to be a few miles down the trail before you can set up camp. Additionally, each trail has quotas for overnights. For information on trailhead availability and to get your permit ($15, required for all overnight stays) and bear canister, head to **Road's End Permit Station** (Hwy. 180, 559/565-3766, www.nps.gov/seki, 7am-3:45pm daily May-Sept.). You can also make a reservation ahead of time, which is recommended for Paradise Valley and the Rae Lakes Loop.

This section covers some simple out-and-back and loop trips from the western side of the Sierra Nevada. All leave from Cedar Grove.

Paradise Valley

There is no hyperbole in the naming of **Paradise Valley.** Never a more peaceful scene existed than an afternoon here, in the shade of a fresh-leafed alder, listening to the endless run of the river. The water glints aquamarine as the sky is reflected on its riffled surface.

This 11.4-mile (18.4-km) out-and-back trip (1,600 ft/490 m elevation gain) starts from the Paradise Valley/Bubb's Creek trailhead at Road's End. You'll hike 4.6 miles (7.4 km) to Mist Falls, then continue up Paradise Valley Trail, heading north past cascades and across boulder fields to a short set of switchbacks. One mile (1.5 km) above the falls, there are so many emerald pools to dip your legs in, you may find it hard to leave. Looking upstream, you'll see your campsite just 0.1 mile (160 m) ahead: Lower Paradise Valley is located at mile

5.7 (km 9.2). In a cozy valley above Mist Falls, these popular sites can be hard to come by. Sites come with fire rings and access to water. This is where you'll spend the next 1-2 nights, or you can connect to the Rae Lakes Loop for a longer trip.

Rae Lakes Loop

The **Rae Lakes Loop,** the most popular backpacking trip in Kings Canyon, starts with Mist Falls and an overnight in Paradise Valley, then passes lakes that house tadpoles of the endangered yellow-legged mountain frog, and concludes with Vidette Meadows—one of the most serene and beautiful places that I've ever visited. The round-trip journey is 41.4 miles (66 km). Permits can be hard to come by, so plan in advance. Make a wilderness permit reservation online (www.nps.gov/seki/planyourvisit/wilderness_permits.htm). Bear canisters are required on this trail.

The loop can be done in either direction, but most people hike it clockwise, spending the first night in Paradise Valley. You'll take Bubb's Creek Trail back to close the loop. Paradise Valley is a great place to acclimate to the elevation. The starting point at Road's End is at 5,035 feet (1,530 m). Crossing Glen Pass, you'll be over 12,000 feet (3,660 m), for a total elevation gain of nearly 7,000 feet (2,130 m). Pack light to make sure your trip is enjoyable.

The first dozen or so miles of the hike are directly adjacent to the Kings River, surrounded by sheer granite walls, and a lush habitat full of birds. In **Paradise Valley** (mile 5.7-10/km 9.2-16), there are three established camping areas (with bear boxes)—Lower, Middle, and Upper. Lower Paradise Valley is closest to Mist Falls. Camping in Paradise Valley is limited to two nights.

At the northern end of Paradise Valley (your second day of the trip), there is a hazardous crossing of the South Fork of the Kings River. The bridge here has been washed out and won't be fully replaced until 2021 or 2022. Depending on the snowpack levels and how much snowmelt there is, the river may be impassable until mid- or late summer. Check

trail conditions online (www.nps.gov/seki/planyourvisit/trailcond.htm) or call Sequoia and Kings Canyon's **wilderness office** (559/565-3766).

After the Kings River crossing, the trail follows Woods Creek for several miles. Here, sheer granite cliffs show evidence of the glaciers that once dominated the landscape. To the north you'll see the bulbous Castle Domes. There are some campsites with bear boxes on the east end of **Castle Domes Meadow,** approximately 12 miles (19 km) in.

At mile 15.7 (km 25), there's a trail junction. Take the trail to the right and carefully cross Woods Creek. In July and August, this part of the trail will be filled with throngs of long-distance hikers, some of whom are traversing the 212-mile (340-km) John Muir Trail, and others who are traveling some (or all!) of the 2,650-mile (4,270-km) Pacific Crest Trail. Due to this section's popularity, the preferred campsites here fill quickly.

As you continue hiking, the trail moves upward into pine forest. There are a couple of campsites at the confluence of the South Fork of the Kings River and Baxter Creek. In another mile (1.5 km), you will reach the junction with Baxter Pass Trail at the north end of **Dollar Lake.** At 19 miles (31 km) in, you've nearly reached the halfway point. Continue heading south on the trail. For a side trip off the beaten path, you can take Baxter Pass Trail heading north to the secluded Baxter Lakes and spend a night in solitude. This will add 2-3 miles (3-5 km) each way and a climb of 1,000 feet (300 m).

Dollar Lake and its southerly neighbor **Arrowhead Lake** are both lovely, but if you push for another 3 miles (5 km), you'll reach the highlight of the trip, and its namesake: the three **Rae Lakes.** The edges of Upper, Middle, and Lower Rae Lakes are frilled with marshes and mats of summer wildflowers. The lakes offer a beautiful reflection of **Painted Lady Peak** and **Mount Rixford.** On the eastern edge of Middle Rae Lake is a ranger station. If you have enough time, it's worth it to spend one night at each lake (the maximum

allowed). During the day, you can explore the nearby Sixty Lake Basin, as well as go swimming, fishing, and bask in the sun like the local marmots.

As you depart the Rae Lakes, you'll get a closer look at Painted Lady Peak as you climb up and into the Bubb's Creek watershed. When you reach **Glen Pass,** you'll be at 11,798 feet (3,600 m). This day holds a lot of switchbacks and requires some mental toughness as you climb ever upward.

It's worth spending your last full day and night near the perfectly sunlit and verdant **Vidette Meadow.** Camping isn't permitted between Bull Frog Lake and Vidette Meadow, but you can stay up to two nights at Kearsarge Lakes or Charlotte Lake, just 0.8 mile (1.3 km) off the main trail.

The descent down to Bubb's Creek is fairly straightforward from here: It's just 13 more miles (21 km) until you can sip a cold beverage and soak in the river. For this section, composed of dozens of switchbacks, trekking poles come in handy. It's best to get an early start on this day, as the sun can be scalding on this south-facing canyon. Pause in **Junction Meadow** after the first of the massive downhill sections. Along the way, you'll pass a couple of intriguing canyons like East Creek and Sphinx Creek, which you might be inspired to hike some other day.

Continue along the trail and cross the bridge over the Kings River. Head west along Bubb's Creek, two sandy miles (3 km) that should feel familiar—this is where you started. Don't forget to buy your commemorative Rae Lakes shirt at the Cedar Grove Market to celebrate making it all the way around.

Granite Lake

A day of sweating uphill to reach the pristine waters of **Granite Lake** is worth the work. The scene here is reminiscent of Japanese paintings: rock, water, a wisp of cloud, a well-situated tree, and wildflowers fill your vision.

This 21-mile (34-km) out-and-back trip (5,500 ft/1,680 m elevation gain) is best done over three days, so you have plenty of time to explore this remote area.

From Road's End, take the less-traveled Copper Creek Trail north. You will hike up 5,500 feet (1,680 m) over 10 miles (16 km) to reach Granite Lake Basin. After you've finished climbing, the trail levels out for the last 0.5 mile (0.8 km) to the campsites, which are set around Granite Lake. If you get a late start, there's an earlier camp at 4 miles (6 km), Lower Tent Meadows. You'll return the way you came.

CYCLING

Cyclists have called the trip along Highway 180 the most scenic and essential ride in the area. The distance from Grant Grove to Road's End is 34 miles (55 km); to make the full out-and-back trip, you'll traverse 68 miles (109 km) with an elevation change of nearly 8,000 feet (2,440 m). On the return, you'll endure a 3,600-foot (1,100-m) climb in 13 miles (21 km), at an incline of 4-6 percent.

To begin, park at **Grant Grove Village.** Your first 3 miles (5 km) on Highway 180 climb through the forest, then you'll begin a descent. You'll pass **Junction View** (at mile 10.7/km 17); this is an excellent place to rest on the return trip before the final push. From there it is all downhill until **Boyden Cavern** (mile 19.5/km 31). Whenever it's safe to do so, ride the inside of the road to keep your distance from the exposed cliffs. At Boyden Cavern, you can fill up on water at the restroom. At the river, churn uphill for another 9.5 miles (15 km).

When the highway crosses the river, veer left onto **North Side Drive** (following signs for Cedar Grove Village) to avoid a hill and get away from traffic. Turn right at the Hotel Creek trailhead, just before the stables, to arrive at the Cedar Grove Visitor Center. North Side Drive will merge back into Highway 180. Turn left and head east to continue for another 5.7 miles (9 km) of pleasant undulations

1: Zumwalt Meadow **2:** hikers resting near Mist Falls **3:** Upper Rae Lake **4:** Rae Lakes Loop trail

to **Road's End** (mile 34/km 55). Return the way you came for a full-on butt-kicker.

It's safest to ride this route early in the morning, on weekdays, and in spring or fall. In this way, you can enjoy the two-lane road with less traffic. There are few places to get water, so carry extra, especially for the return trip. Highway 180 is closed to vehicles beyond Hume Lake during the winter. Remember: Most drivers are looking for bears, not bikers, so be alert.

FISHING

The South Fork and Middle Fork of the Kings River offer ideal fly-fishing conditions to challenge even the craftiest angler. Rainbow trout are native to the Sierra Nevada and are only catch and release here. There are also wild brown and brook trout, and sometimes golden trout. Though small (8-9 inches/20-23 cm), the fish are wily, energetic, and often brightly colored. Wading is best in early autumn, when the river slows to safer conditions and warms from the frigid snowmelt temperatures of spring.

A few key sites worth exploring with rod and reel are easy to access: **Muir Rock** and across the bridge from **Zumwalt Meadow.** If you'd like to expend a little more effort, head to the **Lewis Creek trailhead** at Highway 180. Fish right at the parking lot on the south side of the highway, or head north up the trail for 0.5 mile (0.8 km). Cut west off the trail to reach Lewis Creek's clear waters, especially from April through June.

You can fish the **Kings River** via the **Yucca Point Trail,** but you'll have to work for it. After hiking for 3.6 miles (6 km) and 1,200 feet (370 m) downhill, you're rewarded with the confluence of the Middle and South Forks of the Kings River. Even if you don't catch fish here, you'll have some solitude. To reach the trailhead, go 14 miles (23 km) north from Grant Grove on Highway 180. There's a narrow parking turnout on the north side of the road.

When fishing in Kings Canyon, plan for heat. If you bring your wading boots, make sure they are fully dry to reduce transporting non-native species like the dangerous zebra mussel. Be sure to clamp down barbs or purchase barbless hooks. Get your California fishing license online (http://wildlife.ca.gov) before you arrive. In person, you can get a license at **Hume Lake General Store** (64144 Hume Lake Rd., Hume, 559/305-7770, www. hume.org) or one of the outdoor stores outside of the park.

Kings River

The Orvis-endorsed **Sierra Fly Fisher** (559/683-7664, http://sierraflyfisher.com) offers advice and guide services in Cedar Grove and other parts of the park and national forest. Half-day outings start from $325 for one person, with $75 for each additional person. Full-day outings start from $450 for 1-2 people (lunch included), with $150 for each additional person.

SWIMMING

The cool water of the Kings River is enticing, especially after a hot summer hike. There's a sandy beach near **Muir Rock,** a large flat boulder that's right in the river. Strong swimmers may enjoy leaping off the rock into the river. To get to Muir Rock, head to Road's End and park at the lot, then walk south toward the river.

The safest way to play in the water in this part of the park is to just dip your feet into the river or one of the many creeks. Use caution when swimming in May and June (and sometimes July), when the river is deceptively swift. Be careful of "strainers," logs that have fallen across the river; these can be deadly if the current pushes you up against the log and its branches. Note that the cold temperature of the water can shock even the strongest swimmers.

ROCK CLIMBING

The big granite walls here are apt to make any climber drool. However, due to challenging approaches and limited notoriety, few sport climbs exist in this area. Additionally, few trad climbs have been described in the park and surrounding area. New routes are being discovered on the two major multi-pitch faces in the canyon: **North Dome,** at 8,717 feet (2,660 m), and **Grand Sentinel,** at 8,518 feet (2,600 m) high.

For more details, check the online resource **SEKI Climbing** (http://sekiclimbing.com), where route options are described, with attention to leave no trace ethics. Also on the site is a list of climbs compiled by a former park employee, with helpful maps and descriptions.

Boyden Cavern

Here you'll find metamorphic limestone (aka marble). Below ground, it's created the beautiful features of Boyden Cavern. Above, it means a combination of crumbly and solid handholds. At the parking lot of Boyden Cavern, there's a wall with three routes ranging in difficulty from a 5.8 to a 5.11c.

rock climbing in Kings Canyon

RECREATION KINGS CANYON AND CEDAR GROVE

Road's End

Granite, which comprises much of Kings Canyon, is one of the hardest rocks. Its unique faces were carved by glaciers, creating ledges and massive vertical cracks, seemingly intended for a human hand or foot to use to climb ever skyward. At **Road's End,** there is everything from bouldering to big wall climbing.

Top roping and bouldering can be found just north of Road's End, 200 yards west of the Copper Creek trailhead, and in the boulder fields below North Dome (4.4 mi/7 km east of the visitors center, on the north side of the road).

HORSEBACK RIDING

One way to access the wilderness of Kings Canyon is via horse. The **Cedar Grove Pack Station** (108300 Cedar Ln., 559/565-3464, off-season 559/337-2413, http://cedargrovepackstation.com, 8:15am-4:15pm daily summer) offers guided horseback tours (1-hour ride $50, 2-hour ride $90) for adults and children 8 and older. No prior experience is needed, but riders must be able to ride alone as well as mount and dismount a horse. The weight limit is 225 pounds. Reservations are recommended. Helmets are included. Other options are possible with advance notice, including daylong and multi-day trips to destinations like the Monarch Divide and Rae Lakes Loop. Longer trips require previous horseback experience.

The pack station can be a little challenging to find. It's located in Cedar Gove Village, at the corner of North Cedar Grove Drive and Motor Nature Trail, near the Hotel Creek trailhead. From Highway 180, follow signs to Cedar Grove Lodge and Market on North Side Drive, between Sentinel and Canyon View Campgrounds, and continue straight on North Side Drive to a T-junction. Turn right. In 0.3 mile (0.5 km), on the north side of the road is the pack station.

You can bring your own stock (horses, mules, burros, and llamas) into the park, but pay careful attention to park regulations to protect your animal and the park resources.

Entertainment and Events

RANGER PROGRAMS

Despite hosting many visitors, there are only a couple of rangers in Cedar Grove. Find them in the Cedar Grove Visitor Center to ask questions about the area's plant and wildlife. You can also join one of the evening campfire programs at the Sentinel Campground amphitheater. Topics range from history to wildlife and geology. Check the visitors center or the campground's bulletin boards for a schedule of ranger-led activities. Most activities run May-September.

Kids (and kids at heart) can get their junior ranger booklet, learn about the park, and do some volunteer activities like picking up litter. Return to any visitors center to take the oath and receive your badge.

EVENTS

At the end of the high season, in mid-October, **Sips of the Sierra Wine Tasting** (www.visitsequoia.org) pairs wines from the local Riffelhof Vineyards with California cheese, fruit, and nuts. With luck, the cottonwoods will have fall color to enjoy as you swirl your glass of Riesling.

Food and Accommodations

In Kings Canyon, a single green building houses all of the food and lodging options: the Cedar Grove Lodge houses the Cedar Grove Grill and the Cedar Grove Market.

INSIDE THE PARK

The **Cedar Grove Grill** (in the Cedar Grove Lodge, North Side Dr., no phone, www.visitsequoia.com, 7am-10am, 11:30am-2:30pm, 5pm-9pm daily, $7-20) is casual in terms of service and space, but the food is fair-trade, grass-fed, cage-free, local, and fresh. Foodies will delight in the grilled trout with butter sauce or a classic tofu and vegetable rice bowl with sweet soy sauce. Sandwiches are made to order or available for grab and go. And the breakfast options range from a light and healthy veggie breakfast burrito to rich and decadent French toast. The grill is 28 miles (45 km) northeast from Grant Grove, just off Highway 180 in Cedar Grove Village. If you pass Canyon View Campground, you've gone too far.

The **Cedar Grove Lodge** (North Side Dr., 855/488-3884, www.visitsequoia.com, from $140) occupies the third floor of the building that also houses Cedar Grove's market and restaurant. There are also two large accessible rooms on the ground level, called patio rooms. These actually are the best rooms because the balcony opens out to the river and they each have a mini-fridge. All rooms are tastefully decorated and clean. The standard rooms have two queen beds and a coffee maker, but no television. All rooms have heating/air conditioning, a private bathroom, telephone, radio, and a table with chairs. There is no cell phone reception or Wi-Fi in this part of the park. Check in by 9pm, before the reception desk closes.

Camping

INSIDE THE PARK

All four of Cedar Grove's campgrounds are fairly close together and within walking distance of the Kings River, as well as the market, restaurant, and visitors center. Sentinel is the most central and has the most ranger programs. A bike trail connects all of the campgrounds to Cedar Grove Village. All campgrounds have flush toilets and drinking water. Each site has a fire ring, a picnic table, a bear-proof food storage box, and a tent pad. The campgrounds are open from spring through fall.

There are no dump stations or RV hookups in Cedar Grove. For firewood, gather dead and down wood near your campsite or buy it at the market. Using bear boxes is crucial for protecting the wildlife.

Reservations (www.recreation.gov) are only possible at Sentinel and Canyon View.

Canyon View only offers group sites. The sites at Sheep Creek and Moraine are available on a first-come, first-served basis.

Sentinel (www.recreation.gov, spring-fall, $22) is the most popular campground. Its 82 sites are fully reservable online 6-12 months in advance. **Sheep Creek** (spring-fall, $18) is first-come, first-served and is the closest campground to the river. Its 111 sites have plenty of shade from pine trees. The 120 sites at **Moraine** (spring-fall, $18) are also first-come, first-served. This campground is well named for its position on one of the hillocks of unsorted sediment left behind by the glaciers. **Canyon View** (www.recreation.gov, spring-fall, $30-60) only offers group sites. Its 16 sites are available by reservation for tent and car camping. No RVs or trailers are allowed. If you show up to Sheep Creek or Moraine when people are leaving (8am-11am), you'll have plenty of options for getting the site of your choice.

OUTSIDE THE PARK

Convict Flat (877/444-6777, www.recreation. gov, spring-fall, free) is a small campground in Sequoia National Forest, nestled under oak trees and within earshot of the Kings River. It has five sites with picnic tables. There is a vault toilet. Bring your own water. Large trailers won't fit in most of the sites. This is a good spot for anglers, as it's close to Redwood Creek, a tributary of the Kings River. This is also a good campground if you're looking for solitude among the yucca blooms. Convict Flat opens in the spring when Highway 180

opens for the season. To get to the campground from Grant Grove, head northeast on Highway 180 for 18 miles (29 km). Stay to the right as you enter the campground; all five sites are on the right side of the road.

Dispersed camping is permitted in the Hume Lake Ranger District of Sequoia National Forest (unless posted otherwise), but you will need a permit for any fire, open flame, or stove. There are camping spots with existing fire rings along the Kings River and the road between Convict Flat and the park boundary at Lewis Creek. You will be able to hear noise from the road, but it's a good balance of achieving solitude while still within a short distance of your car.

Transportation and Services

DRIVING AND PARKING

The narrow two-lane Highway 180 is not for everyone. Due to occasional rockfall, animals, and decreased visibility, it's best to drive this road in the daytime. Save your brakes by downshifting and use turnouts when others want to go faster than you do.

Traffic is heaviest during summer weekends, especially holidays. Parking is generally not an issue except at Grizzly Falls and Roaring River Falls. If the parking lots are full, wait at the side of the road or visit on your way back from elsewhere in the park. You can also hike to Roaring River Falls: It's accessible by trail and is within a couple miles of all the campgrounds in Cedar Grove. Traffic is considerably reduced during the shoulder seasons of spring and autumn. The highway is closed just past the Hume Lake turnoff in the winter.

SERVICES

If you want to prepare your own food back at camp, or need some basic toiletries, camping

gear, ice cream, or wine, stop into the **Cedar Grove Market** (in the Cedar Grove Lodge, North Side Dr., no phone, 7am-10pm daily June-Sept., 9am-5pm daily Apr.-May and Oct.-Nov.), adjacent to the restaurant in Cedar Grove Village. The market carries the essentials without too much of a markup. If you're heading out to Road's End at the end of the peak season (late Sept.), the market holds an excellent end-of-summer sale of their gift and souvenir items. There's an ATM available on-site.

It's best to fuel up before entering the park, in Squaw Valley or Dunlap. There are two **gas stations** near Grant Grove, though, if you're running low. About 13 miles (21 km) past the Big Stump entrance, **Stony Creek Lodge** (65569 Generals Hwy., 559/565-3909) has 24-hour credit card gas pumps in the summer. There are also pumps at **Hume Lake,** but hours vary based on when this private camp is operating and when the seasonal road is open.

Mineral King

Named to the National Register of Historic

Places, Mineral King preserves a storied past. The Yokuts people summered here for centuries before settlers discovered silver in the 1870s. Residents of the 3,000-person boomtown Beulah sought their fortunes in the mines. Avalanches and limited returns led to a bust and the end of the town. The area, which encompassed the former Beulah and is now known as Mineral King, was named for the variety of precious ore found in the rocks here. At one point, Disney planned a ski resort where the small Cold Springs Campground now stands, but was thwarted by a famous legal battle with the Sierra Club.

Though it's rich with interesting history, the real prize for making the journey to Mineral King is the landscape. Stunning Black Wolf

Highlights

Look for ★ to find recommended sights, activities, dining, and lodging.

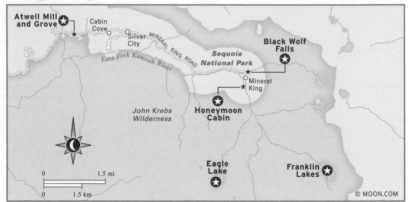

★ **Go Back in Time at Atwell Mill and Grove:** This quiet glen that was once a working timber mill offers visitors a look at Mineral King's mining history (page 154).

★ **Stroll to Black Wolf Falls:** Just minutes from the road, you will find a perfect cold, white waterfall set amid yellow wildflowers (page 154).

★ **Revisit the Past at Honeymoon Cabin:** Stop by the remains of an early 1900s cabin and learn about the area's surprising history (page 154).

★ **Hike to Franklin Lakes:** Pass cascades and plenty of wildflowers on this climb to a wonderous alpine scene (page 159).

★ **Trek to Eagle Lake:** The hike to this quintessential Sierra lake is an adventure that hikers of all ages will enjoy (page 162).

Mineral King

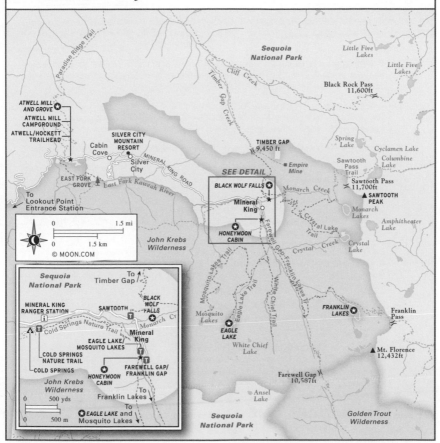

Falls and Crystal Falls can be seen throughout the valley. Sawtooth Peak glows pink at sunset, standing as a sentinel above the valley. Eagle Lake's views and wildlife will transport you to nature's version of a dream world.

Today, Mineral King's untrammeled wilderness is one of the best places for visitors with more time and less tolerance for crowds. Those who brave the harrowing drive (about 1-2 hours from the Foothills region) to get here will be rewarded with stunning views from easier hiking trails in the high country. For rock hounds, there are alpine caves and beautiful banded marble among metamorphic folds of rock.

For your visit, pack your own food, fill up on supplies (especially gas), and watch out for marmots (they chew exposed wires on vehicles, searching for rare salts). Your time in Mineral King will be unlike any other in California: remote, wild, and peaceful.

Previous: wildflowers in Mineral King; Eagle Lake; tree stump at Atwell Mill.

Where Can I Find...?

- **Accessible campgrounds:** The only accessible campsite in this remote area is at the **Atwell Springs Campground.** You must have a disability parking placard to claim this first-come, first-served site.

- **Accessible services:** Unfortunately, the only way to enter the Mineral King Ranger Station is by climbing a set of eight stairs. However, there is an **accessible bathroom** at the Lookout Point Entrance Station on Mineral King Road.

- **ATM:** There are no ATMs in this part of the park. In **Three Rivers,** there's an ATM at **Valley Oak Credit Union** (40870 Sierra Dr., 559/561-4471, http://valleyoak.org) and at the **Three Rivers Market** (41729 Sierra Dr., 559/561-4113), part of a Shell gas station.

- **Electric vehicle charging stations:** There are no EV chargers in this part of the park.

- **Gas:** There are no gas stations inside the park. Before entering the park, you can fill up in **Three Rivers** at **Shell** (41729 Sierra Dr., 559/561-4113).

- **Showers:** At **Silver City Mountain Resort** (Mineral King Rd., 559/561-3223, www.silvercityresort.com, 9am-5pm Tues.-Wed., 8am-8pm Thurs.-Mon. May-mid-Oct.), you can take a shower for a fee, payable at the gift shop. Soap is available for purchase. There's one wheelchair-accessible shower stall.

- **Supplies:** Load up on groceries in **Fresno, Visalia,** or in **Three Rivers** at the **Three Rivers Village Market** (40869 Sierra Dr., 559/561-4441, https://threeriversvillagemarket.com, 8am-8pm daily). For camping supplies like firewood, there is a small selection at **Kaweah General Store** (40462 Sierra Dr., 559/561-3475), also in Three Rivers.

- **Telephones:** There is **no cell service** here. There are **pay phones** outside of the **Mineral King Ranger Station** and at the **Sawtooth trailhead parking area** on the south side of the road.

- **Wi-Fi:** For $5, you can connect to Wi-Fi at **Silver City Mountain Resort** (Mineral King Rd., 559/561-3223, www.silvercityresort.com, 9am-5pm Tues.-Wed., 8am-8pm Thurs.-Mon. May-mid-Oct.).

PLANNING YOUR TIME

Like most of the High Sierra, Mineral King is inaccessible during the long winter season. Roads open around Memorial Day and close at the end of October. Services like potable water are suspended even earlier in October. Spring, summer, and fall are busy as tourists come for wildflowers, animals, hiking, and fishing. Mineral King is home to some of the park's coolest temperatures as well as the highest-elevation trailheads and campgrounds.

Mineral King is a high-elevation valley, nestled at 7,800 feet (2,380 m) elevation, and the weather can be temperamental. Cloudless skies and exposed trails can make for exhausting hiking conditions. Be prepared for afternoon thunderstorms and frigid nights. Snow can persist at some of the passes through June. Mineral King Road opens in May and closes in October. Early- and late-season visits can be chilly, with highs in the 40-60s (4-16°C) and lows in the 20-30s (-6 to -1°C). From June through September, the valley warms up. Temperatures can reach the 90s (32-37°C) during the day, but campers will enjoy a cool evening in the 40-50s (4-10°C).

Just south of Mineral King, sequoia groves like Atwell Mill sit about 1,000 feet (300 m) lower in elevation. The groves tend to be sunny and warm—over 70°F (21°C) during summer days. Campers at Atwell Mill Campground will also enjoy slightly warmer temperatures at night compared to Cold Springs Campground.

Three days in this part of the park will give you a chance to acclimate to the high elevation, try a hard hike, and enjoy dipping your toes in the creek before heading home. But you can hunker down for a **full week** to make the most of the picturesque landscape. If you're just coming for a weekend, aim to arrive early on a Friday to ensure a campsite and head out by 2pm on Sunday for the safest driving conditions.

If Mineral King is your only stop in Sequoia and Kings Canyon, you can experience a sequoia grove at **Atwell Mill** or **East Fork Grove.** If you're venturing into the **backcountry,** reserve a permit beginning March 1 in order to pick your favorite trailhead.

Exploring Mineral King

VISITORS CENTERS
Mineral King Ranger Station
The **Mineral King Ranger Station** (mile 24/km 39, Mineral King Rd., 559/565-3768, 8am-3:45pm daily late May-mid Oct.) issues wilderness permits, rents bear cans, and sells water bottles and hiking maps, including detailed quadrangle topographic maps. You can also get your national park passport stamped at the station.

ENTRANCE STATIONS
The vehicle entrance fee is $35 for Sequoia and Kings Canyon National Parks. The **Lookout Point Entrance Station** (Mineral King Rd. and Hwy. 198, 559/565-3341, late May-mid Oct.) does not have much in the way of services, but it is a good spot to stop and stretch your legs. Restrooms and some information about the park are available. RVs and trailers should turn around at this point.

SCENIC DRIVES
This exciting drive along **Mineral King Road** spans from its western junction off Highway 198, to its eastern terminus, a distance of 25 miles (40 km). Budget about 1.5 hours to do this one-way drive. With a combination of pavement and gravel, this drive is not ideal for low-clearance vehicles. It's also not for the faint of heart, featuring hairpin curves and exposed cliffs.

From the town of Three Rivers, the turnoff for Mineral King Road is 3.8 miles (6 km) northeast on Highway 198. The turnoff is hard to see; take the first right after the sign that reads "Sequoia Nat'l Park 2." If you get to the Ash Mountain entrance, turn around and go back 2 miles (3 km) on Highway 198 to find Mineral King Road.

After 6.5 miles (10.5 km) on Mineral King Road, stop at a pullout before you cross the **cement bridge,** built in 1923 to allow passage over the East Fork of the Kaweah River. Peer into the canyon and admire the view. In spring, a waterfall is visible upstream.

Hop back in the car and continue along Mineral King Road, now running parallel to the East Fork of the Kaweah River. When you reach the **Lookout Point Entrance Station,** pull over and take in one last view of the foothills.

From here you'll notice the composition of the forest changing from buckeyes to pines. Severe droughts in recent decades have changed the composition of southern Sierra conifer forests more drastically than in other areas. Continue your drive and climb through the forest. There are a couple roadside **picnic areas** that make nice stops along the way.

Nine miles (14 km) past the entrance station, **Atwell Mill Campground** marks the center of this giant forest. Pull off the road here and pause for a moment to take in the big trees before continuing uphill.

As you continue along the road, you'll spot great **Sawtooth Peak** with its unmistakable profile above many other mountains. Next, you can stop at the **Mineral King Ranger Station** and stay for a program. At the end of the day, take in the peaceful sunset alongside a small creek near the **Eagle Lake trailhead.** You've reached the eastern end of Mineral King Road. To return, go back the way you came.

Sights

★ ATWELL MILL AND GROVE

At the western edge of Atwell Mill Campground, there is an unnatural glen. Here you'll find the unmarked **Atwell Mill,** a structure once used by the Kaweah Commonwealth Colony, a group of would-be utopians, after they were kicked out of Giant Forest. Unfortunately, lumber milling was impractical in the glen, so they resorted to logging the nearby sequoias. The remaining metal infrastructure and surrounding stumps you see here can help you imagine a much louder and busier time in Mineral King, when hundreds of people would have been milling timber. Today, you can see new sequoias are springing skyward.

To access the unmarked mill and meadow, follow the Atwell Mill Campground road to the end, near site 17. A dirt trail takes you downhill 50 yards to the old mill site. If you aren't staying at the campground, you can park at the end of the road.

★ BLACK WOLF FALLS

Throughout the valley, **Black Wolf Falls** is visible. It's beautiful from a distance, but it's even better up close. The water forms a stout, asymmetrical cascade that's dense and frothy on its right side and a gentle, shimmering trickle on its left. Interrupting the flow are occasional rocky ledges where clusters of vibrant yellow mountain monkeyflower bloom. At the end of the season, when other waterfalls dry up, Black Wolf keeps running. The trail to the waterfall has no clear start, but a short walk brings you to the sight and sounds of water dancing on rock.

Near the end of Mineral King Road is a fork that diverges to the Franklin Lakes trailhead on one side and the Eagle Lake trailhead on the other. Park near the trailhead for Franklin Lakes. (On busy weekends, it can be hard to find a spot.) Walk back the way you came, about 150 yards (toward the ranger station).

On a straight stretch of the road that's bordered by cottonwood trees, you come across a dry riverbed. Walk east for about 200 yards on any of the informal trails that depart from either side of the riverbed. There's really no wrong way to approach the falls, as the informal trails all converge into one short dirt path along the hillside that brings you through the brush and to the misty waterfall. Stay and swim in the small pool beneath the waterfall or admire (but do not enter) the mining tunnel to the right of the falls. Return the way you came, keeping an eye out for warblers and chickadees.

★ HONEYMOON CABIN

Honeymoon Cabin (dawn-dusk daily late May-mid-Oct.) is a free, open-air museum maintained by the Mineral King Historical Society (http://mineralking.org). At the eastern end of Mineral King Road, near the parking area for the Eagle Lake trailhead, is this one-room cabin built around 1914. Photographs and artifacts offer a glimpse of life for the miners and their families who once lived in this area starting in the late 1800s. The displays are updated annually by the museum's passionate curators.

1: ferns and sequoias at Atwell Mill **2:** Black Wolf Falls **3:** Honeymoon Cabin

Mineral King Hikes

Trail	Effort	Distance	Duration
Hockett Trail	easy	3 mi (5 km) rt	1.5 hr
Cold Springs Nature Trail	easy	2.3 mi (3.7 km) rt	1 hr
Timber Gap	moderate-strenuous	9.8 mi (15.8 km) rt	6 hr
Monarch and Crystal Lakes	moderate-strenuous	9 mi (14 km) rt	6 hr
Franklin Lakes	strenuous	11.4 mi (18 km) rt	8 hr
White Chief Trail	moderate	7.1 mi (11.4 km) rt	4 hr
Eagle Lake	strenuous	6.8 mi (11 km) rt	4 hr
Mosquito Lakes	strenuous	6.4 mi (10.3 km) rt	4 hr

It may be hard to believe, but the land that this cabin resides on is technically owned by the Walt Disney Company. A swath of what's now Mineral King was purchased in the 1960s by Disney with the goal of developing a ski resort. The idea was eventually abandoned after preservationists like the Sierra Club stepped in.

Recreation

DAY HIKES

Every hike in Mineral King has some elevation gain. The area is bookended by Timber Gap and Farewell Gap, and surrounded by Mineral, Sawtooth, Florence, and White Chief Peaks.

Hockett Trail

Distance: 3 miles (5 km) round-trip
Duration: 1.5 hours
Elevation Change: 600 feet (180 m)
Effort: Easy
Trailhead: Hockett, Atwell Mill Campground
Directions: From the Lookout Point Entrance Station, drive 9 miles (14 km) northeast along Mineral King Road to the Atwell Mill Campground. The trailhead is near site 16. Parking is available in the lot on the east side of the campground.

Named for John B. Hockett, who helped design Mineral King Road, the full length of the popular Hockett Trail is 10 miles (16 km). This 1.5-mile (2.5-km) section is an easy walk that dips into the canyon, reaching a small waterfall beneath big trees, and a little wooden bridge.

In Atwell Mill Campground, follow the dirt road heading southeast, passing a variety of trees, including some giant sequoias. At 1.5 miles (2.5 km) from the trailhead, you'll reach a **giant sequoia grove.** Stop at the footbridge that crosses the East Fork of the Kaweah River and admire your surroundings. When you're done, return the way you came.

Cold Springs Nature Trail

Distance: 2.3 miles (3.7 km) round-trip
Duration: 1 hour
Elevation Change: 460 feet (140 m)
Effort: Easy
Trailhead: Cold Springs Campground
Directions: From the Lookout Point Entrance Station, drive 13 miles (21 km) northeast along Mineral King Road. Pass the road to Cold Springs Campground on the right and park near the Mineral King Ranger Station. You'll need to walk from here into the campground to start the hike. The trailhead is near site 6.

This dirt path is accessible to most, with few

Hockett Trail

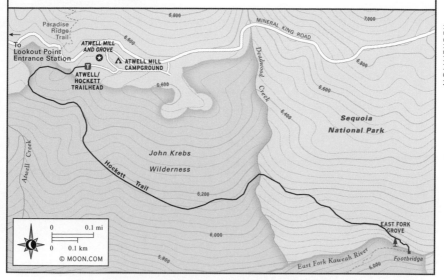

stairs and many wildflowers as you meander upstream from Cold Springs Campground into the Mineral King Valley with Sawtooth Peak above and Black Wolf Falls below.

Follow the lightly traveled trail east from the campground, keeping an eye out for deer and marmot. Enjoy the interpretive signs, which help identify native plants and trees. At the end of the trail, you'll find private cabins. They sit on the remains of **Beulah,** the mining town that thrived in Mineral King until the 1906 San Francisco earthquake. When you're ready, return the way you came.

Timber Gap

Distance: 9.8 miles (15.8 km) round-trip
Duration: 6 hours
Elevation Change: 1,400 feet (430 m)
Effort: Moderate-strenuous
Trailhead: Sawtooth
Directions: From the Lookout Point Entrance Station, drive 13 miles (21 km) northeast along Mineral King Road to the Mineral King Ranger Station. Continue 1 mile (1.5 km) farther east to reach the Sawtooth trailhead, on the north side of the road. Start your hike from the Sawtooth trailhead,

walking through sagebrush-lined switchbacks and stopping to view **Black Wolf Falls** along the way. Continue northward on this old mining route. At 0.2 mile (0.3 km), you'll reach a fork with the Monarch Lakes Trail. Keep left to continue north on the trail to Timber Gap. As you continue to climb steadily through a mix of sun and shade, the views improve. Look to the south, all the way across the valley, and spot Farewell Gap as you trek along the switchbacks that cut through red fir forest.

At mile 4.9 (km 7.9), cresting a hill, you'll reach **Timber Gap,** the pass between Mineral King and the Middle Fork of the Kaweah River Canyon. Stop and enjoy the shaded view. To the south, all of Mineral King is laid out before you, including the canyon that houses the East Fork of the Kaweah River. To the north, the top of a massive exposed plume of granite marks Alta Peak. When you're finished catching your breath and taking in the views, return the way you came.

Adventurous hikers may want to traverse to the right from the top of Timber Gap, approximately 0.75 mile (1.2 km) along a historic

Timber Gap Trail

Directions: From the Lookout Point Entrance Station, drive 13 miles (21 km) northeast along Mineral King Road to the Mineral King Ranger Station. Continue 1 mile (1.5 km) farther east to reach the Sawtooth trailhead, on the north side of the road.

This out-and-back trail is one of the easier ones in the valley, but it is still challenging because of its mileage and the elevation gains. Spend the night if you can: Stargazing up here will blow your mind. Crystal Lake is less crowded than Monarch, but Monarch offers access to the lovely and remote Columbine Lake via a backcountry trip over Sawtooth Pass. Whichever lake you choose, you'll be glad you made the trek—these lakes are why people come to Mineral King.

From the Sawtooth trailhead, trek along sagebrush-lined switchbacks, pausing on a rusty rock that overlooks **Black Wolf Falls.** After 0.2 mile (0.3 km), the trail will split: Keep right to stay on Monarch Lakes Trail. Continue to **Groundhog Meadow,** named for the yellow-bellied marmots who sun themselves here. Deer are also common in this area.

After a quick pause at the meadow, continue climbing for 2.2 miles (3.5 km), darting back and forth across a hillside with little exposure along an even grade. You'll come to a fork in the trail. To reach the Monarch Lakes, take the more traveled northern path (to the left). After 1 mile (1.5 km), you will reach the **Lower Monarch Lake,** cradled beneath Sawtooth Peak. Continue an additional 200 feet (60 m) south to **Upper Monarch Lake** to get a better feel of the place.

To reach the Crystal Lakes from the fork with the Monarch Lakes Trail, take the southern (right) trail. Hike for 1.7 miles (2.7 km) until you reach the base of Mineral Peak, formerly named Little Matterhorn, and home to three mines: Silver Tip, Buckeye, and Crystal. The trail is well worn, though not officially maintained, so loose rock makes it a challenging trek. Continue your ascent until you reach **Lower Crystal Lake. Upper Crystal Lake** is accessible via a northwest spur trail just before the Lower Crystal Lake dam.

wagon road to the ruins of the Empire Mine and its camp. Backpackers can link Timber Gap to Bearpaw Meadow.

Monarch and Crystal Lakes

Distance: 9 miles (14 km) round-trip
Duration: 6 hours
Elevation Change: 2,600 feet (790 m)
Effort: Moderate-strenuous
Trailhead: Sawtooth

Monarch and Crystal Lakes Trails

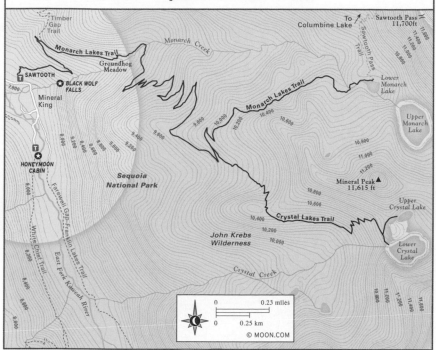

From either the Monarch or Crystal Lakes, you'll return the way you came to the Sawtooth trailhead.

★ Franklin Lakes

Distance: 11.4 miles (18 km) round-trip
Duration: 8 hours
Elevation Change: 3,460 feet (1,050 m)
Effort: Strenuous
Trailhead: Franklin Lakes/Farewell Gap
Directions: From the Lookout Point Entrance Station, drive 14.3 miles (23 km) northeast along Mineral King Road, passing the Mineral King Ranger Station, to a fork in the road. The eastern fork is where you'll find the trailhead for Franklin Lakes. You can park here, but don't block the driveway to the stables. If there's no room to park, go back and take the western fork across a bridge to a gravel parking lot (also the location of the Eagle Lake/Mosquito Lakes trailhead). Retrace your path across the bridge and to the eastern

fork to start hiking. There's a restroom between the two trailheads, next to the river.

This exposed trail on the eastern side of the valley climbs gradually to the reward of the Franklin Lakes and **Farewell Gap.** Following the East Fork of the Kaweah River, you'll meander among sagebrush, with plenty of wildlife like green tailed towhees to keep you company. There are great camping options here if you wish to backpack and stay the night by the lakes.

Heading south from the trailhead, you'll pass the old corrals and Mineral King Pack Station. Continue straight for 1 mile (1.5 km), climbing 200 feet (60 m) in elevation, an ideal height for viewing a **waterfall** at **Crystal Creek.** At a small fork, keep left and take the uphill route. After 0.5 mile (0.8 km) you'll encounter switchbacks beginning at Franklin Creek. At 3.7 miles (6 km) from the trailhead,

Franklin Lakes Trail

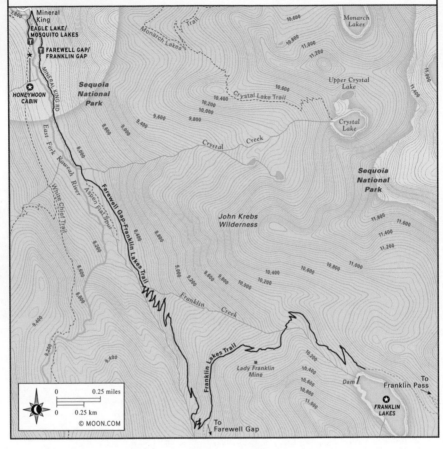

a short set of switchbacks takes you on a path departing from the Farewell Gap Trail. At this fork, take the high road and stay to the left to reach the Franklin Lakes.

The Mather Mountain Men Party entered the valley via Timber Gap, visible for the last time as you cross the Lady Franklin Mine. These pioneers of protected public lands walked their stock up the slippery, snowy hillside. As you climb, consider that at least you're not pulling a horse. When you reach the top, you'll be rewarded with beautiful **Lower and Upper Franklin Lakes.**

Adventurous climbers may enjoy a

scramble up the scree to Florence Peak or Rainbow Mountain. Return the way you came to get back to your car.

White Chief Trail

Distance: 7.1 miles (11.4 km) round-trip

Duration: 4 hours

Elevation Change: 1,500 feet (460 m)

Effort: Moderate

Trailhead: Eagle/Mosquito

Directions: From the Lookout Point Entrance Station, drive 14.3 miles (23 km) northeast along Mineral King Road, passing the Mineral King Ranger Station, to a fork in the road. Take the western fork and

Mather Mountain Party

Though Mineral King wasn't preserved until 1973, the man who became the first director of the National Park Service, Stephen T. Mather, thought it was worthy of preservation when he and a posse of conservation leaders toured Sequoia in the early 20th century.

On July 14, 1915, they left Visalia for Giant Forest and just three days later arrived by mule in Mineral King Valley. They entered from the north via Timber Gap, paused to admire Sawtooth Peak before spending a raucous night in the valley near what we now call Honeymoon Cabin. Mather's tall tales of bears and mountain lions scared two of the party off, and the next day, only 17 of the influential men and their support team attempted to hike up the steep, grueling trail of granitic sand, climbing 4,000 feet (1,220 m) in 5 miles (8 km) to Franklin Lake. They opted out of leaving via Farewell Gap, selecting to walk their horses up to a snowy and icy Franklin Pass instead. Reaching the Great Western Divide, the party peered across the many granite peaks of the Sierra to their first sight of Mount Whitney.

a plaque depicting Stephen T. Mather

This trip was more than a travel adventure. Gilbert Grosvenor, the first publisher of *National Geographic* magazine, dedicated an issue to the protection of what would become the national parks. This issue was placed on the desk of every member of Congress. Mather and his mountain party's journey, in part, led to the passage of the Organic Act, establishing the national park service and preserving the park lands.

cross a bridge to reach a gravel parking lot. The Eagle Lake/Mosquito Lakes trailhead is accessible from the parking lot.

This trek occupies the western flank of the mountains that also house Eagle Lake and the Mosquito Lakes. The trail gradually climbs an east-facing slope and is more shaded than most of the other day hikes in the area. As the trail rises into a red fir forest, across the canyon you can see a wide waterfall. Views of an old mine provide a fun bit of history.

Beginning at the end of the road, start a steady, slow climb heading south. At 0.2 mile (0.3 km), you're treated to a wildflower-encrusted gem of a waterfall, **Tufa Falls.** Across the canyon, looking east, is **Crystal Creek Falls,** an ethereal cascade running the length of the mountainside. It's most photogenic starting at mile 0.8 (km 1.3).

At 1 mile (1.5 km), the junction for Eagle Lake and Mosquito Lakes will reduce most of the foot traffic, and you will be left alone to continue southward, climbing a tough second mile into White Chief Canyon. The views and fewer people make it worth the walk.

This trail is rich in history. At mile 1.5 (km 2.5) are the barely discernible remains of **Crabtree's Cabin,** which was built by farmers trying to escape the summer heat. You'll have to use your imagination: a century of winter weather has reduced the cabin to just a few scraps of metal.

Continue uphill, among the rare Foxtail Pines, until the trail opens up into White Chief Canyon. Just above the trail, you'll see the remains of the **White Chief Mine.** The mine is over 100 feet (30 m) deep, and you can see inside the passageway miners made, but it is not safe to explore. Instead, gaze upon an unnamed dense and frothy waterfall, which appears from a band of white marble just east of the mine. When you're ready, return the way you came.

★ Eagle Lake

Distance: 6.8 miles (11 km) round-trip
Duration: 4 hours
Elevation Change: 2,200 feet (670 m)
Effort: Strenuous
Trailhead: Eagle/Mosquito
Directions: From the Lookout Point Entrance Station, drive 14.3 miles (23 km) northeast along Mineral King Road, passing the Mineral King Ranger Station, to a fork in the road. Take the western fork and cross a bridge to reach a gravel parking lot. The Eagle Lake/Mosquito Lakes trailhead is accessible from the parking lot.

Parts of this trail are steep and a little tricky to navigate and the elevation gain adds the feeling of several more miles; plan for an all-day affair. The challenging trek to Eagle Lake is the most popular trail in Mineral King, and it's easy to see why: It boasts waterfalls, wildflowers, huge views, cool rocks, wildlife, and a big, gorgeous lake to boot. Embrace the crowds and revel with your fellow hikers in what could be the most perfect day of your life.

From the trailhead, start with a gradual climb south up the shady, east-facing side of the canyon, where you can set your gaze on Farewell Gap. Pass **Tufa Falls** at the 0.2-mile (0.3-km) mark and continue chipping away at the elevation along the dirt trail. Continue around a couple of bends and you'll be treated to an elegant wisp of a waterfall: **Crystal Creek Falls** tumbles down the eastern side of the valley. As you turn and ascend the trail, the angle and light on the waterfall changes, making for different and interesting photos.

At about 1 mile (1.5 km), the view opens up: Eagle Creek cuts through a meadow full of lupine, larkspur, horsemint, and more. This is a perfect place to stop and smell the flowers. When you're ready to resume your hike, follow the creek for 0.5 mile (0.8 km) and admire the beautiful crimson columbine and orange leopard lily. (You might even see a coyote sipping water from the creek.) Hike along the trail until you reach a fork. Turn right to continue on Eagle Lake Trail (White Chief Trail continues straight) and follow it along until you reach another fork, where Mosquito Lake Trail ventures off to the right. With Eagle Creek on your left, continue your progress on the trail until you reach Eagle Lake.

Stop to admire the panoramic views from Eagle Cap to Farewell Gap to Mineral King. Swim in the lake, fish for tiny trout, or bask on the lakeshore. Return the way you came; the downhill trek goes much faster.

Eagle Lake

White Chief, Mosquito Lakes, and Eagle Lake Trails

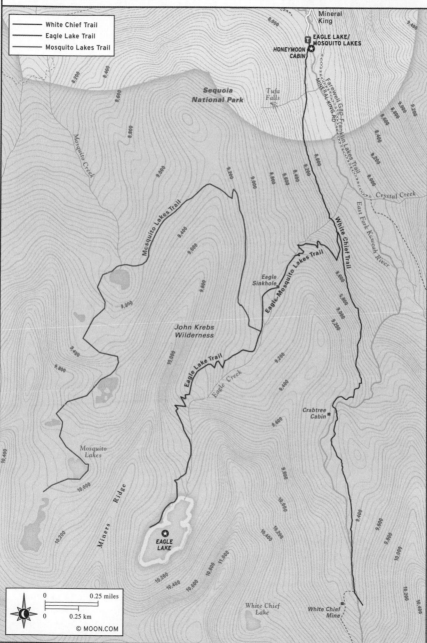

White Chief Trail
Eagle Lake Trail
Mosquito Lakes Trail

Mineral King

EAGLE LAKE/
MOSQUITO LAKES

HONEYMOON CABIN

Sequoia National Park

Tufa Falls

Farewell Gap-Franklin Lakes Trail

MINERAL KING RD.

East Fork Kaweah River

Crystal Creek

Mosquito Creek

Mosquito Lakes Trail

White Chief Trail

Eagle Sinkhole

Eagle-Mosquito Lakes Trail

John Krebs Wilderness

Eagle Lake Trail

Eagle Creek

Crabtree Cabin

Mosquito Lakes

Miners Ridge

EAGLE LAKE

0   0.25 miles
0   0.25 km

White Chief Lake

White Chief Mine

© MOON.COM

Susan Thew, Photographer and Preservationist

At the age of 40, Susan Thew took her first horsepacking trip into the wilderness and high country of what is now Sequoia National Park. With one companion, a small pack train, and her considerable determination, passion, and wit, Thew set out each summer from 1918-1926 to photograph a landscape few would ever be able to reach in person.

The largest and most complete photographic record of the region to date, Thew's gazetteer *The Proposed Roosevelt-Sequoia National Park* was shared with members of Congress in 1926. Later that year, due to Thew's research and hard work, the park boundaries were extended to include the lands surrounding Mineral King: the Great Western Divide, the Kaweah Peaks, Kern Canyon, and Sierra Crest, tripling Sequoia National Park's acreage.

Thew wrote of her experiences, "If you are weary with the battle, either of business or the greater game of life, and would like to find your way back to sound nerves and a new interest in life, I know of no better place than the wild loveliness of some chosen spot in the High Sierra in which, when you have lost your physical self, you have found your mental and spiritual re-awakening."

Susan Thew at Muir Pass, Kings Canyon National Park

Mosquito Lakes

Distance: 6.4 miles (10.3 km) round-trip
Duration: 4 hours
Elevation Change: 2,200 feet (670 m)
Effort: Strenuous
Trailhead: Eagle/Mosquito
Directions: From the Lookout Point Entrance Station, drive 14.3 miles (23 km) northeast along Mineral King Road, passing the Mineral King Ranger Station, to a fork in the road. Take the western fork and cross a bridge to reach a gravel parking lot. The Eagle Lake/Mosquito Lakes trailhead is accessible from the parking lot.

Following the trail marked for both Eagle Lake and Mosquito Lakes, start with a gradual climb south through a shady area with a great view of Timber Gap. Pass **Tufa Falls** and continue your upward trek. After turning right at the junction with White Chief Trail, you'll progress along the peaceful switchbacks of Eagle Lake Trail, cutting back and forth across a meadow brimming with pennyroyal,

horsemint, lupine, and the occasional larkspur. Take a break in the meadow (created by an avalanche!) to admire the view.

When you're ready to continue, resume your hike as the trail continues to climb. When you reach the junction with Mosquito Lakes Trail, marked by a subtle sign just after the Eagle Creek sinkhole, take a sharp right. Most hikers will take the Eagle Lake turnoff, so you'll enjoy more peace and quiet for the remaining portion of the trail.

Follow the trail as it continues upward. When you reach the first of the beautiful Mosquito Lakes, you can stop and turn back or continue on to access the upper lakes. The fishing is better and the lake views more stunning the higher you go. You cannot camp at the first lake, but it is allowed beginning with the second one. There is no official trail between the lakes, but enough people travel this route that you can follow informal trails through the brush. Return the way you came.

BACKPACKING

Most of the listings in the *Day Hikes* section can be made into lovely overnight or two-night backpacking trips. Particularly nice for beginner backpacking trips are **Franklin Lakes** and **Monarch Lakes,** but both are popular on weekends. You may find more privacy on the **Mosquito Lakes** or **Timber Gap.** Camping zones are clearly designated for each lake.

Because of the easy access for backcountry experiences, with relatively painless approaches, Mineral King is a popular starting point for backpacking. It is also easy to link with other trails, including Lodgepole and Mount Whitney. Permit quotas for each trailhead often fill up on weekends. Make a reservation at least two weeks in advance and be prepared for alternate routes if you don't have a reservation.

FISHING

Although the cold waters here are not suitable for larger creatures, the fish make up for their small size with vibrant color and energy. Many of the alpine lakes in Mineral King basin contain trout populations, and the **East Fork of the Kaweah River** (which was once stocked) sustains naturalized populations of brook and rainbow trout.

Eagle Lake and both **Franklin Lakes** are popular, reliably fruitful fishing places. Fly-fishing below Silver City Resort can be good but it's a bit hit-or-miss. Though Soda Springs, the creek running through Farewell Canyon, is closed to fishing, try plying some of the small pools below Cold Springs Campground or Silver City Mountain Resort—but stay in the shadows; the fish can spot an angler through the crystalline waters. Other decent fishing access points include the **East Fork Trail** and the **Lookout Point Entrance Station.**

Get a California fishing license online or at the **Three Rivers Mercantile** (41152 Sierra Dr., Three Rivers, 559/561-2378) before driving up to Mineral King.

Entertainment and Events

RANGER PROGRAMS

Mineral King's rangers know how to put on a show. With axe in hand, rangers will start a campfire and spin a yarn to tell listeners all about the area's storied history. Schedules for the campfire talks, as well as other talks and guided hikes are posted at the Mineral King Ranger Station.

EVENTS

Mineral King is a living community, having been continuously occupied for over 130 years. The dedicated volunteer staff of the **Mineral King Preservation Society** (www.mineralking.org) host **educational picnics** and a variety of programs throughout the high season, including **Music on the Mountain** in early August, and spooky **ghost story presentations** in late October. Visit their facebook page for information about specific events

SHOPPING

The **Mineral King Ranger Station** (mile 24/km 39, Mineral King Rd., 559/565-3768, 8am-3:45pm daily late May-mid Oct.) sells a small selection of maps (including topographic quadrangles for backpackers), water bottles, and a few souvenirs. Proceeds go to the park. You can also get a tarp to protect your car from hungry marmots in May and June.

A visit to the gift shop in the lobby of **Silver City Mountain Resort** (Mineral King Rd., 559/561-3223, www.silvercityresort.com, 9am-5pm Tues.-Wed., 8am-8pm Thurs.-Mon. May-mid-Oct.) might help you find rare books about hiking and history, as well as locally made artistic wares that are not available anywhere else. Even if you're not looking for a souvenir, the shop's original architecture and rustic-chic decor make it worth a stop.

Food and Accommodations

OUTSIDE THE PARK

The only restaurant in the area is at the **Silver City Mountain Resort** (Mineral King Rd., 559/561-3223, www.silvercityresort.com, 8am-7pm Tues.-Wed., 8am-8pm Thurs.-Mon. May-mid-Oct., breakfast $8-18, lunch and dinner $10-20). Surrounded by trees and twinkling lights, the resort's dog-friendly porch doubles as a casual restaurant. Grab a fresh-squeezed mimosa or a pint of California craft beer and start a horseshoes match or conversation with your neighbor. The atmosphere is light, friendly, and family-oriented and the food is just as delightful. The menu highlights local, Central Valley ingredients, like beef from Harris Ranch and produce from Flora Bella Farms. The greatest treat to end brunch, lunch, or dinner is a slice of home-made pie: chocolate walnut, berry, and apple are all part of the rotation. The resort also offers clean and comfortable **cabins** ($125-400) that are best described as logger chic: wooden cabins with modern bathrooms, fresh linens, and a forest-based color palette of dark greens and warm tans. The cabins are set close together on a hillside, but there's still privacy. About half of the cabins have private bathrooms and electricity. The shared bathrooms have hot water, and the resort provides any toiletries you may have forgotten.

Camping

INSIDE THE PARK

Mineral King is a tent camper's paradise: serene and quiet. Whether you choose to pitch your tent at Atwell Mill or Cold Springs, you'll be minutes from world-class hiking. Both sites have potable water, vault toilets, fire pits, picnic tables, food lockers, and pay phones. No RVs can make the trip into Mineral King, which means no generators will be whirring and echoing throughout the campgrounds. Pets are permitted on leash at both campgrounds. There are no reservations accepted for either campground; all sites are first-come, first-served. For holiday weekends, arrive early on Friday. You can self-register for a campsite at the entrance to Mineral King, Lookout Point. (Be sure to clip the ticket from your registration to the post at your driveway to show that your site is paid for and occupied.)

The only campground where you can sleep beneath the stars *and* the sequoias is **Atwell Mill** (mid-June-late Oct., $12). At 6,600 feet (2,010 m) of elevation and 6 miles (10 km) from the end of Mineral King Road, 21 sites sit in a forest of sequoias away from the winds of Mineral King Valley and nestled into a pocket of meadows. This is one of the quietest places to sleep in the front country. It also provides great access to the Hockett Trail (near campsite 16). Site 11 is a wheelchair-accessible site. Site 12 is tucked away and overlooks a meadow. The nearest supplies are 1.5 miles (2.5 km) away at Silver City Mountain Resort.

As you camp along a creek with great views of all of Mineral King's majesty, you'll feel luckier than a miner striking pay dirt. **Cold Springs** (May or June-late Oct., $12) is close to the Mineral King Ranger Station and offers access to fly-fishing in the East Fork of the Kaweah River. Choose from the 31 sites with drive-up access or the 9 walk-in sites, which are 100-200 yards from the parking area, and offer more privacy. This campground opens

1: lunch at the Silver City Mountain Resort
2: outdoor dining at Silver City Mountain Resort

1

2

later than Atwell; the opening date is dependent on the snow levels. Some of the best sites are available by turning right after the bridge. The nearest supplies are 2.5 miles (4 km)

away at Silver City Mountain Resort. From site 6, an easy, wildflower-filled nature trail offers views of the whole valley while following the river.

Transportation and Services

DRIVING AND PARKING

Be cautious while driving in Mineral King. Take your time along the partially paved, single lane roads with blind curves and steep hillsides. Don't brave the roads at night.

It may sound strange, but when the area's marmots emerge from winter hibernation in spring and early summer, they're known to chew car wiring and hoses in order to sate an instinctual craving for salt and minerals. They can cause a lot of destruction, so if you're planning to park in the area, protect your car in wrapping it with a tarp. Be sure to cover the undercarriage and wheel wells in particular. A few tarps are available to borrow at the Mineral King Ranger Station, but it's best to buy your own in advance before entering the park. It is possible for marmots to crawl in, even if you've used a tarp. When you first turn on your car, listen for any strange noises; report marmot-caused damage to the rangers.

SERVICES

The only way to enter Mineral King is through **Three Rivers,** making it the best place to

stock up on food and ice. The main grocery store in Three Rivers, **Three Rivers Village Market** (40869 Sierra Dr., 559/561-4441, http://threeriversvillagemarket.com, 8am-8pm daily), has the best selection and prices in the area. It's on the north side of Highway 198 as you enter town. **Visalia** and **Fresno** both have large chain grocery stores near the highway and en route to the park.

If you need some lip balm or pain relievers, **Silver City Mountain Resort** (Mineral King Rd., 559/561-3223, www.silvercityresort.com, 9am-5pm Tues.-Wed., 8am-8pm Thurs.-Mon. May-mid-Oct.) probably has it in their small souvenir shop. The **Mineral King Ranger Station** (mile 24/km 39, Mineral King Rd., 559/565-3768, 8am-3:45pm daily late May-mid Oct.) carries some resources for campers beyond maps, books, and bear cans. Unfortunately, the ranger station does not have a wheelchair-accessible entrance.

There is no gas in Mineral King. Before entering the park, you can fill up in Three Rivers at **Shell** (41729 Sierra Dr., 559/561-4113).

Background

The Landscape

Sequoia and Kings Canyon National Parks preserve important ecosystems, diverse plant communities, and rare geologic features. Much of the parks are managed as wilderness, protected from logging, grazing, and other unsustainable uses. Kings Canyon National Park is 98 percent wilderness. Between the two parks, 808,000 acres (311,000 ha) of land are protected.

GEOGRAPHY

Some mountain ranges are higher, longer, or steeper, but there truly is no place like the **Sierra Nevada.** The "Range of Light," as it was dubbed by naturalist John Muir, is 400 miles (644 km) long, spanning much of the length of California, and 70 miles (113 km) wide from east to west. It is part of the **American Cordillera,** an igneous chain of mountains along the Pacific Rim, stretching from Alaska to the Andes and Antarctica. Rising from near sea level in the San Joaquin Valley and the Tulare Basin to the highest peak in the contiguous United States, Mount Whitney at 14,505 feet (4,420 m), the southern Sierra includes the highest peaks and greatest area of alpine terrain.

Covering 1,353 square miles (3,480 sq km), Sequoia and Kings Canyon National Parks occupy the southern Sierra, including the Tule, Kaweah, and Kings River watersheds. These rivers are largely designated as Wild and Scenic Rivers, with over 80 miles (129 km) of protected waters.

The Sierra Nevada supplies most of the water for California's Central Valley. On the eastern side of the range are the dry and low deserts of Death Valley and Owens Valley. The Sierra catches most of the precipitation as clouds cross over, leaving a rain shadow (a dry area) on the eastern side and across Nevada.

GEOLOGY

Sequoia and Kings Canyon offer some of the best geological examples in the world. From limestone caverns to glittering granite peaks, you need only look beneath your feet and up at the mountains to experience them for yourself.

The Sierra Nevada are among the most seismically active mountains in the world. This slender chain of glacier-carved peaks extends 400 miles (644 km) from Kernville in Southern California to Klamath and Shasta at the northern border of the state, before connecting with the Cascade range. **Mount Whitney,** the highest peak in the continental United States, sits at 14,505 feet (4,420 m) above sea level. On the eastern side of the Sierra, where little rain falls, Death Valley is the lowest point in North America. Between the highs and lows are, in the words of poet Gary Snyder, "mountains and rivers without end." From glittering granite peaks to limestone caverns, this superlative place offers an expansive study in geology.

The Sierra Nevada is composed primarily of former ocean bed that was uplifted repeatedly by volcanic activity. These rocks were eventually worn away and refined by erosion from glaciers and rivers. The rock that composes the Sierra Nevada piled up in miles-thick layers of sand, silt, and fossilized organisms, also known as **sedimentary rock.** These layers can be seen today throughout the **Mineral King** region.

The Sierra Nevada was formed by plate tectonics, and the endless action of the plates are why the range is still growing today (though notably, it erodes at almost the same rate as it forms). As far back as 215 million years ago, this mountain range began to form, when an oceanic plate dove under the North American plate. Chambers of magma formed underneath the plates. The magma then penetrated the rock there, becoming what's known as a **pluton** or **plutonic rock.** The rock pushed its way upward over millions of years. The plutonic rock that forms the Sierra came to the surface and is visible today thanks to tectonic movement and erosion.

The Sierra plutons each have a unique chemical composition. The older ones are darker colored; the younger ones are lighter in color. As you traverse the parks, pause and closely examine the ratio of white rock to black. The lighter rocks are quartz (a very hard silica that appears shiny), potassium feldspar (a pink, rectangular-shaped mineral), and plagioclase feldspar (a gray and

---

Previous: elderberry blooming in Mineral King.

sometimes shiny mineral). The dark rocks are rich in iron and magnesium, but also aluminum. Beautiful salmon-pink phenocrysts (whose name means "showy crystals") can be found near Lodgepole, on the way to **Pear Lake.**

The most extensive Sierra glaciation took place one million years ago. **Glaciers** made their way into the region's valleys, retreated, then advanced again two more times (though to a lesser extent). Today, several glaciers exist above 10,000 feet (3,050 m) elevation in the parks, but they are retreating. On the flank of North Palisade, the third-highest peak in the Sierra Nevada at 14,242 feet (4,340 m), is the **Palisade Glacier.** The Sierra's glaciers have shrunk rapidly and now hide in cirques on the northern side of mountains high above where most visitors will ever go.

Instead, visitors will be more likely to encounter what the glaciers have left behind, like the stunning **paternoster lakes**—a string of glacier-formed lakes that resemble a rosary—or **glacial erratics,** which are tremendous boulders that are stranded far from their original formation. There are several vantage points (along Highway 180, heading into Cedar Grove, and on the deck of the Wuksachi Lodge) where you can see the V-shaped river valley transition into a **U-shaped valley,** evidence of where a glacier once stood. My personal favorite is **glacier-polished granite,** which has a smooth-as-glass veneer. This mirror-like surface developed thanks to the immense weight of a glacier.

Sequoia and Kings Canyon also contain interesting features that are still buried under the earth. The parks are home to more than 270 **caves.** This rock started as layers of limestone; over time, it compressed and became marble. For a rock, marble is soft. Small amounts of acid in water can erode it. As the marble dissolves, water moves through the cracks and crevices, dripping off underground ledges and ceilings into ponds. As the water slowly evaporates, calcium carbonate is left behind. Thus, over millennia, a solid band of marble can transform into a cave.

In **Crystal Cave** and **Boyden Cavern,** the two caves in the parks that are open to the public, the marble appears yellowish white and has formed into large features: Massive stalagmites erupt across the floor, and chandeliers and waves populate the ceiling. Tiny straws of rock are the youngest of the formations. Home to 20 species that live nowhere else on earth, these caves are a world unto themselves.

CLIMATE

In the Sierra Nevada, the region's **Mediterranean climate** is altered by the mountains themselves. Mediterranean climates occur between 30-45 degrees above and below the equator, and are defined by warm, sunny, and dry summers and wet, cool winters. Across the globe, these are agriculturally rich regions. Sequoia and Kings Canyon National Parks are no different.

In the **low-elevation foothills,** the Mediterranean climate is largely intact. The foothills receive, on average, less than 30 inches of rain per year, mostly between November and April. It rarely snows or freezes in this area. Many species of bird migrate down from higher in the mountains in the winter. As you enter the park, notice the abundant citrus groves that have thrived in the area for a century. The daytime and nighttime temperatures are markedly different because there is no insulating blanket like the ocean. Even in the middle of summer, the nights are cool.

Though summer afternoon **thunderstorms** are frequent, they typically drop no rain in the foothills. The air is too warm and what does fall from the clouds is evaporated before it reaches the ground. Instead this air mass will be pushed eastward, colliding with the wall of the Sierra Nevada. Thus, thunderstorms occur, usually around 3pm above 5,000 feet (1,525 m) elevation. If you happen to be on an exposed granite dome like Moro Rock or Little Baldy, it's best to leave when the clouds come through to avoid risk of being struck by lightning.

The **mid-elevations,** where pine forests inhabit grassy slopes, make the most of rain and snow throughout the year, but predominantly in the winter. The upper pine belt, dominated by red fir, is dependent on the deep snows that accumulate from November to February. Patches of snow often persist into June. The forests only receive the equivalent of 15 inches more precipitation annually than the foothills, with an average of 42-46 inches per year. Snow sustains the forests far longer than rain.

The **high elevations,** also called the **subalpine** and **alpine zones,** occur above 9,500 feet (2,900 m). Subalpine typically has a climate temperate enough for trees. Above the treeline, however, the harshness of the environment prohibits even the hardiest of junipers, whitebark pines, and lodgepole pines from growing. Powerful winds, sometimes called **katabatic winds,** result in trees with a krummholz (stunted) shape, unable to grow branches in any direction besides the predominant wind direction. Though some are just 2 feet (0.6 m) tall, they may be hundreds of years old.

ENVIRONMENTAL ISSUES
Climate Change

Climate change disproportionately affects alpine and high latitudes. Whereas a global temperature increase of 1.8-3.6°F (1-2°C) is anticipated by 2100, in mountainous regions the increase will be more like 9-12.6°F (5-7°C). This is like taking the climate of the foothills, with all its heat and dryness, and mapping it onto the Giant Forest.

The snow that defines the Sierra Nevada serves as a source of water not only for plants and animals during the dry summer, but for many Californians. The **Sierra Nevada snowpack** typically constitutes two-thirds of California's annual surface water use. (The snowpack is monitored in part by remote stations that are located throughout the

backcountry of Kings Canyon.) Warmer temperatures in the spring have especially detrimental effects on the snow storage: Warmer temperatures melt snow and heat up exposed soil which in turn holds more heat and melts more snow. This is known as the **snow albedo feedback loop** (albedo means reflectivity of light). A little warming can cause disproportionately large amounts of snowmelt earlier in the season.

Changes to snow- and rainfall, increased intensity and frequency of wildfires, and higher temperatures will affect all the plant communities in the Sierra Nevada. The **giant sequoia,** although a survivor of millennia of changes to the climate thus far, may be the least equipped to adapt to the increased heat. This is partly due to an inability to migrate—most of its seeds fall close to the parent tree—and due to the increase of insects and diseases. Sequoias are carefully monitored throughout the parks and preserved lands.

Climate change is also affecting many of the animals who live in mid- and high-elevation areas. These animals have no way of finding a similar habitat if their home area is impacted by climate change. Take the **American pika:** This herbivorous mammal, the size of a human fist, dwells among shattered rock fields in the mid-elevations of the Sierra. Pika numbers may be decreasing because it's getting too cold in the winter. Because pikas do not hibernate, they spend all summer gathering and storing grasses and flowers for winter. Without a blanket of thick snow covering and insulating their burrows, they may get too cold to reproduce and have sufficient offspring the following year.

The endemic **mountain yellow-legged frog** (of which there are two different species: the southern mountain yellow-legged frog and the Sierra Nevada yellow-legged frog) is well adapted to the short growing season of the high elevation lakes, most of which have ice floating on them into July. The large tadpoles clump together in dark clusters in the warm, sandy shallows of glacial lakes like those between LeConte Canyon and Muir Pass or

1: layers of sedimentary rock 2: massive boulder

above Vidette Meadows on the Rae Lakes Loop. The frogs are endangered due to several threats, including climate change.

Drought and Wildfires

The historic drought of 2012-2016 radically altered the forest of the southern Sierra Nevada. By the end of the drought, 100 million trees had died. In some places, 90 percent of the trees died. Entire plant communities have changed in a short time period. Hillsides of ponderosa pines turned orange as their needles desiccated, then became grey and ghostly. Within the parks, aggressive removal of dead trees occurred in areas where there was risk to humans, but most of the habitat is too steep for mechanical thinning. **Prescribed burns** are slowly being introduced, as the dead trees also pose significant fire threats because they add easy fuel to the ground—and where they stay standing, the trees can act as a ladder, as fire moves from the ground to the crown of living trees.

Fire suppression has been a commonplace practice in western U.S. forests for over a century. Lookout stations, like the one at Buck Rock, provided long views for fire scouts throughout the summer. Lightning strikes would ignite dry forests, but were immediately doused if they were within reach of infrastructure. Therefore, across the Sierra Nevada, fire was suppressed when the forest would have otherwise undergone regular, low-intensity ground fires. This means that when fire does strike these areas, there's a higher amount of fuel. These high-intensity fires are wind-drive and often affect the crowns of trees, resulting in highly devastated areas. Fortunately, the parks are developing new **fire management techniques.**

Air Pollution

Despite coming to the parks for fresh mountain air, you may notice an apparent haze from the top of Moro Rock. The San Joaquin Valley and Tulare Basin are agricultural areas that produce significant amounts of dust during harvest season. Additionally, diesel trucks and other vehicles produce exhaust and particulate matter. The air of the Central Valley is channeled between the Coast Range and the Sierra Nevada, and pushed south and east by westerly winds. This air is comprised of smog from the San Francisco Bay Area as well as large Central Valley cities like Fresno, and it has no way of exiting from the Tulare Basin, blocked by surrounding mountains. The only way it can go is into the Kaweah Canyon. For this reason, the **air quality** of Sequoia National Park consistently ranks among the worst of the national parks.

Even on a morning after a rainstorm, when the air is pristine and clear, you can see the impacts of air pollution. From the Giant Forest, find a pine or fir tree. Look on its older needles (the ones closer to the trunk). White pocks and streaks on the needles are the telltale sign of **ozone-stressed trees.** Ozone is a colorless, flavorless, odorless gas that naturally occurs—many know it best as a protective layer in the atmosphere. However, ozone close to the surface of the earth is caused by humans, mostly personal vehicles and power plants. Exposed to ozone, pines show declines in their needle health. Combined with dry and hot conditions and damage caused by insects, the stress of ozone exposure may reduce the capacity for these pines to grow needles and recover from drought.

Plants and Animals

Due to the exceptional remoteness and diversity of Sequoia and Kings Canyon, several plant and animal species live here and nowhere else. Some 300 species of wildlife are native to the parks; several are endangered or threatened, including the California condor, bighorn sheep, mountain yellow-legged frog, Sierra Nevada yellow-legged frog, the little Kern golden trout, and the Yosemite toad.

PLANTS

Trees

The sunny westerns slopes of the Sierra Nevada offer among the greatest tree diversity and height in all of North America's forests. From oak-populated scrubland to the magnificent forests of the giants (sequoias, pines, and firs) and the High Sierra's hardy conifers (lodgepole, whitebark, and foxtail pines), each species is perfectly adapted to their present situation.

GIANT SEQUOIA

In Sequoia and Kings Canyon you can see the two largest trees in the world. **Giant sequoias** are the largest trees by volume on earth, measuring 26 feet (8 m) wide at the base and nearly 300 feet (90 m) high. They are also among the oldest and tallest. The girth at ground level for the world's largest tree, **General Sherman,** is 102.5 feet (31.2 m); the second largest, **General Grant,** measures 107.5 feet (32.8 m) around. Though Grant is wider at its base, Sherman is taller by almost 7 feet (2.1 m), measuring 274.9 feet (83.8 m) in height. Even the branches of these trees are mind-boggling. One of General Sherman's branches, when it broke off in 1978, measured 6.5 feet (2 m) in diameter and 150 feet (45.7 m) long. Each year, adult sequoias add another foot in diameter to their trunks. These giants can live up to 3,000 years and weigh as many as 2.7 million pounds.

Giant sequoias are found in just one place: a narrow band that runs 260 miles (419 km) from north to south on the western side of the Sierra Nevada. They sit at an elevation of 2,700-8,900 feet (820-2,710 m) in snow-fed canyons and hillsides. They require a specific amount of water, thanks to their shallow

giant sequoias

roots, which extend about a third as wide as the tree is tall. If the soil is too wet, the tree falls over. If it's too dry, the sequoias cannot survive under the hot summer sun.

Sequoias are known for their red bark, the tannin of which works as a natural deterrent against insects. This bark can be thicker than 2 feet (0.6 m) and insulates the tree's inner layers, protecting it from fire. Oddly, it's fire that helps it reproduce: The tree's cones release seeds only after the heat of a fire dries them out.

Sequoias provide a home to a countless number of animals and plant life. Woodpeckers, chickadees, and squirrels raise their young in the trees' cavities. Frogs reproduce in the pools formed in the crux of branches. Dancing around the base of the trees are western dogwoods, with their white bracts.

INCENSE-CEDAR
Shade-dwelling **incense-cedar** trees can be deceptive: The red bark that peels vertically and the long, scaly needles can make you think you're looking at a sequoia, but the yellow-green foliage is much brighter and shinier and forms flat, rather than in brushy clusters. Additionally, the overall shape of the incense-cedar is conical, rather than the hulking cylindrical shape of the sequoia. Though not a true cedar, the incense-cedar is the mark of a mature Sierra forest, overtaking fast-growing pines and filling the area with a sweet, citrusy odor. These beautiful trees grow in the lower montane elevations, from 3,500-6,500 feet (1,070-1,980 m).

RED FIR
With its deeply furrowed bark and a sparsity of branches, the **red fir** fills the snowiest part of the Sierra's western flank (6,500-9,000 ft/1,980-2,740 m elevation). Also known as the silvertip fir, these trees have parallel, flat branches that house tufts of upward-curving needles. The red fir is most notable for its sizeable barrel-shaped cones that point skyward at the tips of its branches. So snow-adapted is the red fir that its seeds can germinate on the late snowpack, though these seedlings rarely survive. Red fir snags (standing trees that are dead or dying) are a popular site for many forms of forest life, especially woodpeckers, owls, and squirrels.

SUGAR PINE
Known for its giant cones, the **sugar pine** cuts a stunning silhouette against the sunset. Their height is magnificent, soaring up to 275 feet (84 m) when undisturbed. The long, sprawling branches elegantly unfurl like ferns, extending 50 feet (15 m) or more. They can be found perched on sunny hilltops. You can see spectacular specimens entering Grant Grove at the Big Stump Entrance Station.

PONDEROSA AND JEFFREY PINES
The **ponderosa** and **Jeffrey pines** (collectively called **yellow pines**) are famous for their beauty, adaptability, and pleasant odor. Although red-barked Jeffrey pines can be found throughout the southern Sierra, they are more common on the eastern side of the range and grow in groves in the middle of the volcanic ash soils near Mono Lake and Mammoth Lakes. The ponderosa is usually found lower in elevation and its bark is a warmer orange color.

Most of the mid-elevation (4,500-7,000 ft/1,370-2,130 m) yellow pines (defined by needles in bundles of three and cones 10 inches in diameter) will be the ponderosa, which forms a symmetrical cylinder over 200 feet (60 m) in height. The 2012-2016 drought and the ongoing practice of fire suppression killed 100 million of these trees. Swaths of forest turned orange with dead needles, then umber with bare trunks, and eventually an ashy gray as they have started to weather. Some survivors have made it through due to extensive root networks. A massive Jeffrey pine can be seen next to Knapp's Cabin in Cedar Grove. Along the Generals Highway between Grant Grove and Lodgepole you will find many groves of ponderosas on southwest-facing slopes.

LODGEPOLE PINE

The most abundant and adaptable of all Sierra trees is the **lodgepole pine.** Growing in dense thickets, these trees can be found at the edges of or inside meadows. They grow in the mid- to high-elevation range, up to 11,000 feet (3,350 m). Lodgepoles are easy to identify: They are the only pine in the region with two needles to a bundle. Sometimes, the needles form the two perpendicular lines of the letter "L"—for lodgepole. Their thin bark is also distinctive, resembling the pieces of a jigsaw puzzle. Their cones are approximately 2 inches in diameter, and make great camouflage for the bird that calls this tree home—the dark-eyed junco's head is the same color as the lodgepole's cone.

GRAY PINE

The **gray pine,** also known as foothill pine or bull pine, is shorter than other pines, around 36-45 feet (11-13.5 m). It's likely the first pine you'll see as you enter Three Rivers or as you drive into Grant Grove. The sweet, rich nuts of this pine were once a major food source for the region's Native Americans. This tree, with its lacy, sage green needles, fills the foothills of the Sierra Nevada, growing nowhere else in the world. While most conifers have one main trunk, the gray pine can have several. Its cones are dense and very sharp, weighing up to 2 pounds.

OAKS

The **California black oak** occupies the foothills of the Sierra Nevada. It produces acorns that were once used as a food source by Native Americans; they considered the acorns of the black oak to be the best-tasting. They are abundant in wetter areas that see around 25 inches of annual precipitation. The species has a broad open crown and low branches. The bark is ashy gray and becomes ridged with age. The vibrant green leaf is deeply lobed and about six inches long. California black oaks serve as habitat to the acorn woodpecker, mountain quail, and Steller's jay.

In addition to black oaks, look for the lobed leaves of the endemic, drought-resistant **blue oak** and the pointy, ovate leaves of the evergreen **California live oak,** found among the dusty slopes of most foothill trails.

Flowers

With more than 1,550 species of flowering trees, shrubs, and wildflowers, Sequoia and Kings Canyon National Parks are among the most diverse preserved plant communities in North America. Ten percent of these plants are protected as threatened or endangered species.

The low-elevation foothills erupt in rapturous fields of color in the winter and spring, starting in February. Poppies and fiddlenecks paint the land in golden hues, while showy white blooms emerge from large buckbrush shrubs, buckeye trees, and pearly everlasting plants. During the summer in the mid-elevation range, mountain pride (a species of penstemon) bursts forth from overhangs of granite and the scarlet gilia makes itself at home on sunny slopes. Some flowering plants survive on decay rather than sunlight, like the snow plant and the pinedrops, both found on the floor of the Giant Forest. A host of ethereal orchids, some with burgundy and orange stripes or spots, are also found on the shaded forest floor.

In the high-elevation range, above 7,000 feet (2,130 m), the show starts when the snow melts: Flowers bloom from June and July into September. Look for purple shooting stars and towering corn lilies in the meadows and cerulean sky pilots on the top of granite peaks. Several tiny orchids also dot this ecosystem.

LOW TO MIDDLE ELEVATIONS

The yellowish-white, 18-foot-tall (5.5-m) **chaparral yucca** grows in the steep slopes of Kings Canyon. Yucca moths, highly specialized, spend their entire lives on this plant. Native Americans used the yucca for many things, from cloth and rope to food and soap. It often takes several years for this plant to bloom, with a cluster of pale whitish-yellow blossoms. The fruits are light green balls, one inch in diameter.

The **California poppy,** in addition to being the state flower, was also a medicine for toothaches and headaches among California Native Americans. The four petals float on a filigree of lacy leaves. From February through May, poppies wash the foothills in pure gold. The plant is about 6-12 inches in height.

Starting in May and lasting until October, the descent into Kings Canyon is accompanied by the blooming of **blazing stars,** a riot of pure sunshine on the sides of the road. The shrub grows 24 inches tall with five large yellow petals comprising its flower.

The plant known as the **live-forever** fades from pale green to crimson, then to gold. It can be found on bright rocky slopes and in granite cracks. Thick rounded leaves at the base support a firecracker of scarlet blooms from April to June. Look for it while hiking on sunny arid slopes throughout the mid-elevation parts of the parks.

Whether sprouting from the sandy soil of a burned area or lining roadsides in the spring, **lupines** are a constant sight throughout the Sierra Nevada. Half of California's 80 species of lupine reside in Sequoia and Kings Canyon. Deep purple petals sheath their pollen in a pea-like enclosure. The individual flowers encircle thin stems, which appear in clusters. The compound leaves are formed from smaller leaflets, which are often hairy. The **harlequin lupine** is unmistakable, with its yellow and hot-pink petals. The plant's name came from *lupus,* the Latin word for wolf, because it was thought to steal nutrients from the soil. In reality, though, lupines add nitrogen to the soil.

MIDDLE TO HIGH ELEVATIONS

The showy **crimson columbine** blooms from April to August. Sometimes the plants can be quite robust, up to 42 inches tall. Its slender neck arcs over streams, seeps, and meadow edges. Its cousin, with whom it sometimes cross-pollinates, is the **Coville's columbine,** with large cream flowers, found in rocky areas in higher elevations. Both hummingbirds and bees feed on the nectar of these two flowers.

Similar to columbines, the **Sierra shooting star** nods toward the ground on a slender, bowed stem. This delicate purple to indigo flower can be found mostly along streams or in bogs and meadows. A yellow ring highlights its pollen. There are six species of this plant in the Sierra.

Throughout the Giant Forest, the fuchsia **mountain pride** drips from rocky outcroppings, as if raspberry jelly were seeping out of the earth. These stunning flowers bloom for several months throughout the summer, and can be found from the foothills up to 12,000 feet (3,660 m). The individual flowers are inch-long tubes, which attract pollinators with proboscises, like hummingbirds and butterflies. Mountain pride are a type of **penstemon,** of which there are more than 25 species in the Sierra Nevada. They are recognizable by their tubular flowers that form two lip-like halves.

The **leopard lily** is an especially beautiful Sierra flower. The color of the petals is striking, fading from crimson to golden orange, with the brown spots that give the flower its name. As many as 30 blossoms can populate a single plant, bending into a backward bell shape, exposing the stamen. The plant can grow as high as 8 feet (2.5 m) tall. It's often found in the mid-elevation range like the Giant Forest. Other lily species, like the **Sierra tiger lily** and **Kelley's lily,** reside on higher ground.

Stands of statuesque **corn lilies** fill mountain meadows with their broad, parallel-veined leaves, which often overpower the plant's blossoms. When enough moisture is present in the soil, the corn lily blooms, becoming coated in inch-wide white blossoms with purple streaks. This plant is toxic to humans and livestock. It blooms from July to August, after which its stalks turn golden. It can be found in places like Crescent Meadow.

Above 11,000 feet (3,350 m) lives the aptly named **sky pilot,** a type of phlox. The electric purple blooms grow in clusters of five petals and the fuzzy leaves rustle in the Sierra wind. To find these lovely flowers, you'll need to head up high from July to August.

ANIMALS
Mammals
AMERICAN BLACK BEAR
Despite their name, **black bears** range in color from cinnamon to blond to jet black. They hibernate in the winter, emerging in spring to feed on grass and carrion. In late summer, black bears feast on nuts that have fallen to the forest floor. They have a powerful sense of smell, and can walk long distances, even on steep mountain terrain.

Evidence of black bears can be seen in shredded logs and standing trees; sometimes you might see some fur stuck in the splinters of wood. For the best chances of seeing a bear, visit meadows in the early morning and stay quiet. Some of the trails of the Giant Forest that are farther from the road are excellent opportunities to see a bear. For information on bear safety precautions, see the *Essentials* chapter.

MOUNTAIN LION
Roaming expansive territories of over 100 square miles (259 sq km), mostly alone, the **mountain lion** is the ultimate stealthy predator. They live in the parks' canyons and are extremely furtive. Their padded paws, as wide as an adult human hand, are designed for silence. They hunt deer and smaller mammals from rocky ledges, their yellow-brown coats blending in well with their surroundings. They are known for their quick sprints and pounces, which kill their prey by suffocation. Mountain lions can weigh up to 250 pounds. They're 2.5 feet (0.8 m) tall at the shoulder and 5-8 feet (1.5-2.5 m) long, including their long, black-tipped tail, which can serve as a rudder to help them make tight turns.

If you encounter a mountain lion, try to appear larger by standing up tall with your arms overhead and loudly shouting. Do not turn your back or run. If you go hiking in the quiet parts of Cedar Grove, take at least one other

person with you. Keep an eye out for scratching posts with a foul urine smell or for prints in dusty trails.

MULE DEER
Often found in quiet meadows, mule deer were once a critical resource for Indigenous people who hunted them for sustenance throughout the year. The mule deer can be identified by its large ears and black-tipped tail. Female deer, or does, mate in the fall. Fawns are born in the spring, camouflaged with white spots. They will stay with their mothers until fall.

AMERICAN PIKA
Few animals delight like the high-elevation, chinchilla-like **American pika.** It settles in scree, gathering hay for winter, separating the stashes for eating and sleeping. Pika emerge on hillsides throughout the park, notably in Mineral King and along the trail to Pear Lake. You may hear or see them screeching at each other and at hikers. Hardly the size of a softball, these chubby-cheeked critters are very cute: They're a gray poof of fur with rounded ears on top of their heads.

YELLOW-BELLIED MARMOT AND OTHER RODENTS
The yellow-bellied marmot is a large rodent with mottled gray fur on its back and a yellowish chest and belly. More than 2 feet (0.6 m) long, marmots have a dark tail that's about a quarter of their length. Marmots communicate with each other using their tails and by vocalizing with loud, piercing squeaks and chirps. They live in groups, foraging montane meadows and resting in rocky dens, where they hibernate. They feed on wildflowers, including lupine and cow-parsnip, enabling them to grow up to 11 pounds (5 kg). In Mineral King, marmots emerge from hibernation starved of minerals. They are known to cause damage to vehicles during this time, as they chew engine wires and other materials, looking for the salt and other minerals they need.

Several other species of rodent grace the sequoia forests, like the **golden mantle ground squirrel,** five **chipmunk** species, shrews, voles, mice, the Douglas squirrel (also called a chickaree), the western ground squirrel, and the seldom seen **flying squirrel.** You're most likely to encounter squirrels in your campsite and in the forested areas.

WEASELS

Among the carnivores of this region are eight species of mustelid, the mighty-jawed weasel family. You're most likely to encounter a tiny **long-tailed weasel** loping among the slopes, but keep an eye out for the **American marten** and the **fisher.** These fearsome predators are capable of climbing high into trees to attack nests of squirrels and birds.

Birds

Over 200 species of bird reside in Sequoia and Kings Canyon, including the state bird, the **California quail.** Bird life abounds in every area of the park. In the low elevations, winter sees mixed flocks of **juncos, chickadees, white-winged doves,** and **American robins.** In the high elevation, you might spot rarities like the **pine grosbeak, Clark's nutcracker,** the **rosy-finch,** and the **red crossbill.** In the mid-elevation range are the passerines: golden-crowned and ruby-crowned **kinglets, finches** and **sparrows,** three types of **nuthatch,** and the **hermit thrush.**

On a spring or summer evening, just after the sun sets, **owls** of many kinds hoot in the distance, including the largest of all owl species: the **great grey owl.**

Famously, the Sierra Nevada is home to 12 different types of **woodpecker**—one or two species for every habitat! In Giant Forest, you might find the **white-headed woodpecker** flying through the trees or hear the thump

of a **giant pileated woodpecker** in the distance.

Crows are clever and noisy, and among the most noticeable animals in the park. In the foothills you'll see the **western scrub jay,** and in Giant Forest, crested **Steller's jays** aggressively alight on picnic benches and caw from live oaks and pines. **Ravens** also parade through the park.

The **songbirds** of Sequoia and Kings Canyon are often heard before they are found in the foliage. You might spot a singular **brown creeper** as it descends a ponderosa pine. You're sure to hear the rustling, peeping, and squeaking of the miniscule **dark-eyed junco,** which hop among the pine needles. Look for lovely crested **cedar waxwings** filling the high canopy or **bushtits** attacking pests on an elderberry.

Western tanagers, a stocky songbird that sounds like (but is smaller than) a robin, are noticeable from far away: The bright red head coupled with a lemon-yellow body and striking black wings make this bird utterly unique in the Sierra. The male will strut his stuff with dancing and acrobatics to impress the muted yellow-green female. They nest across the pine belt.

John Muir's favorite bird was the **water ouzel,** or **American dipper.** This swimming bird has a sort of ballast system to keep it underwater despite the buoyant air trapped in its feathers. Hunting in the shallows, the dark gray dipper snaps caddis flies from their rocky nests before taking off to sing and flit along the water.

Fish, Amphibians, and Reptiles

In the Sierra Nevada, there are 24 native species of fish, including salmon and specialized species of trout. There are 30 non-native fish species that have been introduced to this ecosystem or have made their way into its waters due to climate change.

The **California golden trout,** the state fish, is found only in tributaries of the Kern River at the southern end of Sequoia National

---

1: black bear 2: raven 3: mountain pride, a type of penstemon 4: tadpoles of the mountain yellow-legged frog

Park, accessible from Mineral King. It is truly a special sight, featuring a black-dotted tail, crimson neck, sunshine-yellow belly, and a streak of pinkish red. These fish are not big, but they are fighters. In Mineral King and in Cedar Grove, fishers will encounter the elegant **rainbow trout,** the most widely distributed fish in the Sierra. Transplantation introduced this species to the highest reaches, areas where they would not have otherwise lived. The Kings River is arguably one of the finest wild rainbow trout fisheries in the state. These fish have an important role in the ecosystem, serving as dinner for raccoons, osprey, and bears.

High in the backcountry, the tadpoles of the **mountain yellow-legged frog** reside for 2-4 years in alpine lakes near Kearsarge and Muir Passes. The tadpoles and frog range 1.5-3 inches long, and are mostly dark mottled brown. The frogs get their name from their yellow-colored belly and back legs. A specialized high-elevation species, these frogs are threatened due to introduced species, an invasive fungus, and climate change. Look along high-elevation lakeshores for a gray or brownish frog. It hunts by sitting quietly and whipping out its long tongue when prey is in range. When threatened, they emit a deterrent that smells like garlic.

There are 14 species of snake in the Sierra Nevada, including the muted brown **rubber boa** and the elegant **garter snake.** The ruler of them all is the **California mountain kingsnake.** This snake has no venom but instead uses its powerful constriction—the strongest squeeze relative to its size—to suffocate prey. They are so named for their ability to hunt and eat other snakes, including rattlesnakes. First described in 1835, the kingsnake spans California, but appreciates the woodland chaparral of the Foothills and Cedar Grove. Look for its striking black-and-white stripe pattern with a few red stripes on the tail and near the neck.

The **western rattlesnake** is often heard before it's seen, shaking its namesake rattle to warn off potential predators. Rattlesnakes use their retractable fangs to inject venom into small mammals and birds, but they will also eat eggs. Late in the day or along sunny slopes in the early morning is when you will most likely encounter this light brown snake, usually 3 feet (0.9 m) in length, with dark brown blotches on the back that change to stripes toward the tail. The head shape and scale patterns of **gopher snakes** resemble that of the western rattlesnake, helping to protect them from predators.

History

EARLY HISTORY

Several groups of Indigenous peoples dwelled in and around the area that would eventually become Sequoia and Kings Canyon National Parks. In the area that's now the town of Three Rivers, in the foothills of the Sierra Nevada, lived the largest populations of the **Yokuts people,** including the **Wukchumni.** Starting from around 3,000 years ago, there were around 15,000-20,000 Yokuts people in the area. Their main source of food was the acorn, ground into meal by granite mortars and pestles next to the river. Once ground, the flour had to be leached, often in big pits. Women

prepared flour, soup, mush, and bread, preferably of black oak acorns. The acorns that were shaken from the tree were said to taste the best. Berries, deer meat, and other game filled out the Yokuts' diet. The liver of the deer, dried in the sun, was the most common toxin for covering arrow points.

The **Western Mono people,** descendants of the Shoshone-Paiute, eventually moved into the forests and foothills of the Sierra. At Hospital Rock, over 500 **Patwisha people** resided. The Patwisha were a subgroup of the Western Mono (also called Monache) and lived throughout the area that was fed by the

A Day in the Life of a Yokuts Woman

BACKGROUND
HISTORY

The historical information presented below was collected from *The Sierra Nevada Before History* (Louise Jackson, 2010), *Indians of Sequoia and Kings Canyon National Parks* (A. B. Elsasser, 1988), and *Indian Tribes of Sequoia National Park Region* (Julian H. Steward, 1935). To learn more about the Indigenous people of the Sierra Nevada and foothills, stop by the Foothills Visitor Center in Sequoia National Park.

As sunlight pours over the mountain peaks and fills the deep river valley, the day begins for a Yokuts woman. She unwraps her baby from deerskin coverings and props her against her body. A smoothed piece of willow, used for fishing hot items out of baskets, entertains the baby for now. The young mother folds the family's bedding and runs a brush made of soapbush through her raven hair before standing in the dappled morning light.

The family's central granary, a platform with two wooden huts, holds plenty of food and keeps rodents at bay. She carries dried manzanita berries and shreds of smoked venison back to the fire. She takes heated rocks from the fire and tosses them into a special pine-pitched basket full of fresh water. Her husband holds the red feather of a flicker above the baby's face. Over breakfast, the couple discusses last night's dreams and today's journeys.

Yokuts basket maker, Tule River Reservation near Porterville, California, circa 1900

They are preparing for the summer, when relatives will visit. The woman straps the baby upright to a flat board backpack inside a burden basket. After some adjustments, she pulls a milkweed cord across her forehead and the baby rests comfortably between her shoulder blades. The baby's eyes are shaded by a small awning, and she soon coos herself to sleep.

With her husband's female relatives, the woman heads to the river to gather redbud bark in the warming afternoon, preparing to weave baskets with it. Her mother-in-law compliments her work. She hopes her husband will trade these baskets for the salty snacks of dried fly larvae and pine nuts.

Hours later, the woman returns home and serves dinner to her family. The stars come to life as her husband's father tells stories. Everyone holds the baby, lifting her to stand on her leather-wrapped feet in the soft dirt. Firelight and laughter fill this small corner of the Gaweah River canyon.

Marble, Middle, East, and South Forks of the Kaweah River. Like the Yokuts, the Mono also subsisted on various preparations of acorns.

Though the groups of people that lived throughout the region spoke different languages, trade between them was healthy. It would have flowed even more steadily, if not for the distance (about 70 mi/113 km) and mountain peaks between them. In the summer, the **Owens Valley (or Eastern) Paiute** used trails to reach the Western Mono in places like Lodgepole, near what's now the

Wuksachi Lodge, as well as the **Tübatulabal people** in the White Chief Mine area of Mineral King and along the Kern River. The Paiutes transported critical goods: brownware pottery, pinyon pine nuts, edible fly larvae from saline lakes, and hunting tools from the volcanically active region, including obsidian arrow points. Families blended. These same trade routes were in use for centuries.

Note: The last native speaker of Wukchumni, a language of the Yokuts people, resides in the San Joaquin Valley today.

She is creating a dictionary and recording her voice to preserve the language of her people. About 200 Wukchumni Yokuts also live in the area. They have resided near the Kaweah River (often spelled "Gaweah" by the Yokuts), for at least 3,000 years.

EXPLORATION, COLONIZATION, AND THE LUMBER INDUSTRY

Early European explorers came to this region looking for resources, territory, and souls to convert to Christianity. The Kings River was named in the early 1800s when an expedition of Spanish conquistadors and friars encountered it on the religious holiday known as El Día de los Reyes (Three Kings Day). The area otherwise remained relatively undisturbed. It would be another 40-50 years before Europeans settled in the southern Sierra.

California's gold rush exploded in 1849. In the early 1850s, gold was discovered in the Kern River, but it didn't last long. Throughout the area, silver and gold mines, including some in what's now Mineral King, busted even before they were built. The state recognized the potential value of minerals in the Sierra. Surveying these incredible mountains took the California Geological Survey and a team of adventurers years to map. The mountains bear their names today: Mount Clarence King, accessible from Cedar Grove, stands 12,905 feet (3,930 m) tall, commemorating the author of the book *Mountaineering in the Sierra Nevada*. Mount Brewer, at 13,570 feet (4,140 m), is named for William Brewer, Yale professor of agriculture, leader of the expedition team, and the first person to climb it (in 1864). Brewer is situated between the front country and the highest peaks in the Great Western Divide, accessible from Cedar Grove and Bubb's Creek. Brewer also found the highest peak in the Sierra and named it after his boss, Josiah Whitney, director and Harvard professor of geology. Mount Whitney is the highest peak in the contiguous United States, at 14,505 feet (4,421 m) in elevation.

As settlers began to occupy the nearby San Joaquin Valley and Tulare Basin, farmers and ranchers began to search for summer grazing land. In 1858, a rancher from the town of Three Rivers, named Hale Tharp, took a hunting trip up the Kaweah River and found Giant Forest. He grazed cattle and lived in a cabin formed by a fallen sequoia for 30 summers, building relationships with the area's Indigenous people.

Timber seekers, lured by the groves of giant sequoias, imported equipment and teams of men and mules into the forests. Enterprising lumber workers from the Central Valley, in partnership with the Southern Pacific Railway, built shipping and transport infrastructure. In order to move the lumber from the mountains, at 8,000 feet (2,440 m) elevation, down to the train station, vast hydraulic systems were built, including a 79-mile (127-km) flume that ran from Hume Lake to the town of Sanger. Sequoia Lake and Hume Lake, both near Grant Grove, are artifacts of this logging infrastructure.

From 1893 to 1907, the Sanger Lumber Company operated Converse Mill, cutting down 200 sequoias in Indian Basin Grove and clear-cutting the Converse Basin, which had been the largest of all the sequoia groves in the world. When logging operations were finally restricted in 1920, 200 million board feet of sequoia wood had been harvested, accompanied by many other species of trees.

CONSERVATION, PROTECTION, AND TOURISM

After seeing the decimation caused by the lumber industry, preservationists and other advocates took action to protect the biodiversity and natural resources of the Sierra Nevada. Several groups and individuals worked in every way they knew how to protect this special place. The effort of Tulare, Hanford, and Visalia residents, where the impacts could most easily be observed, led to several newspaper articles and aggressive lobbying of state legislature.

John Muir, the father of the modern conservation movement, led the Sierra Club in a charge against the desecration of the massive ancient sequoias. Muir held talks from the pulpit of Kings Canyon and wrote extensive essays expounding the importance of wilderness to the soul of humanity.

On September 25, 1890, President Benjamin Harrison created Sequoia National Park. America's second national park, Sequoia was the first area formed to protect a living species: the giant sequoia. One week later, the park was expanded from the foothills to the Giant Forest, likely for the purpose of preventing logging along the way to the big trees. The area around the General Grant Tree was also added as General Grant National Park.

From 1891 to 1913, the focus was on protecting park resources from destruction and connecting visitors to their new park. The first protectors of the park were U.S. Army Calvary troops, including the Buffalo Soldiers. Four regiments of African American soldiers build the first wagon road into Giant Forest, completed in 1903. This new accessibility led to more visitors wanting a firsthand look at the giant sequoias.

The invention of the car made visiting the parks even more accessible. Tourists photographed their cars being dwarfed by the trees. Some industrious folk even cut into the fallen logs, making it so cars could drive right over or through them. An example that still exists today is Auto Log.

Hiking also became a popular activity in the parks. In 1917 Moro Rock's wooden stairs were built, allowing visitors to more easily reach the top. In 1932, workers from the Civilian Conservation Corps developed the High Sierra Trail, cutting tracks at the upper edge of the Middle Fork of the Kaweah River, into the backcountry, and all the way to Mount Whitney.

Photography also proved a valuable resource for conservation. Susan Thew, a woman from Visalia, photographed the Sierra on horseback in the early 1920s. Her photographs became the most complete visual record to date of the backcountry. The same method was employed by famed national park photographer Ansel Adams. He dragged an 8x10-inch negative camera, lens, and tripod, which weighed some 30 pounds, into the backcountry of Kings Canyon, capturing rare and iconic views of the present-day John Muir Trail and the wilderness of Cedar Grove.

Once the public had physical and virtual access to this wonderland, the park was expanded. In 1940, under President Franklin Delano Roosevelt, a new national park was formed, extending to protect the wild Kings River canyon. In 1978, Mineral King was officially added to Sequoia National Park after a revival of the conservation movement. Nearly 20 years prior, this same section of land was owned by Walt Disney Productions. The company had plans to build a ski resort here, but was opposed and eventually defeated by the Sierra Club, due to the potential for negative environmental impact.

Today, park managers, scientists, and rangers continue to work toward the protection of the parks. This includes revising their stance on fire suppression (which has led to devastating wildfires), managing visitor use and crowds, and coordinating conservation efforts with adjacent agencies and landowners.

Essentials

Getting There

FROM FRESNO OR VISALIA

Air

If you are arriving by air, the **Fresno Yosemite International Airport** (FAT, 5175 E. Clinton Ave., Fresno, 559/621-4500 or 800/244-2359, www.flyfresno.com) is the closest airport to the parks, with reasonable connections to major airlines and excellent customer service. The main airlines that serve Fresno are Alaska Airlines and Delta, but AeroMexico, Allegiant, American, Frontier, United, and Volaris also

fly here. Two hotels directly across the street make early morning departures easier.

Rental cars are in the same building as the terminal. Companies include **Alamo** (559/251-5577), **Avis** (559/454-5030), **Budget** (559/253-4100), **Dollar** (866/434-2226), **Enterprise** (559/253-2700), **Hertz** (559/251-5055), **National** (559/251-5577), **Payless** (559/253-9937), and **Thrifty** (559/458-7337).

The **V-Line shuttle** (877/404-6473, http://ridevline.com, $10 single ride, $9 students, seniors, veterans, and people with disabilities) provides access from the airport to Visalia, where you can take the **Sequoia Shuttle** (877/287-4453, www.sequoiashuttle.com, May-Sept., $20 round-trip) to Giant Forest and Lodgepole.

Train and Bus
From Fresno, you can take **Amtrak** (www.amtrak.com) to the town of Hanford on the **San Joaquins route.** From Hanford, you'll transfer to a connecting bus that heads east to Visalia. From there, you can take the **Sequoia Shuttle** (877/287-4453, www.sequoiashuttle.com, May-Sept., $20 round-trip) to Giant Forest and Lodgepole. You can also take the **V-Line shuttle** (877/404-6473, http://ridevline.com, $10 single ride, $9 students, seniors, veterans, and people with disabilities) from the Fresno airport to Visalia, then board the Sequoia Shuttle. The V-Line runs six trips a day, seven days a week.

Public transit does not run between Fresno and Grant Grove. You'll need a personal vehicle to vist the northern parts of the parks.

Driving
SUGGESTED ROUTES
From Fresno, it's 100 miles (160 km), a drive of about 2.5 hours, to reach Lodgepole. You'll take Highway 99 south, then Highway 198 until you reach Visalia. From here, it's just 55 miles (90 km) to reach Lodgepole, a drive of about two hours. Continue following Highway

198 to the town of Three Rivers. This is your last chance to pick up supplies before entering the park.

As you continue on Highway 198, you'll enter the Foothills region via the Ash Mountain Entrance Station. From here, keep driving the scenic Generals Highway to reach Lodgepole. Grant Grove is about 30 miles away, which takes an hour to drive.

To get to Grant Grove directly from Fresno, take Highway 180 east for 55 miles. This drive takes a little less than 1.5 hours.

Tours
Sequoia Sightseeing Tours (559/561-4189, www.sequoiatours.com, adults $79-159, children under 12 $59-99) offers educational and fun guided tours that feature all the hits of the parks. Full-day and half-day tours of Sequoia and Kings Canyon are available, depending on group size and timing. Full-day tours depart from Three Rivers. Half-day tours meet at Wuksachi Lodge.

Crossroads Tours (559/658-8687, www.yosemite1.com, from $109 per person) offers tours of Sequoia and Kings Canyon from Fresno and other points of origin in SUVs, vans, and minibuses. Tours include entrance fees.

Viator (888/651-9785, www.viator.com, $249 per person) has a couple options for touring Sequoia National Park from Visalia. They also offer a half-day snowshoe tour in the winter.

FROM YOSEMITE NATIONAL PARK
Driving
SUGGESTED ROUTES
From Yosemite Valley to Grant Grove is 3.5-4 hours and 150-175 miles, depending on the route. There are two viable routes that each have a couple of benefits.

Traveling from Yosemite Valley to Grant Grove via **Highway 41** is the shorter and faster route. Take Highway 41 south out of the valley, through the Wawona area of Yosemite, and into Fresno. Pick up Highway 180 and head east into Grant Grove for a total of 150 miles and 3.5 hours of driving. The views on this route are stunning. Highway 41 can get crowded with traffic, however. Travelers with longer RVs (over 22 ft/6.5 m) will need to take this route.

Take **Highway 140** out of Yosemite Valley and you'll trace the path of the Merced River. This route covers 175 miles (280 km) and takes around four hours to reach Grant Grove. There are plenty of places to stop for a dip in the river or a photo of the gorgeous spring wildflowers that decorate the river canyon. It's not uncommon for there to be construction on Highway 140, which may cause delays of 15-30 minutes. After leaving the park, you'll go through the town of Mariposa; from here to Fresno, the drive is straightforward and mostly downhill. Vehicles longer than 22 feet are not recommended on Highway 140.

FROM SAN FRANCISCO
Air

There are several Bay Area airports, so be sure to consider each when looking for the best price and most convenience for your trip. Oakland's airport is technically the closest to the parks, approximately four hours from Grant Grove. Commuter traffic can be gruesome throughout the Bay Area, starting around 3pm Monday through Thursday and even earlier on Fridays.

SAN FRANCISCO INTERNATIONAL AIRPORT

San Francisco International Airport (SFO, 650/821-8211 or 800/435-9736, www.flysfo.com) is 15 miles south of San Francisco. It is the second-busiest airport in California, after Los Angeles, and spans four terminals with rich entertainment, shopping and dining options, including an art museum. The airport is a hub for United Airlines and Alaska Airlines. It has international connections from Europe and Asia.

SFO's rental car center is accessible via the blue line of the AirTrain (24 hours daily). Rental agencies typically close their desks overnight. **Alamo** (650/616-2400), **Avis** (650/877-6780), **Budget** (650/877-0998), **Dollar** (650/244-4131), **Enterprise** (650/697-9200), **Fox** (800/225-4369), **Hertz** (650/624-6600), **National** (650/616-3000), and **Thrifty** (650/283-0898) are all at the rental car center. **NU Car** (800/556-8227), **Payless** (650/548-5161), **Silvercar** (650/273-7110), and **Sixt** (415/658-9800) are off site, requiring an additional shuttle from the rental car center upon request. Call ahead to ensure a shuttle will be available.

OAKLAND INTERNATIONAL AIRPORT

Oakland International Airport (OAK, 1 Airport Dr., Oakland, 510/563-3300, www.oaklandairport.com) is a hub for Southwest Airlines and is connected to BART, the San Francisco Bay Area's rapid transit system. It is the smallest of the area's airports, but it's also the closest to Grant Grove. Rental cars are accessible by shuttle that runs every 10 minutes.

OAK is also served by the major rental companies. Just outside the airport, the rental car center is accessible by a shuttle (every 10 minutes 4:30am-1:30am, on-demand 1:30am-4:30am). **Alamo** (800/462-5266), **Avis** (800/331-1212), **Budget** (800/527-0700), **Dollar** (800/800-4000), **Enterprise** (800/261-7331), **Fox** (800/225-4369), **Hertz** (800/654-3131), **National** (510/877-4507), **Payless** (510/638-1000), and **Thrifty** (800/847-4389) all have desks at the rental car center.

MINETA SAN JOSE INTERNATIONAL AIRPORT

Mineta San Jose International (SJC, 1701 Airport Blvd., San Jose, 408/392-3600, www.flysanjose.com) is easily navigated and hosts many restaurant options with simple fare. The rental car center is on site near Terminal B. If you are considering a trip to Sequoia and Kings Canyon that ends with cruising the California coast, this airport may be the most convenient. To reach Grant Grove from San Jose takes approximately four hours over scenic mountains, wetland habitat, and the heart of San Joaquin Valley.

To get to the rental car center at SJC, just walk across the main road at Terminal B. Terminal A passengers can take the airport shuttle bus (blue route) to the rental car center. All of the major rental car companies are there: **Alamo** (800/327-9633), **Avis** (800/831-2847), **Budget** (800/527-0700), **Dollar** (800/800-4000), **Enterprise** (800/736-8222), **Fox** (800/225-4369), **Hertz** (800/654-3131), **National** (800/227-7368), **Payless** (800/729-5377), **Sixt** (888-749-8227), and **Thrifty** (800/367-2277). The desks close for a few hours in the middle of the night, but you can call in advance for after-hours service.

Train and Bus

From the San Francisco Bay Area, it's possible to take a train to within an hour of the parks. **Amtrak** (www.amtrak.com) offers the **San Joaquins route,** which runs from several stations in the Bay Area to Fresno. This journey takes four hours and chugs through agricultural areas. To continue to Grant Grove and Kings Canyon from Fresno, you'll need to rent a car.

To reach Sequoia, you can take the San Joaquins route one stop farther, to Hanford. From Hanford, Amtrak operates a connecting thruway bus to Visalia. This trip takes around 6.5 hours. From Visalia, hop on the **Sequoia Shuttle** (877/287-4453, www.sequoiashuttle.com, May-Sept., $20 round-trip), which will take you to the Giant Forest and Lodgepole areas.

Driving
SUGGESTED ROUTES

To get to Grant Grove from San Francisco, it's 245 miles (395 km) via I-580, Highway 99, and Highway 180, which takes a little over four hours. To reach Lodgepole via the Ash Mountain Entrance Station, you'll continue on Highway 99, going through Visalia to Highway 198, for a total of 280 miles (450 km) and a little over five hours of driving.

Tours
Take Tours (www.taketours.com, $258-450 per person) offers bus tours from the San Francisco Bay Area to Sequoia, Kings Canyon, and Yosemite in a two-day, one-night trip. Guides speak English and Mandarin. **Tours4Fun** (www.tours4fun.com, $228 per person) is a similar two-day bus trip that shares the highlights of Sequoia, Kings Canyon, and Yosemite in English and Mandarin.

FROM LOS ANGELES
Air
Los Angeles International Airport (LAX, 855/463-5252, www.flylax.com), the third-busiest airport in the world, is massive. In addition to the international terminal, there are eight domestic terminals. Leave plenty of time for layovers, as LAX is notorious for last-minute gate changes. Thankfully, countless creature comforts and a world of food options are here, including an organic tea and coffee shop.

To reach the rental cars, pick up your rental company's shuttle outside the arrivals area. Companies include **Alamo** (844/357-5138), **Avis** (800/352-7900), **Budget** (800/214-6094), **Dollar** (800/800-4000), **Enterprise** (855/266-9289), **Fox** (323/593-7486), **Hertz** (800/654-3131), **National** (844/393-9989), **Sixt** (888/749-8227), and **Thrifty** (800/847-4389).

Train and Bus
It's technically possible to take **Amtrak** (www.amtrak.com, from $30) from Los Angeles to Visalia, but your train ride, which goes from Bakersfield to Hanford will be sandwiched between two bus rides, from Los Angeles to Bakersfield, then from Hanford to Visalia, for a travel time of around five hours. The simpler, faster, and cheaper option is to take **Greyhound** (www.greyhound.com, $21) directly from Los Angeles to Visalia. This bus journey takes only 4.5 hours. From Visalia, hop on the **Sequoia Shuttle** (877/287-4453, www.sequoiashuttle.com, May-Sept., $20 round-trip), which will take you to the Giant Forest and Lodgepole areas.

Driving

SUGGESTED ROUTES

To get to Giant Forest and Lodgepole from Los Angeles, it's 240 miles (385 km) via I-5, Highway 99, and Highway 198, which takes about 4-6 hours, depending on how much traffic you hit leaving L.A. To continue on to Grant Grove, it's 30 miles (50 km) on the Generals Highway, which takes an hour to drive.

Getting Around

DRIVING

The parks' curvy roads require slow and careful driving. Focus on what's around the next turn, as wildlife on the road is not uncommon.

Winter driving conditions can be dangerous, even in the Foothills area. Bridges are susceptible to black ice, which is hard to see but very slippery. If conditions become too dangerous due to snow, ice, or rockfall, the park service will close the roads. More often in winter conditions, the park service will require that your vehicle have snow tires, four-wheel-drive, or chains.

Chains are only helpful when there is snow on the road. Use a turnout or parking lot to install chains. Install thick chains by laying them flat and then driving over them before clipping. A newer and easier style may be available for your vehicle, where you do not have to drive over the chains, but instead clip and bungee them around the tire. Test your chains by driving slowly for about a quarter of a mile and make sure they are secure. Keep a pair of gloves with your chains, which will make installing them more comfortable in cold weather. Driving below 30 mph (50 kph) is recommended when your vehicle has chains on.

If your car breaks down, expect a long wait for a tow truck; some are coming from as far away as Fresno. Several towing companies service the parks.

- **AAA South** (800/678-3839)
- **AAA North** (800/408-2225): for Cedar Grove
- **Michael's Towing** (Reedley, 559/638-4101)
- **Abel's Towing** (Reedley, 559/978-6232)
- **Active Towing** (Reedley, 559/643-0911)
- **Allstar Towing** (Dinuba, 559/591-3492)
- **Action Towing** (Fresno, 559/498-9999)
- **Herndon Towing** (Fresno, 559/431-3334)

SHUTTLE

If you want to explore Giant Forest and Lodgepole, there's a **free park shuttle** that services these parts of Sequoia National Park in the summer. It runs every 15-20 minutes from 8am to 6pm every day. Major stops include Dorst Creek Campground, Wuksachi Lodge, Lodgepole Village, the General Sherman Tree, and Moro Rock. The shuttles get crowded during the last hour of service, when everyone is trying to get back to their car or campground at the same time. Take an earlier shuttle to ensure you get a seat.

It's also possible to take the **Sequoia Shuttle** (877/287-4453, www.sequoiashuttle.com, May-Sept., $20 round-trip) into the park from Visalia and surrounding towns. Reservations are required. The shuttle fare includes the park entrance fee.

RV

No RVs are allowed on Crescent Meadow Road (the road to Moro Rock) or Crystal Cave Road. Vehicles over 22 feet (6.5 m) are not advised between Potwisha Campground in the Foothills region and Giant Forest. If you have a large RV, you can get to Giant Forest and Lodgepole from the north, via Grant Grove and the Big Stump Entrance Station. RVs and trailers are not advised on Mineral King Road.

Ideal campgrounds for RVs are Azalea,

Crystal Springs, and Sunset Campgrounds in Grant Grove, where there are several sites that are large and flat. In Cedar Grove, Sheep Creek and Moraine Campgrounds have good RV sites. Finally, in Lodgepole, Lodgepole and Dorst Creek Campgrounds have dump stations and paved sites. Generator use is limited at Lodgepole and Dorst to 8am-11am and 5pm 8pm daily. In the Foothills, you can stay at Potwisha Campground, which has a nearby dump station, but the road is a little narrow. Quiet hours in Potwisha are from 10pm to 6am daily, which means you can't run a generator during this time.

Recreation

DAY HIKING

Sequoia and Kings Canyon have some of the best hiking trails in the country. Sadly, the air quality in the parks is among the worst in California. To get the best views, hike early in the morning when the pollution is more likely to be at lower elevations. Always tell someone where you are going and when you expect to return. In addition, you can also leave a note in your car at the trailhead. Packing for a day hike in this area can be tricky, but it's possible to be well-prepared and still sport a light pack.

Sources of water can be scarce, and what water you do come across is likely contaminated with bacteria. Bring all the water you'll need for the day, or save wright by carrying a pump or water-purification system. Pack some snacks. Even if you don't normally get hungry while you hike, eating something can help relieve nausea caused by altitude sickness.

At elevation, you're more likely to get sunburned. Wear a hat, sunscreen, sunglasses and perhaps long-sleeves to protect your skin, especially on a long hike. Wearing long sleeves and pants will also help prevent tick and mosquito bites and exposure to poison oak.

The weather can be unpredictable and change rapidly, especially in the higher elevations. If you're tackling Alta Peak or another granite dome, have a protective, warm layer to put on when you take in the views at the top.

Trekking poles are a great help for hikers, no matter the size of your pack. They help with balance and take some of the pressure off weary knees on downhill stints.

It's never a bad idea to brush up on your map-and-compass skills. Cell reception is poor in Sequoia and Kings Canyon, so having a map and compass to guide you can be a lifesaver if you get lost. Buy topo maps when possible, like the *National Geographic Sequoia Kings Canyon National Parks Trails Illustrated Topographic Map* ($12). Study your map before, during, and after a hike. Use your compass to see what peaks are around you.

Pack a flashlight or headlamp; either will help you navigate if you're hiking before dawn or after sunset—or if you just need to get to the campground bathroom in the middle of the night. Some headlamps have a red light setting, which helps protect your night vision. This setting is also good for looking for animals in the wilderness at night.

BACKPACKING

Backpacking is a great way to leave the stress of the world behind and explore these wild parks. Most backpackers visit the High Sierra in the summer, where they enjoy long days, starry nights, and cooler temperatures. The glorious alpine peaks and granite bowls are easily accessed from Lodgepole and Mineral King. These areas both start at higher elevations, so that means less climbing on the trail. The best backpacking in the park can be accessed from Cedar Grove, but requires a steep first day getting out of Kings Canyon and into the high country.

Spring, fall, and winter are great times for roaming the lower elevations of the parks. Grant Grove and some of the less visited sequoia groves, like Redwood Mountain Grove, are great in spring, after the snow has cleared, and in fall, when the leaves change color. The Foothills offer a year-round escape, especially from December through March. Wherever you go, always let someone else know your planned destination and when to expect you back.

All overnight trips require a wilderness permit (from $15). Submit your application for a permit by email (seki_wilderness_reservations@nps.gov) in order to reserve your trailhead and date. Apply at least two weeks in advance. From September to May, self-register at Foothills Visitor Center, Kings Canyon Visitor Center, and the Giant Forest Museum for free.

If you're not sure what trail might be right for you, call and talk to a park ranger. Rangers are also great at offering alternative options if your preferred route is booked. Use the dedicated **wilderness permit phone line** (559/565-3766) or check out the Wilderness Permit section of the parks' website (nps.gov/seki/planyourvisit/wilderness_permits.htm).

Most backcountry areas have bears and thus require backpackers to carry a bear canister (which can be rented at Lodgepole Visitor Center and in Grant Grove). Buying or borrowing one in advance helps your packing process go smoother. They run $35-100. With a little planning and preparation, you can spend a night in perfect solitude in Sequoia and Kings Canyon.

FISHING

Idyllic, crystalline waters make fishing here a stunningly beautiful challenge. Fish have been introduced to the waterways and are savvy to fishers' ploys. Fly-fishing along the Kings River in Cedar Grove is a good bet, as well as in the alpine lakes of Mineral King. The primary species is rainbow trout, but you can also find the California golden trout in the Kern River watershed. For simpler angling, get your bait and tackle and head to Hume Lake, then park yourself in a boat or on the edge of the lake.

Get your California state fishing license online (http://wildlife.ca.gov) before you arrive, if possible. Otherwise, you can get a license at a sporting goods store in Visalia or Fresno, or at Hume Lake.

SNOWSHOEING AND CROSS-COUNTRY SKIING

When the snows come to the Sierra Nevada, they pile up several feet thick and persist into early spring. During winter, Cedar Grove and Mineral King are inaccessible. Fortunately, the Generals Highway up to and between Giant Forest and Grant Grove remains open and accessible. This is the primo winter adventure area. Snowshoe along trails around Giant Forest or go with a ranger on a nighttime snowshoe tour of Grant Grove.

In between Grant Grove and Giant Forest is the Montecito Sequoia Lodge, which has maintained and marked trails for snowshoeing and cross-country skiing. Rent simple-to-use snowshoes from Grant Grove Market and Wuksachi Lodge; free gear is often available on ranger walks.

Travel Tips

INTERNATIONAL TRAVELERS

International travelers are required to show a valid passport upon entering the United States. The U.S. government's **Visa Waiver Program** (VWP) allows tourists from many countries to visit without a visa for up to 90 days. To check if your country is on the list, go to http://travel.state.gov. To qualify, you must apply online with the **Electronic System for Travel Authorization** (ESTA, cbp.gov) and hold a return travel ticket to your country of origin dated less than 90 days from your date of entry. All other temporary international travelers are required to secure a nonimmigrant visa before entering the United States. Wait times vary, so plan ahead.

PARK FEES AND PASSES

To cruise through the park entrance stations without waiting in a long line, buy your entrance pass online in advance. Passes last for up to seven days and cost $35 per vehicle, $30 for motorcyclists, and $20 for pedestrians and bicyclists. Other options include:

- an **annual pass** to Sequoia and Kings Canyon, which costs $70 and covers all passengers in your car
- the **America the Beautiful pass,** which costs $80 for a year and covers all passengers in your car
- a **senior pass** ($20 for a year or $80 lifetime), if you're a U.S. citizen or permanent resident and 62 or older
- the **Access Pass** (free), which is available to U.S. citizens and permanent residents with disabilities
- the **Every Kid Outdoors Annual 4th Grade Pass** (free), which is available to children in fourth grade (and their families) and lasts the length of the school year

Fee-Free Days

There are several days each year when entry to all national parks is free. These days may vary each year, so check ahead of time to verify.

- Martin Luther King Jr.'s birthday (third Mon. in Jan.)
- the first day of National Park Week (mid-Apr.)
- the National Park Service's birthday (Aug. 25)
- National Public Lands Day (last Sat. in Sept.)
- Veterans Day (Nov. 11)

Sequoia and Kings Canyon also offers visitors free admission in mid-December, for Trek to the Tree, a yearly event that honors the General Grant Tree.

ACCESS FOR TRAVELERS WITH DISABILITIES

Visitors to Sequoia and Kings Canyon may find the park resources lacking. Inconsistent signage, fluctuating campsite numbers, and challenging doors on vault toilets impact the experiences of all visitors, but are most egregious for people with mobility and sensory disabilities. However, the National Park Service is aware of the need to improve its inclusivity of services and it continues to make improvements throughout the park system.

Before You Go

Obtain a National Parks **Access Pass,** which is available to U.S. citizens and permanent residents with disabilities. The free pass gains you (and anyone else in your vehicle) access to 2,000 federal recreation sites, including national parks, preserves, forests, and wildlife refuges and is good for life. The application form can be filled out online. You'll need identification that proves you are a U.S. citizen or permanent resident, and medical documentation (such as a note from your physician).

Visit the accessibility section of the Sequoia and Kings Canyon website (www.nps.gov) for updated information on barrier-free attractions in the park. This section also contains the numbers for wheelchair-accessible campsites in the parks.

Getting There and Around

In Fresno, **Mobility Works** (120 N. Diamond St., 559/408-5835, www.mobilityworks.com, 8am-5pm Mon.-Fri., 9am-1pm Sat.) rents out wheelchair vans, with an option for delivery. They offer weekday specials and discounted monthly rates, as well as rates for veterans. Most vehicle are newer than the 2014 model year. Rental prices vary by time of year.

It's also possible to reach Sequoia National Park via wheelchair accessible public transportation. From Fresno, take the **V-Line shuttle** (877/404-6473, http://ridevline.com, $10 single ride, $9 students, seniors, veterans, and people with disabilities) to Visalia. The shuttle, which can accommodate two wheelchairs, runs from the Fresno airport to the Visalia Transit Center six times daily. The journey takes 1.75 hours. From the transit center in Visalia, board the **Sequoia Shuttle** (www.sequoiashuttle.com, $20 round-trip). This 16-passenger shuttle has room for two wheelchairs. Advance reservations are required.

In Visalia, **Wyndham Visalia** (9000 W Airport Dr., 559/931-2117, www.wyndhamhohtels.com, $117-200) and **Visalia Marriott at the Convention Center** (300 South Court, 559/636-1111, www.marriott.com, $125-250) both have comfortable roll-in accommodations.

To access Grant Grove and Cedar Grove without your own vehicle, you can take a guided tour with **Sequoia Sightseeing Tours** (559/561-4189, www.sequoiatours.com). Note, though, that their vehicles do not have ramps or spots for wheelchairs; they can only accommodate collapsible wheelchairs

and walkers. There is no public transit access to Mineral King.

Park Resources

At the Lodgepole Visitor Center, Kings Canyon Visitor Center, and Giant Forest Museum, several resources are available. **Free rental wheelchairs** are available to borrow from each of these visitors centers on a first-come, first-served basis.

Visitors who do not already have a disability parking placard may request a park-specific one to access closer parking spots. These **temporary accessible parking placards** do not require documentation. Having a placard is especially useful in Giant Forest, where two **accessible parking lots** at the Big Trees Trail and General Sherman Tree provide closer and more level access to these wheelchair-accessible attractions. At these lots, accessible restrooms and water-bottle filling stations at dual heights are also available.

There is **limited braille signage** in the parks, most of which can be found along the trail for the General Grant Tree. **Audio interpretive** and **assistive listening devices** are available upon request for park films. **Closed captions** are also available on some films. **Audio assistive devices** are available for some campfire programs. The Crystal Cave tours offer **American Sign Language (ASL) translations** via tablets that you take into the cave on your tour. Some rangers and guides are experienced in ASL and **interpreters** may be available. You can request an interpreter for any scheduled park program at no cost by calling (559/565-3729) or emailing (seki_information@nps.gov) two weeks ahead of your trip.

Accessible Park Features

Each area of the parks have varied accessibility. However, the park lodges, restaurants, and main visitors centers are all wheelchair-accessible. Campgrounds typically have 1-3 sites designated as accessible. Only some campgrounds have accessible amphitheaters for ranger programs.

FOOTHILLS

The **Foothills Visitor Center** is accessible. The **Potwisha** and **Buckeye Flat Campgrounds** each have accessible sites that are reservable. Both campgrounds only have vault restrooms; the doors of these can be challenging to operate for visitors in wheelchairs or with other mobility issues.

GIANT FOREST AND LODGEPOLE

Lodgepole and Giant Forest have several accessible features. **Wuksachi Lodge** has eight accessible rooms (request at time of reservation), but the approach and travel between the lodge's buildings can prove challenging when ice and snow are present.

Lodgepole Campground has two accessible sites. Its amphitheater is reachable via a paved path at the eastern end of the parking lot (unmarked). **Dorst Creek Campground** has several accessible sites but some of the sites are on less even ground than others. To ensure a level space, book an RV site.

There's an accessible parking lot for the **General Sherman Tree.** To park here, you'll need a DMV- or park-issued disability placard. This parking lot is in a different location from the main lot for General Sherman, and avoids steep descents and stairs on the way to the tree. The **Big Trees Trail** also has designated accessible parking at the entrance to Round Meadow. This 1-mile (1.5-km) trail is flat and mostly paved. The parts that aren't paved are a boardwalk. Adjacent to the **Giant Forest Museum** is a designated accessible parking lot. Across the street from the museum is a paved path to Beetle Rock. The picnic areas with the best options for mobility are **Wolverton** and **Pinewood.**

GRANT GROVE

Grant Grove's lodging and restaurant are comfortable for most visitors. During winter, some of the area's paths might be icy or unplowed. At the **John Muir Lodge,** there's an unmarked wheelchair-accessible entrance behind the main entrance. The lodge does not have an elevator, so be sure to request a room on the first floor.

The **Grant Grove Cabins** generally don't have running water (with a few exceptions) and require climbing a few stairs to enter. The **Azalea, Sunset,** and **Crystal Springs Campgrounds** all have designated accessible spaces. Of these, Crystal Springs is probably the best for ease of parking and proximity to Grant Grove Village.

The **Kings Canyon Visitor Center** and the **Grant Grove Restaurant** are both accessible, with electric doors, spacious restrooms, and ramps. The **Grant Grove Market** and the **Grant Grove Gift Shop** have narrow aisles, so are a little hard to maneuver around.

The **General Grant Tree** has a mostly accessible paved interpretive trail. (The pavement can be a little uneven and the trail is not entirely level.) The road to **Panoramic Point** opens when the snow melts, usually in April, and stays open through November. The view from the driveway is nice, but there is also a 0.5-mile (0.8-km) paved, moderately steep trail that leads to an overlook of Kings Canyon. The grade is mostly 6.5 percent, but goes up to 8.5 percent.

KINGS CANYON AND CEDAR GROVE

Cedar Grove has excellent accessibility resources. The best room in **Cedar Grove Lodge** is the accessible room with a roll-in shower and riverfront views. The **Cedar Grove Grill** and the **Cedar Grove Market** are both accessible via ramps and have wide aisles inside. Several sites at **Moraine, Sentinel,** and **Canyon View Campgrounds** are accessible and include extended picnic tables.

The **Cedar Grove Amphitheater** has an accessible pathway. The **Cedar Grove Visitor Center** is accessible. There are not many paved paths in this part of Kings Canyon.

Roaring River Falls is a popular attraction accessed by a paved path. The steepest slope is a 10 percent grade, but there are level landings along the way, and the short path concludes at a paved landing where you can gaze upon the falls.

MINERAL KING

The remote area of Mineral King has just one accessible campsite at the Atwell Springs Campground, which is available on a first-come, first-served basis. To claim the site, you must have a disability parking placard. The Mineral King Ranger Station has eight stairs, making it inaccessible to wheelchair users. There is an accessible bathroom at the Lookout Point Entrance Station on Mineral King Road. Note, though, that the ground leading up to the bathroom is a little rough and uneven.

Other Resources

- TTY Federal Relay Service (800/877-8339)
- Voice Carry Over (VCO, 877/877-6280)
- Speech-to-Speech (877/877-8982)
- Spanish translation services (800/845-6136)
- TeleBraille (866/893-8340)

TRAVELING WITH CHILDREN

Sequoia and Kings Canyon offer plenty of entertaining and educational opportunities for kids. There's a seemingly endless number of activities for families to do together in these parks, but I've listed some of my favorites here.

Join a ranger on a hike. Free ranger-led walks and talks are appropriate for children. Some are even specifically aimed at kids of different ages. Many of these hikes will stretch your child's imagination and curiosity about nature, whether the topic is living history or a sunset bat walk. The bear talk at Lodgepole is a classic. Especially fun for kids are the campfire programs, which enliven many evenings in the campgrounds. Check online (www. nps.gov/seki) or on the bulletin boards at the parks' campgrounds and visitors centers for updated events.

Get sprayed by a waterfall. Grizzly Falls and Roaring River Falls are the closest waterfalls in the parks to the road. If your children are up for a short hike, visit Tokopah Falls, which is especially thrilling in May and June.

Hike up a granite dome. Whether they're conquering the 400 steps to the top of Moro Rock or summiting another of the parks' domes, kids will love the feeling of being on top of the world.

Explore underground. Take your child on a tour of Crystal Cave. If your little one is 10 or older, you can even go on one of the extra-fun adventure tours of the cave. Note that tours of Crystal Cave aren't intended for children 2 and younger.

Watch for wildlife. Head to a quiet meadow at dawn or dusk with a headlamp and spend some time looking for the deer, chipmunks, and birds that call these parks home.

TRAVELING WITH PETS

Traveling in a national park with your four-legged friend can be challenging. Luckily, national forest land surrounds Sequoia and Kings Canyon, which means you'll have a few more options than you would otherwise.

In the parks, dogs must be on a leash at all times. They are not allowed on trails, in public buildings, or in the backcountry. Leashed pets can be walked 100 feet from roads in developed areas (picnic areas, campgrounds, and roads). Pets are not allowed on the paved or dirt paths within the parks, including the trails for the General Grant and General Sherman Trees. You cannot leave your dog unattended in your hotel room or your car. Pet-friendly lodging in the parks include John Muir Lodge, Grant Grove Cabins, Cedar Grove Lodge, and Wuksachi Lodge. There's a non-refundable $25 fee (per night) for each pet.

The surrounding Sequoia National Forest provides you and your dog access to excellent hiking and wilderness, with 60 miles (95 km) of trails. Here are a few tips for hiking with dogs that will make your trip safe for your pet and for the area's wildlife:

- A leash is a must; this is mountain lion country. In addition, do not hike alone, for the safety of your pet—and yourself.

- Protect the local wildlife. Pets must not be allowed to chase or disturb wildlife. Dogs can put undue stress on fledgling birds, lizards, and young deer and other small mammals.

- Pick up and dispose of all waste. There are sensitive plant species and ecosystems all around you.

From easiest to hardest, these dog-friendly trails require pets to be on a leash or under voice control:

- Near Grant Grove, the **Indian Basin Grove Interpretive Trail** is a flat 1-mile (1.5-km) loop through a recovering sequoia grove that leaves from Princess Campground.

- The **Boole Tree Loop** is 1 mile (1.5 km) with 500 feet of elevation gain. It leads to one of the largest of all sequoias, a gnarled survivor of logging in the Converse Basin. It's near Grant Grove, down a dirt Forest Service road.

- **Yucca Point Trail** leads to a good fishing spot, but it's also a steep, exposed hike of 3.6 miles (5.8 km). It's located 14 miles (23 km) into Kings Canyon, accessible from Grant Grove.

A safer alternative is to leave your pet at a local kennel in Fresno or Visalia. Highly rated kennels include **Elaine's Pet Resorts** (http://elainespetresorts.com) in Fresno, and **Visalia Country Kennel** (http://visaliacountrykennel.com), **Visalia's VIP Pet Boarding and More** (http://visaliasvippetboardingandmore.com), and **Your Best Friends Inn** (http://yourbestfriendsinn.com) in Visalia. Online services like Rover.com can also help you find pet sitters in Three Rivers and beyond.

CELL PHONES AND INTERNET ACCESS

There's little to no cell phone reception in Lodgepole, Cedar Grove, and Mineral King. Some areas of the parks, like Grant Grove, have limited service.

Wi-Fi is available at Wuksachi Lodge, the Grant Grove Restaurant, and the Foothills Visitor Center. Pay phones are available at several spots in Sequoia and Kings Canyon, including Lodgepole Market, Stony Creek Lodge, and Mineral King Visitor Center.

Health and Safety

WILDERNESS AND HIKING SAFETY

Most Search and Rescue (SAR) Operations could have been prevented by better planning and communication. Tell people where you are going and leave a copy of your itinerary with someone who will know to contact the park if they do not hear from you by a certain date and time. Do not deviate from your plan without communicating. Be sensitive to your physical and mental limitations. Practice a measured approach to exploring and know when to turn back. Take care of yourself in the summer's hot and dry conditions by carrying

and consuming the appropriate amounts of water (eight ounces for every hour of hiking). A little bit of salt and sugar can help stabilize your body, but remember that the heat, dryness, and elevation can affect even the most attuned athlete's body.

Personal trackers that communicate via satellite to emergency workers or family are excellent tools for emergencies, and have become fairly refined and sophisticated, with the ability to target messages to particular recipients. One example is the **SPOT personal tracker** (www.findmespot.com).

Only use a **personal locator beacon** (a

device that sends an SOS signal and your location to rescue agencies) in the case of an emergency. If you are uninjured and call for help, you'll still have to walk your way back to the nearest trailhead, even though you'll be accompanied by a ranger.

HEAT STROKE AND ALTITUDE SICKNESS

Temperatures in Cedar Grove and the Foothills regularly reach above 90°F (32°C). High temps and strenuous activity are a recipe for **heat stroke.** Symptoms include a high temperature, incoherent thoughts, nausea, and a racing heart rate. Get into shade or cool down in a stream. Alcohol consumption and dehydration can make heat stroke worse.

The symptoms for **altitude sickness** are similar to heat stroke and include headache, nausea, fatigue, muscle aches, and dizziness. Altitude sickness can happen to anyone. It takes the body several days to adapt to reduced oxygen levels at 8,000 feet elevation and higher. Mitigate altitude sickness by drinking water, sleeping at a lower elevation, and cutting out alcohol and tobacco.

An important note for parents of babies under three months: Infant lungs are underdeveloped and going to high elevations can put your baby at risk of high altitude pulmonary edema, a buildup of fluid in the lungs. Infants who regularly live at low elevations should not spend time above 8,000 feet elevation. Return to low elevations and go to the doctor if your child seems listless.

LIGHTNING

A thunderstorm rolls up the mountains and collides with the Great Western Divide. The mountains glow against the stunning dark backdrop. Atop Moro Rock, the hairs on the back of your head start to tingle. **Lightning** is a major risk for hiking on exposed high-elevation peaks and domes. Be aware of the sudden summer storms and descend when the weather takes a turn for the electrically charged.

WATER SAFETY

Every year, **swimmers** drown in Sierra Nevada rivers. In the heat of the summer, nothing beats a dip in the Kaweah or Kings Rivers. However, these are not simple streams. Practice caution: The currents can be deceptively strong, the temperature of the water can be shockingly cold, and underwater hazards like tree branches can pin swimmers between the current and the hazard. Safer options include the lakes near the Montecito Sequoia Lodge and Hume Lake. The rivers are safer to swim in when the water levels have receded, in late summer and fall.

DISEASES

Giardia

This bacterial infection initially causes diarrhea and can complicate a digestive tract for years after exposure. You may not know that you have it for a few weeks. Exposure to *Giardia lamblia* occurs when you drink unclean, unfiltered water. Do not be lulled into false security by the remoteness of the area: All of the parks' rivers are contaminated with bacteria. Always boil, filter, or sterilize water from streams and lakes before consuming it.

Options for cleaning your drinking water can be as inexpensive as a $6 bottle of iodine tablets (plus a couple dollars for something to cover up the taste), but you can also purchase more expensive gravity-fed filter bags or lasers that use ultraviolet light to kill bacteria. Carrying a water filter is often worth the expense and backpack space compared to carrying as much water as you will need for a full day of hiking. Boiling water at high elevations can take a long time and use up costly fuel. Filters and lasers are the best option and have come a long way! Look for Platypus gravity filters, Katadyn pocket filters, and Steripen laser purifiers.

Hantavirus

Hantavirus occurs in and around Sequoia National Park, though cases are rare. Hantavirus is the result of an exposure to rodents and their waste matter. Avoid rodents and their homes to protect yourself.

Plague

Every few years the plague rears its head in the Sierra Nevada. Yes, this is the same plague that once killed a third of the world's population. The biggest threat of plague in this area comes from fleas that feed on local rodents like chipmunks and squirrels. Avoid potential exposure: Don't feed any rodent, even if it's cute!

ANIMAL ENCOUNTERS
Mountain Lions

Some areas of the parks have higher populations of **mountain lions,** though the risk of being attacked by one is extremely low. Still, it is safest to hike with at least one other person, especially on remote trails in Cedar Grove and the Foothills. If you come across a mountain lion, make yourself look big. Shout and wave your arms. Do not turn your back or run.

Bears

A restful night in the campground, stargazing or sitting by the fire, can go rapidly awry thanks to inappropriate food storage. Bears have an extremely sensitive sense of smell. They are able to smell food from miles away. Bears that live around campgrounds begin to associate the presence of people with food. They are very smart and know how to procure food: by charging a table and scaring away campers, waiting until your food is left unattended, or even by breaking into cars. Store everything with a smell in a bear-proof food locker. And don't abandon your picnic table—scare the bear away with loud sounds. Deposit all garbage in trash cans and make sure they are shut properly.

If you encounter a bear in the Giant Forest or while hiking in other parts of the parks, watch from a great distance—over 100 yards. Bears can be very protective of their young, so do not approach a cub if you see one—the mother is probably close by. If a bear is following you, shout and wave your arms. Do not turn your back or run away. In the rare case that a bear charges or attacks, do not play dead.

TICKS

These tiny arachnids move swiftly from trails to the tops of brush and grasses and onto your clothes. Ticks are present wherever there are deer, but especially in the Foothills, in wooded, brushy, and grassy areas. They are active throughout the year, but especially in spring. Ticks live on the blood of deer, mice, birds, and humans, and carry serious diseases, including Lyme disease. The parasites favor warm crevices and folds: armpits, groins, and sometimes the hairline of the neck.

There are several species of ticks in the Sierra Nevada. Deer ticks are brownish red and can carry Lyme disease, a crippling autoimmune disease. Black ticks, glossy and opaque, are the most common kind. The larger the tick, the older it is. Each meal it has, the parasite grows and molts its prior skin and enlarges.

To avoid ticks, use insect repellant containing DEET, wear long-sleeved shirts and pants (lighter colors are better), and treat clothes in permethrin-based products. Take precautions to reduce exposure to ticks and remove ticks before they bite if possible. Hike in the center of trails and avoid brushing up against plants. Inspect your clothing and body upon return, before entering your car, including hard-to-see spots such as scalp, groin, and underarms. Bathe within two hours of exposure to wash off ticks. If you notice a fever or rash, you may have a tick bite. Keep away from wildlife, which might host ticks.

POISON OAK

Just a brush of bare skin against this plant results in raised bumps, blisters, and painful itching within a day or so of exposure. The oils from the plant can remain on exposed clothing and continue to infect the skin.

To identify poison oak, look for lobed leaves that grow in sets of three. Depending on the season, leaves can be green, orange, or red. In spring, greasy, oak-like leaves emerge from bare brown sticks along hillsides in the Foothills. In summer, the plant appears in dense patches along trails. In autumn, the leaves change to a slick red or orange, then drop their leaves to become plain brown sticks once again. In winter, poison oak's bare stems still carry the oils that cause the rash, and are much harder to identify. Look for poison oak on less-maintained trails, including Marble Falls, Middle Fork Falls, and Dorst Creek Trail.

Many of the same techniques for preventing ticks also reduce exposure to poison oak. Wear long sleeves and pants. After suspected exposure, washing your body with soap and warm water is the best way to remove the oils quickly. Wash any clothing that may have been exposed separately with warm water and detergent. Products like Tecnu are effective at cleaning both clothes and the body. They even come in the form of wipes, which are handy for wiping down your trekking poles and shoes.

Resources

Suggested Reading

GEOLOGY

Brewer, William H. *Up and Down California in 1860-1864: The Journal of William H. Brewer*. Berkeley, CA: University of California Press, 2003. In this travelogue, Brewer describes his experiences in the Sierra Nevada as part of the newly born California Geological Survey, including his first view of giant sequoias, in vivid, transportive language, including some colorful dialogue.

Hill, Mary. *Geology of the Sierra Nevada*. Berkeley, CA: University of California Press, 2006. The quintessential geology guide offers such clarity on the topic that even a novice can become a rock hound overnight. Its words are so valuable and the story so riveting that I have carried its two pounds on backpacking trips because the wisdom was worth the weight.

Hoff, Emily. *Scenic Science of the National Parks*. New York: Ten Speed Press, 2020. Fun exploratory narratives and questions on the Sierra Nevada connect young scientists to deep geological and climatic processes.

King, Clarence. *Mountaineering in the Sierra Nevada*. New York: Penguin, 1989. Originally published in 1872, this book comes from another member of the California Geological Survey. King details a more extravagant and puffed-up account of the mountains the team encountered.

Muir, John. *Studies in the Sierra*. San Francisco: Sierra Club, 1950. This reprint of the original 1874 text has careful illustrations of each of the Sierra's glacial features. It's Muir's finest scientific work: methodical and sparse in its prose, yet classically curious, and a delight for anyone interested in the history of discovery in the Sierra.

Wise, James M. *Mount Whitney to Yosemite: The Geology of the John Muir Trail*. Create Space, 2008. This textbook-like study of geology is organized by sections of the John Muir Trail. With careful description of sights and over 45 geologic formations, hikers and backpackers will delight in reading the lexicon of the land. The section on glaciers is particularly excellent.

ZOOLOGY

Gaines, David. *Birds of Yosemite and the East Slope*. Lee Vining, CA: Artemesia Press, 1988. Written with poetic passion and an attention to phenology, this is easily the most beautiful book about birds you will ever encounter. Although the book is now out of print, many libraries carry it.

Laws, John Muir. *The Laws Field Guide to the Sierra Nevada*. Berkeley, CA: Heyday Books, 2007. This impeccably illustrated, lightweight volume is the Rosetta Stone to understanding Sierra fauna. The author is especially skilled at creating interest in invertebrates and amphibians. The section on birds covers distinguishing features between similar species as well as habitat descriptions.

Peterson, Roger Tory. *Peterson First Guides: Birds.* New Yor: Houghton Mifflin Co., 1980. An economical beginner's volume that is always in my backpack (I leave the big one in the car), this guide includes many of the most common birds while also training you on gestalt identification, so that you can know a bird by its location and shape.

BOTANY

Arno, Stephen F. *Discovering Sierra Trees.* Yosemite Association and Sequoia National History Association, 1973. Light, simple, and exquisitely written, this book is with me whenever I visit the Sierra. Thanks to its woodcut drawings and artful descriptions I can narrow down and eventually identify each plant I see and inevitably learn something new.

Bryant Logan, William. *Oak: The Frame of Civilization.* New York: W.W. Norton, 2005. California oaks figure initially in this short socio-environmental history of the acorn-bearing family of trees that is the center of the Foothills ecosystem.

Lanner, Ronald M. *Conifers of California.* Los Olivos, CA: Cachuma Press, 1999. The key to understanding a place is knowing what species grow there and why. With beautifully deep descriptions, maps, and unmistakably clear illustrations, this book will help you see the forest for all of the trees in Sequoia and Kings Canyon.

Stocking, Stephen and Jack A. Rockwell. *Wildflowers of Sequoia & Kings Canyon National Parks.* Three Rivers, CA: Sequoia Natural History Association, 2013. Arranged by color, this is the easiest book to carry along for flower identification. It contains some of the most interesting tidbits about each plant.

Stocking, Stephen. *The Giant Sequoias of Sequoia and Kings Canyon National Parks and the Giant Sequoia National Monument.* Three Rivers, CA: Sequoia Natural History Association, 2014. This brief pamphlet on interesting individual sequoias and their life cycle is a good introduction to the parks. It's usually available at the parks' museums and visitors centers.

Wiese, Karen. *Sierra Nevada Wildflowers: Including Yosemite, Sequoia, and Kings Canyon National Parks.* Helena, MT: Falcon Rowman & Littlefield, 2013. Organized by color and annotated for location, ecosystem, and bloom dates, this go-to volume can help amateurs jump into botany and plant identification. It also serves as a great resource for the entire range with excellent interpretation of Latin and Greek name roots.

WILDERNESS TRAVEL AND CLIMBING

Albright, Horace Marden, Marian Albright Schenck, and William C. Tweed. *The Mather Mountain Party of 1915 and the Founding of the National Park Service.* Three Rivers, CA: Sequoia Natural History Association, 2014. This is a rollicking journey through the high country with the men who contributed to the campaign to establish the national parks and preserve this special place.

Arnold, Daniel. *Early Days in the Range of Light: Encounters with Legendary Mountaineers.* Berkeley, CA: Counterpoint, 2009. The exploration of the Sierra Nevada happened late by Gold Rush standards: Explorers ascended remote mountain peaks with no rain gear, maps, or chance of rescue. This selection of firsthand accounts is prefaced with Arnold's expertise, and organized with an image and story per peak.

Blehm, Eric. *The Last Season.* New York: HarperCollins, 2006. This book relates the mystery of how a ranger "who knew the country better than the map did" disappeared in the roadless wilderness of northern Kings Canyon with hardly a trace. It will take you on a journey through places that few visitors ever see.

Gisel, Bonnie J., ed. *The Wilder Muir: The Curious Nature of John Muir*. San Francisco: Yosemite Conservancy, 2017. This collection of Muir's writings includes his ascent of Mount Whitney and adventures throughout the American West.

Harrington, Candy B. *Barrier-Free Travel: Yosemite, Sequoia and Kings Canyon National Parks for Wheelers and Slow Walkers*. C&C Creative Concepts, 2017. Harrington holds parks to the letter of law, tape measure in hand, and pushes park managers to implement inclusive designs. This book contains photographs of accessible trails and hotels in the parks. The author shares the best resources for accessibility in this book.

Muir, John. *My First Summer in the Sierra*. San Francisco: Sierra Club, 1911. This is an account of the several months in 1869 that Muir spent with shepherds in the Sierra Nevada. It contains illustrations, prose, and poetry.

Roberts, Suzanne. *Almost Somewhere: Twenty-Eight Days on the John Muir Trail*. Lincoln, NE: University of Nebraska Press, 2012. Three young women make the life-altering journey of 211 miles from Mount Whitney, through Kings Canyon, to Yosemite in this short, clear memoir.

Stetson, Lee, ed. *The Wild Muir: Twenty-Two of John Muir's Greatest Adventures*. San Francisco: Yosemite Conservancy, 1994. This volume of Muir's writings includes his adventures exploring the Sierra and beyond.

Umemoto, Hank. *Manzanar to Mount Whitney: The Life and Times of a Lost Hiker*. Berkeley, CA: Heyday Books, 2013. Manzanar, one of the internment camps that imprisoned Japanese Americans during WWII was in the shadow of Mount Whitney, on the east side of the Sierra. With lyricism and clarity, Umemoto describes his climb of Whitney at age 71 and his life in Manzanar.

HUMAN HISTORY

Eldredge, Ward. *In the Summer of 1903: Colonel Charles Young and the Buffalo Soldiers in Sequoia National Park*. Three Rivers, CA: Sequoia Natural History Association, 2003. The roads of Sequoia and Kings Canyon were designed and built by the parks' first protectors, the African American Cavalry and Infantry, also known as the Buffalo Soldiers. This brief history covers their journeys and the lasting impact.

Elsasser, A. B. *Indians of Sequoia and Kings Canyon National Parks*. Three Rivers, CA: Sequoia Natural History Association, 1988. The most interesting descriptions in this text are on hunting and fishing methods, crafts, and games, each illustrated with a pen and ink drawing. The booklet depicts the park land as it once was, when Native American groups lived here. Note that the text contains some problematic language.

Farquhar, Francis P. *History of the Sierra Nevada*. Berkeley, CA: University of California Press, 2007. Farquhar, a former president of the Sierra Club, describes in riveting detail each wave of exploration to the mountain range, with good coverage of sequoias and conservation.

Jackson, Louise A. *Mineral King: The Story of Beulah*. Three Rivers, CA: Sequoia Parks Conservancy, 2006. Full of details about the hard-knock life of mining camps and the troubles of extracting the parks' natural resources, this is a must-read for anyone curious about the history of Mineral King.

Jackson, Louise A. *The Sierra Nevada Before History: Ancient Landscapes, Early Peoples*.

Missoula, MT: Mountain Press Publishing Company, 2010. Organized by tribe, this book offers exemplary stories, illustrated with images and maps, of the Indigenous peoples who once lived in this area.

Mayfield, Thomas Jefferson. *Indian Summer: A True Account of Traditional Life Among the Choinumne Indians of California's San Joaquin Valley.* Berkeley, CA: Heyday Books and California Historical Society, 1993. This book shares the factual and fascinating life of a young boy who spent 10 summers with a group of Choinumne Yokuts people in the 1850s. There's also a version of this book for young readers, called *Adopted by Indians.*

Tweed, William C. *King Sequoia.* Berkeley, CA: Heyday Books and Sierra College, 2016. A former park historian and ranger weaves an astounding tale. This must-read book is a painful history of logging as well as the catalyzation of the preservation movement.

Internet Resources

SEQUOIA AND KINGS CANYON

Sequoia and Kings Canyon National Parks
www.nps.gov/seki
You'll find everything there is to know about Sequoia and Kings Canyon on the parks' official website, from live webcams to road construction updates. Summer ranger programs are updated weekly. Rangers also provide updates on trail conditions throughout the summer. There's also a free smartphone app available for download, which offers offline access for when you're in the parks and don't have reception. Look for "NPS Sequoia and Kings Canyon National Park app" in the app stores for both Android and Apple devices.

Sequoia National Forest
www.fs.usda.gov/sequoia
The US Forest Service operates Sequoia National Forest, which you will inevitably pass through as you traverse the parks. Information on campfires, wilderness permits, and dispersed camping are all updated regularly on this site.

Sequoia Parks Conservancy
www.sequoiaparksconservancy.org
Sequoia Parks Conservancy is the official nonprofit partner of Sequoia and Kings Canyon National Parks. This website is where to purchase Crystal Cave tour tickets, check on the weather via their webcams, or find general information about the parks.

Visit Sequoia
www.visitsequoia.com
This site, run by the parks' concessioner, Delaware North, has tons of information about things to do in Sequoia and Kings Canyon. It's also where you can make lodging reservations for the parks' cabins, hotels, and wilderness huts.

RESERVATIONS

Recreation.gov
www.recreation.gov
This website lets you book any reservable campsites in the national parks or national forest up to six months in advance. Some other recreational reservations are also available on this site.

NATURE

Blossom Trail
www.goblossomtrail.com
Most visitors will enter the parks on either Highway 180 or Highway 198. From spring to fall, both routes are a corridor of blossoming fruit trees. This website shares information about special events and timing for photography and adventures.

The Gymnosperm Database
http://conifers.org
This website provides detailed information about tree species in the parks. It also provides links to key research, so you can do a deep dive on whichever trees you're curious about.

Index

List of Maps

Photo Credits

Acknowledgments

For joyful explorer, beer-taster extraordinaire, and naturalist Amelia Johnson.

For my greatest gift, bright companion for all seasons, and wild, wonderful daughter, Phoebe Ruth.

For my wise, kind, brave, and loving parents, Leslie and Dean Bernacchi.

Thank you.

Craft a personalized journey through the top national parks in the U.S. and Canada with Moon Travel Guides.

MOON

USA NATIONAL PARKS

THE COMPLETE GUIDE TO ALL

62 PARKS

BECKY LOMAX

MOON

ACADIA NATIONAL PARK

HILARY NANGLE

MOON

ARCHES & CANYONLANDS NATIONAL PARKS

W. C. MCRAE & JUDY JEWELL

MOON

BANFF NATIONAL PARK

HIKE·CAMP SEE WILDLIFE

ANDREW HEMPSTEAD

DEATH VALLEY NATIONAL PARK

JENNA BLOUGH

MOON

GLACIER NATIONAL PARK

HIKING · CAMPING LAKES & PEAKS

BECKY LOMAX

MOON

GRAND CANYON

HIKE·CAMP RAFT THE COLORADO RIVER

TIM HULL

MOON

GREAT SMOKY MOUNTAINS NATIONAL PARK

HIKING · CAMPING SCENIC DRIVES

JASON FRYE

MOON

MOUNT RUSHMORE & THE BLACK HILLS

Including the Badlands

LAURAL A. BIDWELL

MOON

ROCKY MOUNTAIN NATIONAL PARK

HIKE·CAMP SEE WILDLIFE

ERIN ENGLISH

MOON

SEQUOIA & KINGS CANYON

HIKING·CAMPING WATERFALLS & BIG TREES

LEIGH BERNACCHI

MOON

YELLOWSTONE & GRAND TETON

HIKE, CAMP, SEE WILDLIFE

BECKY LOMAX

MOON

YOSEMITE SEQUOIA & KINGS CANYON

ANN MARIE BROWN

MOON

ZION & BRYCE

Including Arches, Canyonlands, Capitol Reef, Grand Staircase-Escalante & Moab

W. C. MCRAE & JUDY JEWELL

MOON SEQUOIA & KINGS CANYON
Avalon Travel
Hachette Book Group
1700 Fourth Street
Berkeley, CA 94710, USA
www.moon.com

Editor: Leah Gordon
Acquiring Editor: Nikki Ioakimedes
Graphics Coordinator: Rue Flaherty
Production Coordinator: Rue Flaherty
Cover Design: Kimberly Glyder
Interior Design: Domini Dragoone
Moon Logo: Tim McGrath
Map Editor: Albert Angulo
Cartographer: John Culp
Indexer: Rachel Kuhn

ISBN-13: 9781640498013

Printing History
1st Edition — January 2021
5 4 3 2 1

Front cover photo: Senate Grove, Sequoia National Park © Steve Satushek / Getty Images
Back cover photo: Mosquito Lakes, Sequoia National Park © Sburel | Dreamstime.com

Printed in China by RR Donnelley